Urban Chroniclers in Modern Latin America

Joe R. and Teresa Lozano Long Series
in Latin American and Latino Art and Culture

URBAN CHRONICLERS IN MODERN LATIN AMERICA

THE SHARED INTIMACY OF EVERYDAY LIFE

Viviane Mahieux

UNIVERSITY OF TEXAS | AUSTIN

Requests for permission to reproduce material
from this work should be sent to:
  Permissions
  University of Texas Press
  P.O. Box 7819
  Austin, TX 78713–7819
  www.utexas.edu/utpress/about/bpermission.html

∞ The paper used in this book meets the minimum requirements of
ANSI/NISO Z39.48–1992 (R1997) (Permanence of Paper).

LIBRARY OF CONGRESS CATALOGING-IN-PUBLICATION DATA
Mahieux, Viviane.
  Urban chroniclers in modern Latin America : the shared intimacy of everyday life /
Viviane Mahieux. — 1st ed.
     p.   cm. — (Joe R. and Teresa Lozano Long series in Latin American and
Latino art and culture)
  Includes bibliographical references and index.
  ISBN 978-0-292-72669-7 (cloth : alk. paper) — ISBN 978-0-292-73544-6 (e-book)
  1. Latin American literature—20th century—History and criticism.   2. Reportage
literature, Latin American—History and criticism.   3. Literature and society—Latin
America.   4. City and town life—Latin America.   5. Literature and society—Latin
America.   6. Marginality, Social, in literature.   7. Latin America—Intellectual life.
8. Latin America—In literature.   I. Title.
  PQ7082.R46M335 2011
  868'.60309—dc23
                                                              2011027162

For Susana Mahieux, mother and friend

Contents

Abbreviations

I use the following abbreviations for frequently quoted works. Unless otherwise noted, the translations cited in the text are mine. The chronicles included in the appendix were translated by Jacinto Fombona.

AS II   Storni, Alfonsina. *Obras: Prosa; Narraciones, periodismo, ensayo, teatro.* Vol. 2. Buenos Aires: Losada, 2002.

RA II   Arlt, Roberto. *Obras.* Vol. 2. Buenos Aires: Losada, 1998.

T   Andrade, Mário de. *Táxi e crônicas do Diário Nacional.* São Paulo: Duas Cidades, 1976.

TA   Andrade, Mário de. *O turista aprendiz.* São Paulo: Secretaria da Cultura, Ciência e Tecnologia, 1976.

VE I   Novo, Salvador. *Viajes y ensayos I.* Mexico City: Fondo de Cultura Económica, 1996.

VE II   Novo, Salvador. *Viajes y ensayos II.* Mexico City: Fondo de Cultura Económica, 1999.

Acknowledgments

This project was, for many years, an important part of my everyday life—too much so, some of those who lived it with me might say. But it was also a process that I was lucky enough to share with many people along the way. The constant advice and encouragement I received from mentors, colleagues, and friends have enriched this book, and my own life, in more ways than I can imagine. My adviser Doris Sommer guided me through the first steps of this project while it was taking shape as a dissertation, and I still count on her ideas and generosity. My readers Joaquim Coelho and Luis Cárcamo Huechante contributed many insights to this project, and Luis remains a frequent interlocutor and a patient reader. At the time, my research benefited from the financial support of the David Rockefeller Center, the Department of Romance Languages and Literatures, and the Nancy Clark Smith Fund, all of Harvard University; as well as the emotional and intellectual support of my friends in graduate school: Wanda Rivera, Susan Antebi, Santiago Morales, Juan Pablo Lupi, Carmen Oquendo Villar, Alexandra Vega, and Claret Vargas.

In New York, where I grappled with the mysterious process of transforming a thesis into a book, I counted on the help of friends and colleagues at Fordham University who had the patience to read drafts and proposals and even toy with possible titles. My thanks go to Hugo Benavides, Andrew Clark, Arnaldo Cruz Malavé, Jeanne Flavin, Javier Jiménez Belmonte, Carey Kasten, Luz Lenis, Chris Schmidt-Nowara,

Lise Schreier, and Cynthia Vich. Numerous conversations in conference hallways, cafés, bars, parks, and even taxicabs gave me stamina and new ideas. I am indebted to Anke Birkenmaier, Jean Franco, Rubén Gallo, Wael Hibri, Alberto Medina, Lina Meruane, José del Valle, Pablo Piccato, Adela Pineda, Nicolau Sevcenko, and Sylvia Saítta, as well as to Julio Ramos, who many years ago put a book of chronicles in my hands for the first time and who also commented on the final versions of this manuscript. Two research fellowships and a faculty fellowship from Fordham University enabled me to complete my archival research and gave me the time to focus on revisions. I would like to particularly thank Jacinto Fombona for his excellent work in translating the appendices.

Much of the research for this book took place in archives abroad. In Mexico City, I counted on the encouragement of Antonio Saborit, Héctor de Mauleón, Michael Schuessler, and Miguel Capistrán, as well as with the patience of the staff of the Hemeroteca Nacional, and the *hemeroteca* of *El Universal*. In Buenos Aires, I received the help of Ana María Amar Sánchez and Matt Cifaldi. In Rio de Janeiro and São Paulo, I counted on the advice of Charles Perrone and Beatriz Resende.

I am especially grateful to Theresa May of the University of Texas Press for her consistent support throughout the road to publication, as well as to Victoria Davis, Nancy Bryan, Rosemary Wetherold, and Laura Young Bost for their expert help. My sincere thanks also go to Vicky Unruh and my anonymous reader; their insightful comments helped make this a better book.

An abridged version of chapter 4 appeared as "The Chronicler as Streetwalker: Salvador Novo and the Performance of Genre" in *Hispanic Review* 76, no. 2 (Spring 2008), pp. 155–177, © 2008 The University of Pennsylvania Press. Sections of chapter 5 appeared in previous form as "Cube Bonifant: Una escritora professional en el México post-revolucionario" in *Revista de Crítica Literaria Latinoamericana*, no. 66 (2007); and in my introduction to the edition of Cube Bonifant's chronicles, *Una pequeña Marquesa de Sade: Crónicas selectas (1921–1948)*.

Finishing this book would have been impossible without the encouragement of Susana Mahieux; the patience and humor of Ricardo Restrepo; and the contagious energy of my many friends who have nothing to do with literary criticism and always remind me of the pleasures in life.

Urban Chroniclers in Modern Latin America

A somewhat unstructured genre that combines literary aestheticism with journalistic form, the Latin American *crónica*, or chronicle, has been surprisingly successful in recent years at consolidating critical recognition with popular appeal. Since the 1970s and 1980s, many of Latin America's most prominent intellectuals have devoted themselves primarily, if not exclusively, to this genre. Such is the case for Carlos Monsiváis and Elena Poniatowska in Mexico, Pedro Lemebel in Chile, and María Moreno in Argentina, writers who command enormous esteem within their respective countries and wield authority on issues ranging from literature and popular culture to public policy and the politics of representation. The importance of the chronicle at the turn of the twenty-first century hinges on its inherent ability to capture urban life in all of its chaotic, fragmented, and often dysfunctional grandeur. At a time when so many cities have reached "postapocalyptic" levels, to borrow Monsiváis' description of Mexico City, chroniclers have become the intermediaries through whom the gritty reality of city streets, like the modest accounts of isolated neighborhoods and ignored public happenings, are recognized and resignified. They write about the characters, cityscapes, and practices that have been left out of official versions of national modernity, highlighting how an increasingly globalized mass culture can be locally and creatively appropriated. More than ever, guides are needed to grasp the overwhelming experience that is the Latin American city, and chroniclers have stepped in as the ironic, irreverent, and indispensable commentators of everyday life.

That the urban chronicle has become such a necessary genre would have surprised a number of its early contributors, who in the late nineteenth century disparaged it as a side job for poets in need of a salary and were pessimistic about its future. Many of the founders of the Spanish American literary movement of *modernismo*, such as José Martí, Rubén Darío, and Manuel Gutiérrez Nájera were also journalists who published chronicles regularly throughout most of their writing lives. Their articles dwelled on the effects of modernity on the city, often revealing the anxieties of writers who felt trapped between a desired creative autonomy and their dependence on a profession limited by commercial norms. Regardless of their doubts, the journalistic chronicle has remained a staple of writers and their publics since the end of the nineteenth century. Many authors, Gabriel García Márquez among them, consider that writing chronicles played an essential part of their formative years. But even if the chronicle played a consistent role in shaping Latin American literature and culture since the nineteenth century, the genre's lasting importance was long undernoted.

It was not until the late twentieth century that the chronicle began to receive the systematic critical attention it so richly deserved. Carlos Monsiváis' volume *A ustedes les consta: Antología de la crónica en México*, originally published in 1980, brought together a selection of chronicles written in Mexico between 1843 and 1979 and provided a crucial first step in establishing the aesthetic continuity of a genre that until then had remained mostly invisible to literary history.[1] Monsiváis' anthology astutely situates the chronicle as a genre that appeals to, and is shaped by, heterogeneous reading publics. The title of the anthology *A ustedes les consta*, loosely translated to "As you can attest," is briefly explained in the blurb at the back of the book: "As you can attest. You, readers of this literary and journalistic genre, the chronicle, are and have been witnesses— and in a very particular way—actors of an admirable creative and informative operation in Mexican culture." From its conception, Monsiváis' groundbreaking anthology establishes the chronicle as a flexible genre that is defined by the collaboration of its public and that has consistently intertwined historical events, minor happenings, and aesthetic traditions to offer readers a unique immersion into their present contexts.

In the years that followed the appearance of Monsiváis' anthology, important scholarly books that focused on the chronicles written by

Spanish American *modernistas* were published. The works of Aníbal González (1983), Julio Ramos (1989), and Susana Rotker (1992) contributed to establishing the literary importance of the chronicle and to situating it as a genre that emerged alongside the consolidation of the newspaper industry in the nineteenth century. Like González, Ramos, and Rotker, I do not trace the origins of the chronicle back to colonial times—as did Monsiváis, in his double function as critic and chronicler, for his introduction to *A ustedes les consta*. There is certainly continuity in the implications of the genre since the colony, especially when considering its status as a nonfictional, chronological rendition of events. However, I consider that glossing over the significant differences between a colonial text, usually addressed to a single person of authority, and a journalistic one, which responds to the interests of a broad public and to the requests of an editor, has often reflected a strategic choice to link the genre to a foundational historical moment. In this case, establishing a colonial genealogy for the chronicle enables Monsiváis to address both a public's everyday concerns and broader questions of a national imaginary.

The past decade has seen a growing interest in the Latin American chronicle among U.S.-based academics. Recent books have focused specifically on the genre's critical dimension in Mexico from the late 1960s onward; I can cite as examples the works of Linda Egan (2001) and Anadeli Bencomo (2002), as well as Ignacio Corona and Beth Jörgensen's edition of essays on the contemporary Mexican chronicle (2002). At the same time, various scholars throughout Latin America have revalued the legacies of diverse chroniclers, publishing anthologies and biographies of figures such as Machado de Assis and Clarice Lispector (Brazil), Roberto Arlt and Enrique González Tuñón (Argentina), to mention just a few.[2] Presses, large and small, have also responded to this increased interest by issuing anthologies featuring the works of various chroniclers, selected according to a surprising variety of criteria.[3] As a result, chronicles are easier to find today than ever before, and they will hopefully form a part of many literary conversations, academic or not, for years to come.

The present book strives to contribute to these ongoing discussions on the urban chronicle by focusing on the 1920s and early 1930s, a period that has yet to be established as a formative moment in the evolution of the genre. I propose that these crucial decades, when modernizing media and avant-garde movements dramatically changed how writers and consumers thought about literature, can help us understand how the chronicle has come to play such an important role in contemporary

Latin America. Because the chronicle responds both to aesthetic influences and to concrete events, it was particularly subject to the changes that affected the lives and tastes of city dwellers in the 1920s. It also absorbed and reflected some of the most urgent issues put forth by the avant-gardes of the period—namely, a questioning of cultural hierarchies, a political engagement, a will to provoke a complacent public, and at the same time, a belief in the role of art and literature in the construction of a modern identity. The chroniclers of the 1920s and 1930s were active participants in the cities they described, and their articles combined erudite knowledge, literary style, and media savvy with street credibility. By embracing a plurality of registers, they transformed the heterogeneity of the chronicle into a unique means of intervening in both literature and society. The discursive fluidity of the genre, especially as written in the 1920s, thus paved the way for the self-fashioning of the contemporary chronicler as a mobile subject whose public status results from an agile balancing act between high culture and the urban popular.[4] The growing relevance of the chronicle during this early period would also foreshadow the urban turn taken by cultural conversations in Latin America since the latter half of the twentieth century.

The writers analyzed in the following chapters—Roberto Arlt, Mário de Andrade, Salvador Novo, Alfonsina Storni, and Cube Bonifant—all interacted with the avant-gardes of their respective cities while earning a living by writing regular columns for the popular, or middlebrow, press. They wrote from three cities with an innovative art scene and a strong press industry: Buenos Aires, São Paulo, and Mexico City. These cities grew immensely in the late nineteenth and early twentieth centuries, each in its own particular way. Buenos Aires and Mexico City were cosmopolitan centers with a tradition in journalism and a press industry that was expanding to meet the demands of a growing educated middle class.[5] Mexico City was still reeling from the 1910 revolution; its print culture was on the rise, but most readers still came from higher social tiers. In Buenos Aires, a healthy economy and strong European immigration ensured readers from a broad social spectrum. In the 1920s, São Paulo, having recently grown into an important commercial center through the boom of the coffee industry in the early twentieth century, was new to the cosmopolitan air that had accompanied the journalistic and publishing industry of Buenos Aires and Mexico City for a few years already. It did not have Rio de Janeiro's long tradition of journalism and letters, yet its commercial effervescence quickly transformed it into a symbol of the nation's aspirations for progress and modernity.

Although the chroniclers examined in this study differ in many aspects, all identified with urban modernity, seemed relatively at ease with new media, and found creative ways to negotiate their participation in an increasingly commodified culture.[6] Roberto Arlt once compared his role as a writer to that of a builder, emphasizing his condition as a salaried worker paid to construct texts (*RA II*, 201). This analogy was apt, for in the 1920s and 1930s Buenos Aires expanded and new neighborhoods were sprouting up on its outskirts. In this manner, Arlt proposed himself as an agent of the change that was transforming his city. He didn't simply adapt to urban novelty; he set down the foundations for his city's future. In São Paulo, Mário de Andrade chose to title one of his most interesting columns *Táxi*, thus associating his writing to movement, commerce, and communication. His links to urban modernity were clear: his column doubled as public transportation, offering new ways of crossing the city and instigating a modern way of seeing, mediated by the speed of a motorized vehicle. A series of six articles called *Rádio* (1931), like an article titled "Zeppelin" (1930), also confirmed his awareness of the parallel between communications, technology, and his role as a chronicler. Salvador Novo, like Mário de Andrade, was a great admirer of the radio (*VE I*, 39). What attracted Novo to the radio was not simply the immediacy of its reception, but that it could link him intimately, even sensually, to his audience: anyone wearing slippers or pajamas could listen to him speak while resting comfortably in the privacy of the home. For the women chroniclers studied in this book, Alfonsina Storni and Cube Bonifant, the modern experience through which they negotiated their public writing personas was undoubtedly the cinema. Films provided models for the risky cosmopolitan femininity of the New Woman and, at the same time, created fodder for debates in which stereotypes of modern female sexuality could be confirmed or refuted. In the particular case of Bonifant, the cinema provided a second wind to her journalistic career, and she became one of the most important Mexican film critics of the 1930s and 1940s.

For all of its unsettling aspects, urban change was, for the chroniclers studied in this book, an opportunity to ensure that their columns became necessary reading. They wrote *for* and *about* their city, describing a modernity that had already arrived, even if it was uneven, out of place, incomplete. Only a few years before, Spanish American *modernistas* had both desired and felt threatened by a modernity that they imagined elsewhere: Gutiérrez Nájera had dwelled on the isolated Parisian frivolity of Mexico City; the exiled Martí had described a monstrous New York for a distant Latin American audience. The chroniclers of the 1920s instead used their columns as a means to link themselves with the changes that were affecting, publicly and privately, every city dweller's life. They were not lone mediators between a distant modernity and a local reading public; rather, they seldom traveled and instead strove to give meaning to local urban life. They were the personal interlocutors who walked with their readers through busy streets, accompanied them to cinemas and cafés, shared streetcar rides, read the same newspapers, and heard the same radio programs. Sometimes they even intruded into family gatherings or eavesdropped on conversations, participating in the shared voyeurism and forced intimacy of urban life at close quarters.

As both members and spokespeople of modernizing communities, the chroniclers of the 1920s guided their publics through a constantly changing cityscape and advised on matters of cultural taste, playing an instrumental role in shaping the identity and collective memory of their cities. They took advantage of the chronicle's ambivalent location between literature and journalism, combining *accessibility* (a versatile public persona that appeals to a broad audience) with *intellect* (literary and artistic knowledge). The concept of an *accessible intellectual*, which guides my analysis throughout this book, thus points to how these modern men and women used the supposed "weakness" of short-lived journalism as an asset. They showcased their urban engagement through the daily practice of the chronicle, highlighting similarities with their readers by participating in the shared routine of everyday life. At the same time, their articles fomented a permeable idea of literature in which aesthetic ambition and a growing media industry could collaborate.

In the 1920s and 1930s, chronicles were short articles that commented on various aspects of city life in a light and anecdotal tone. They were written with a self-conscious literary style, often in the first person, and were framed by a signature, if not also a caricature or photograph of the chronicler who penned it. At the time, these articles were intended only for publication in the daily press, and consequently the works of many chroniclers who were widely read in their day remain forgotten in yellowing newspaper archives. Relatively few articles from this early period have been collected and reissued in book form, and most of the editions that circulate today reflect the canonization of their authors through accomplishments in other, more "literary" genres, such as the novel.[7]

With the exception of Cube Bonifant, the chroniclers grouped here were successful in their ventures as novelists, playwrights, or poets. Most of the articles I analyze have therefore been reedited and published in volumes that tend to highlight literary value by diminishing journalistic origins.[8] This study aims to return the chronicle to the newspaper page and reflect on how the incipient industrial media of the early twentieth century shaped the public roles of chroniclers and the modern urban imaginaries they proposed. Even if the chroniclers analyzed in this book were seldom, if ever, read outside their respective countries, their articles dialogued with each other in surprisingly intimate ways and hence deserve to be read comparatively, bringing together different locations, ideologies, and aesthetic orientations.[9] The heterogeneous unity of Latin America, in the context of both urban development and literary tradition, will serve as a starting point in this study of the evolution of the urban chronicle in the early twentieth century.

I read the chronicle as a forum where long-lasting aesthetic influences and immediate occurrences intersect and interact. What at first glance appears to be a simple and accessible article that merely intends to entertain can also yield complex ideological and literary interpretations. Likewise, a politically charged article can appeal to a specific historical moment, yet shy from the lasting relevance of a more complex intervention. As a result, this book proposes a dual reading of the chronicle. While I approach the genre in a literary manner, tracing influences, common rhetorical turns, and stylistic engagements that encompass broad literary traditions (mostly Spanish American *modernismo* and the Argentine, Brazilian, and Mexican vanguards), I also consider the chronicle as a product that is shaped by its original context of production and reception.[10] I am well aware that one could find an inherent tension in the objectives that guide this book. On one hand, I seek to reconstruct the literary genealogy of a dispersed and minor genre that focuses on capturing a fleeting, localized present. On the other hand, I wish to go beyond a literary reading of the chronicle, to explore the very concrete role played by the genre in the shaping of modern urban cultures during the tumultuous 1920s. Yet doing justice to the complexity of the chronicle demands a flexible approach that, like the genre itself, is open to hetero-geneous influences and objectives.

In the following chapter, I present the chroniclers of the 1920s as accessible intellectuals whose relationship to media and literary culture marked a turning point in the status of the chronicle—and the public vis-ibility of chroniclers—in Latin America. I begin with a glance back at the concerns of late nineteenth-century chroniclers, such as Manuel Gutiérrez Nájera, who saw in the rise of the telegraph the exclusion of literary writ-ing from the newspaper. I then show how new media did not necessarily imply a renunciation of literary aesthetics for the generation of chroniclers who wrote during the avant-garde period. Instead, negotiating with an industrial press and with modern communications led to a more flexible repositioning of the genre as part of a daily practice—both of reading and of writing—that shaped the chronicler's role as a cultural mediator who shared everyday city life with his or her readers.

Chapter 2 looks at Roberto Arlt's *Aguafuertes porteñas*, published in the daily *El Mundo* starting in 1928, to explore his relationship with the space of Buenos Aires and his self-fashioning as a spokesperson for and a mem-ber of his urban community. I trace the tensions that surface between the solitude of the writer and the public availability of the chronicler, between a conceptual approach to the city—privileged by the literary car-tography of Buenos Aires that pitched Boedo and Florida, the city's two avant-garde circles, against each other—and a practical one, which Arlt found in Corrientes, a bustling street where a variety of cultural offer-ings mingled indiscriminately. Arlt's persona as an accessible intellectual hinges around his belonging to the lower-class and lower middle-class communities of Buenos Aires. Although he was not affiliated with class privilege, Arlt built his cultural capital through roundabout means. By defending the value of short-lived cultural products, such as the chronicle, Arlt paradoxically used their transient nature to forge an alternative route toward literary permanence.

Chapter 3 focuses on how Mário de Andrade established in his chronicles a relation between commercial texts, nation building, and the city of São Paulo. For Mário, the chronicle revealed a tension between movement and stability, written text and orality, city and nation. Most chroniclers that make up this study sidestepped nationalist preoccupations and privileged the construction of a sense of urban belonging, but Mário was profoundly invested in Brazilian identity. Although he considered the chronicle (or, more precisely, his aptly named column *Táxi*) a vehicle for cultural movement and change, the opportunities this medium provided were limited by the uneven modernization of a country with a large illiterate rural population. The chronicle could not yet permit him to address issues outside the limited readership of São Paulo, and as a result, this writer hesitated to take full advantage of his public accessibility as a chronicler in the way that Arlt was doing in Buenos Aires, a city with a growing population of literate immigrants and potential readers. Nonetheless, Mário's column *Táxi* would strive to rhetorically bridge the gap between the urban and the rural by bringing oral culture and folkloric traditions into the São Paulo cityscape, using them to imagine a dialogic relationship with his readers.

While chapters 2 and 3 focus on the relationship between the chronicle and the particularities of a specific cityscape, chapter 4 approaches Salvador Novo's chronicles of the early 1920s through the prism of the debates that took place in Mexico on the "feminization" of literature after the revolution. In these polemics, virility was equated to "serious" literature that focused on the revolutionary struggle; effeminacy was associated with literature that privileged aesthetic, frivolous, and cosmopolitan matters. These debates indirectly expressed a concern about the growing presence of a popular press that was often feminized in the discourse of the times, a factor that Novo consciously toyed with by fashioning the chronicle as a genre that performed both the "masculinity" of literature and the "femininity" of mass media. Doubling as a temptress or a prostitute, the chronicler chose to strip literature of its aura, making it desirable, accessible, and public. Novo thus designated his mostly upper middle-class readers as the sexual/textual accomplices that helped him open a space for a cosmopolitan literary style in the public sphere. As a flirtatious intellectual who nonetheless remained politically conservative, Novo used his transgressive sexuality as a means to intervene in the major cultural conversations of 1920s Mexico.

The last chapter expands my reflection on the relationship between gender, media, and the chronicle by focusing on two of the few women writers to develop a significant presence as journalists in the 1920s and early 1930s. I analyze articles by Alfonsina Storni (Buenos Aires) and Cube Bonifant (Mexico City), women writers whose chronicles have received little critical attention, even though they published regularly in the press of their day and developed their public personas as modern writing women through their journalism. I discuss the ways in which Storni and Bonifant undermined the supposedly straightforward accessibility of their articles for female readers, and show how they used the chronicle's rhetorical flexibility to critique and challenge the limitations imposed on them as women journalists. I then return to questions of urban space by reading their narrative "walks" through the diverse offerings of their cities as a means to undermine the restricted discursive space allotted to them on the newspaper page. While both Storni and Bonifant share many of the characteristics of the other chroniclers included in this book, their personas as accessible intellectuals with close ties to their readers had ambiguous implications, for addressing a heterogeneous public as women writers was considered both a transgression of journalistic hierarchies and a sign of a dubious morality.

This book does not intend to be exhaustive; instead, it aims to illustrate a distinctive moment in the trajectory of the urban chronicle through a few detailed examples of writers who engaged with the radical growth of Buenos Aires, Mexico City, and São Paulo during the 1920s and early 1930s. Many other chroniclers who began writing during the same decades could be read with similar questions in mind. Their works, however, fall outside the scope of this present project, mostly because I have chosen to limit my focus to writers who dialogued with avant-garde movements while writing for a broad newspaper audience with whom they shared local urban referents. Avant-garde writers such as César Vallejo (Peru) and Alejo Carpentier (Cuba) wrote chronicles regularly during the period studied here, but they wrote from Paris, describing this cosmopolitan city for the readers they left at home. Renato Leduc (Mexico) was a poet before he was a chronicler, and did not begin writing regularly for newspapers until his stay in Paris during the late 1930s.[11] Rubem Braga (Brazil) wrote numerous chronicles on the gritty underbelly of glamorous Rio de Janeiro, yet he remained aloof from the vanguard happenings in neighboring São Paulo. Tarsila do Amaral and Patricia Galvão (Brazil) played starring roles in São Paulo's dynamic avant-garde, yet for various reasons, they did not write chronicles regularly until later in their lives, and hence their articles do not strongly reflect their contributions to the vanguardist conversations of the 1920s and early 1930s.[12] Mexico's Catalina D'Erzell wrote copiously for the press of the 1920s and 1930s, but her chronicles were of a traditional bent and did not reflect on the complexity of urban modernity with the incisiveness of Bonifant's.[13]

While it would be futile to embark on a comprehensive analysis of the evolution of such a dispersed and heterogeneous genre as the chronicle, it is my hope that the different examples explored in the following chapters can shed light on the crucial role that the chronicle played in the development of modern urban identities in Latin America. This book is therefore an invitation to find, in this analysis of the chronicles that circulated during the dynamic 1920s, clues that can guide us in understanding the multiple ways in which urban chroniclers continue to intervene in contemporary Latin American public life.

Cities, Publics, and Urban Chroniclers in Latin America
1920s–1930s

A young man, recently returned to his city after a serious illness, walks through the streets for the first time since his recovery. He observes his surroundings with a mixture of surprise and recognition, as if rediscovering a familiar book read long ago. He strolls by stores opening their doors in the early morning, breathes in the smell of fresh bread from bakeries, and watches the city wake up around him. Trucks and cars honk at each other. Streetcars zoom by. Chauffeurs wash down Cadillacs or Fords, locally nicknamed Fordcitos. Advertisements spring out at him: "*The Leading Hatters*, anyone who tries them recommends them" and "Do you have corns? Take Tanlac." Later that day, newspaper vendors cry out the headlines of the afternoon editions. Students congregate in the Café América, eager to air their views. Others prefer tea at fashionable cafés such as Sanborns or El Globo. In the evening, people mill around cinemas and theaters. As the city quiets down again, street children wrap themselves in the old newspapers of the day before going to sleep.

This description of Mexico City comes from Salvador Novo's "El joven," a chronicle written in early 1920s.[1] By that time, the sensory overload evoked in this text had become an unavoidable part of urban life. Cities were filled unusual sounds, smells, and sights. Newly commonplace technologies mediated encounters between dwellers and accelerated the rhythm of everyday life: motorized vehicles shortened everyday distances, and an increasing number of people spoke on the telephone, went to the cinema, and listened to concerts broadcast on the radio.[2] Consumers from a growing urban middle class were reading for leisure, keen for novelties from abroad and the latest news in their cities. They found the information they coveted in newspapers and magazines that also show-cased the new necessities of modern life, such as Kodak cameras, Gillette razors, and Remington typewriters.

"El joven" confirms the extent to which Latin American modernity of the early twentieth century was associated with the bustle of urban growth. In the late nineteenth century, most Latin American capitals doubled or tripled in population. This expansion heightened the resemblance between large cities, which became synonymous with mobility, novelty, and the possibility of anonymity.[3] Novo's narrator walks through media, advertisements, and commerce in ways that today seem unremarkable, yet these elements indicated urban norms that were still in transition during the 1920s. Local traditions coexisted with cosmopolitan novelties, and new lifestyles shared the streets with a disenfranchised population that remained untouched by the whirlwind of progress.

Despite being driven by the seemingly endless possibilities of urban modernity, Novo's chronicle evokes the experience of a changing Mexico City in terms clearly linked to a tradition of literary representation. Walking is equated to a process of *reading* that, in turn, leads to a practice of *writing*. As the convalescent youth travels through familiar neighborhoods, he reads the material reality that surrounds him and recalls his literary knowledge of the city, joining disparate elements into a narrative that wanders indiscriminately through literature, history, and popular culture. In stream-of-consciousness mode, the narrator comments on ice cream flavors, newspapers, cars, chauffeurs, streetcar drivers, policemen, adver-tisements, pharmacies, drugs, and so on—all intermixed with unexpected scholarly references to Socrates, Freud, José Vasconcelos, Anatole France, Amado Nervo, Plato, and Gabriela Mistral, among others. His physical and rhetorical mobility suggests that writing the city—like sharing its public spaces—is a means of participating in the renovation of an imagi-nary that spans the arts as well as informal traditions and oral histories. Writing about urban life, in this manner, encompasses both a conscious-ness of the city's past and an engagement with its present.

The journey of Novo's young autobiographical narrator locates the chronicle at the intersection between reading and writing, witnessing and creating. By juxtaposing familiar referents with aesthetic innovations, the fragmented eclecticism of the chronicle recreates the experience of living

in a city that was undergoing a radical process of growth and modernization. Such overarching changes in the fabric of daily urban life in the
1920s were, in many ways, reflected in the very nature of the chronicle,
a genre that was changing as much as the environment it commented
on. Like Novo, many young Latin American chroniclers found themselves
negotiating with literature, commerce, and media in transformative ways,
breathing new life into a genre that a few decades before had been
considered by many as perilously in decline.

The Threat of Technology

Manuel Gutiérrez Nájera, Mexico's most prolific chronicler during the
regime of Porfirio Díaz, can help us understand what was at stake for the
genre in the final decades of the nineteenth century. Gutiérrez Nájera
wrote during the 1870s–1890s, decades of intense change in Mexico. He
witnessed the construction of the railroad, the arrival of electricity and the
telephone, as well as the implementation of another artifact of modernity
that would, according to him, have a disastrous effect on his profession:
the telegraph. Gutiérrez Nájera wrote frequently of his fears for the long-
term viability of the chronicle, attributing the impending demise of the
genre to the telegraph and the telegraphic language it encouraged.[4] In
his column *Crónicas de Puck*, published in the daily *El Universal* from 1893
to 1895, the chronicler declared: "The telegram has neither literature,
nor grammar, nor spelling. It is brutal" (*Puck*, 55). In Gutiérrez Nájera's
view, the chronicle was succumbing to the harsh reality of technological
progress and to the commercial demands of the press. Anonymous
reporters were penning more and more articles, and this meant that
privileged chroniclers—who cultivated a personal writing style, had a set
space on the editorial page, and signed their texts—were being displaced
by raw information and advertising. Now that news could travel across
the world via telegraph, local reading publics were getting accustomed to
a speedy turnover of information. There seemed to be no place for the
leisurely—and literary—pace of the chronicle.

In the face of these changes, Gutiérrez Nájera nostalgically opted to
defend the epistolary form. In contrast to the telegraph, whose speed
made it prone to mistakes and premature announcements, he considered
the letter a slow, crafted, and hence trustworthy medium. "The letter was
more honest," he affirmed, and backed up this statement by emphasizing

its proximity to literature: "Letters have their literature." The literary value of the epistolary form lay precisely in its linguistic excess, in its detachment from the economic value of the telegraphed word. Letters were decorated with "these useless phrases, empty, dictated by affection and that fill the soul" (*Puck*, 55). They provoked emotion and suggested a complicity that could not be transmitted by telegraphic language. More importantly, as Aníbal González explains, the telegram indicated "the very negation of style, and, therefore, of the author" (*Journalism*, 89). If the brutal telegram stood for the cold and anonymous writings of reporters, the letter represented the personalized chronicle. While the former was speedy, current, and impersonal, the latter was outmoded, yet intimate and familiar: "[The letter] resembles that aunt I had, old and white-haired, who gave me candy and a scolding from time to time" (*Puck*, 55). But the cozy femininity embodied by the old-fashioned aunt that stood for epistolary tradition—and by analogy, the chronicle—was hardly a match for the telegram. For Gutiérrez Nájera, the letter represented one of the values that modernization was obliterating; a trustworthy, comforting presence, it was nonetheless a nostalgic tradition whose days were counted.

Gutiérrez Nájera's fear for the future of the chronicle was part of a broader concern shared by the writers of Spanish American *modernismo*, many of whom, such as Rubén Darío, José Martí, Enrique Gómez Carrillo, Julián del Casal, and Amado Nervo, also published chronicles regularly in newspapers like *La Nación* (Buenos Aires) and *La Opinión Nacional* (Caracas).[5] The chronicles penned by these *modernistas* often focused on urban settings as ideal locations from which to explore the constantly changing nature of modern experience. While they differed in writing styles (Gutiérrez Nájera was often humorous and frivolous, Martí tended toward gravity), their articles shared a common tendency to smooth over the distasteful effects of modernity through a crafted and aesthetic prose, a move that Julio Ramos has called "decorating the city" (*Divergent Modernities*, 112–147).

The complex and often contradictory relationship that the Spanish American *modernistas* had with modernity has garnered the interest of many scholars in recent years.[6] An in-depth reflection would lie beyond the scope of this book, but a few points should be addressed here. While the *modernistas* were caught in the feverish desire for novelty and progress of the time and desired to make of Latin America a player in the global market of trade, communication, and culture, there is no doubt that the changes that accompanied modernity provoked in them a deep malaise. This discomfort reflects the flip side of technological modernity that critic Matei Calinescu calls aesthetic modernity: the sense of loss and disenchantment that led writers and artists to feel alienated from the rational idea of modernity as progress.[7] In the particular case of the *modernistas*, this unease reflected that modernity was an ambitious project more than an attainable reality, and that it often heightened existing inequalities not only within Latin America but also between Latin America and metropolitan centers such as Paris and New York. The malaise of modernity also pointed to the changing social place of artists and writers, who for the most part could not avoid being drawn into the laws of the market. As Gutiérrez Nájera's lamentations well show, the speed of the telegraph underscored the tensions between art and commerce embodied by the chronicle. The professionalization of writing implied that articles had to be written quickly and regularly, leaving little time to polish journalistic texts despite the aesthetic ambitions that guided their authors. Gutiérrez Nájera's parallel between the epistolary form and the chronicle was thus more wishful than descriptive. The chronicle was "literature under pressure," as Susana Rotker has aptly pointed out (*Martí*, 43). It served as a daily reminder of the professional writer's dependence on the press, not only to make a living but also to establish a long-lasting relationship with the reading public.

That Gutiérrez Nájera channeled his unease with modernity through the journalistic chronicle can be explained by the origins of the genre, which coincided with the growth of the press during the late eighteenth and early nineteenth centuries.[8] At that time, the press transitioned from being an artisanal project to becoming a systematized commercial industry with a rigidly structured division of labor. Newspapers had been closely associated with the state and state opinions, but they then began to rely on the profit principles of commerce. Writing for the press thus became a profession intrinsically linked to the market and to the informative demands of journalism.[9] In Latin America the transition from a state-run press to an independent commercial press was hardly as clear-cut as in Europe, yet by the 1880s the workings of an industrial media were being established.[10] Spanish American chronicles of the late nineteenth century are considered an offspring of the French *chroniques,* the short, entertaining, and informative articles that described the major happenings of Paris in the newspaper *Le Figaro* during the 1850s, as well as the British sketch of manners. Spanish

American chronicles also take from the genre of *costumbrismo*, practiced by Mariano José de Larra in Spain and Ricardo Palma in Peru, which aimed to document lifestyles and traditions with a realist eye.[11]

In Brazil, Machado de Assis was the most prolific and respected chronicler of the late nineteenth century. He became an indispensable reference for twentieth-century Brazilian chroniclers, such as Mário de Andrade, Carlos Drummond de Andrade, and, later, Clarice Lispector and Rubem Braga, among others. He wrote mostly on Rio de Janeiro and played a crucial role in establishing the strong tradition of chronicle writing now associated with the city.[12] The chronicle had a slightly different evolution in Brazil from that in Spanish America. This can be only partly explained by its isolation from the anxieties of nineteenth-century Spanish American *modernistas,* such as Gutiérrez Nájera, since, at the turn of the twentieth century, chroniclers such as Olavo Bilac had frequently aired similarly disparaging views on the effects of industrial journalism and new technologies on literature.[13] Machado's unique status as a founding father of Brazilian letters, as well as his decades-long dedication to the chronicle, is perhaps most helpful in explaining why the genre was recognized for its literary value earlier in Brazil than in Spanish America.[14] While the tension between journalism and literature embodied by the chronicle might not have been as contentious in Brazil as it was in Spanish America, the genre nonetheless occupied a similarly low place in the literary hierarchy. It was considered a "minor" genre devoid of the permanence and ambition of other literary forms.[15]

The *modernistas* hardly ranked the chronicle at the same level as their "truly" literary endeavors, such as poetry, but the genre arguably played as important a role in their writing lives as it did in Machado's. More than half of José Martí's and two-thirds of Rubén Darío's publications were chronicles (Rotker, *Invención*, 15). In many ways, the daily toil of journalism heightened the *modernistas*' yearning for a protected literary sphere in which they could devote themselves to aesthetic concerns.[16] Ramos has argued that because of the chronicle's dual ties to aesthetics and commerce, the genre became a battleground in which the *modernistas* defended and affirmed the discursive autonomy of literature.[17] This defensive stance was, however, paradoxical, as modern journalism facilitated in many ways the formation of *modernista* literary aesthetics. The maligned telegraph, for instance, enabled the correspondent José Martí to write from New York and publish in Buenos Aires and Caracas. Not only did the newspaper enable the *modernistas* to broaden their readership, but it also served as a sounding board for poetic experimentation.[18] While not all chroniclers opposed the professionalization of writing implied by journalism, those who saw its advantages, as did Martí, considered the chronicle a means to support a literary project that was imagined far from the newspaper page.[19]

The antagonism most *modernistas* felt toward commerce and technology was not without contradictions. They defined themselves in opposition to mercantile interests, even as they contributed to the market of cultural commodities, and they felt that the chronicle, in great part because of its location on the fringes of literature, would be the first to fall as a result of the losing battle that they were waging against the rationalization of writing. These apprehensions were succinctly expressed by Gutiérrez Nájera in another of his oft-quoted laments, this one dating from 1893: "The chronicle is an anachronism" (*Puck*, 7), he affirmed, boldly defining the genre against its name. The term "chronicle," after all, comes from the Greek *chrónos*, or "time," and refers to the relation of events in a chronological manner. Gutiérrez Nájera here purposefully chose to erase the chronicle's journalistic responsibility to inform, privileging the creative, literary side of the genre over its referential and commercial aspect. He thus left the chronicle at a crossroads: it could either keep pace with the industrial modernity of the newspaper and sacrifice its literary voice, or keep its literary autonomy and lose its contemporary relevance. In either case, it seemed as if the telegraph—and the irreversible progress it symbolized—was dramatically broadening the distance between literature and the public sphere.

Yet Gutiérrez Nájera was premature in foretelling the death of the chronicle. The genre might have been frail, like his white-haired aunt, but it did not die on time. How, then, did the chronicle survive the threat of technology? Or perhaps more accurately, how did chroniclers manage to move beyond the rhetorical dead end proposed by Gutiérrez Nájera?

Surviving the Telegraph

The example of Renato Leduc, a Mexican chronicler and a contemporary of the writers studied in this book, offers a possible answer to these questions. Leduc began training for his first job in 1912. At the age of fourteen, he entered the Escuela Nacional de Telégrafos (National Telegraph School) to learn a profession that promised a stable future. This experience opened his interest in communication and language: he later became a poet and a chronicler. The telegraph, which for Gutiérrez Nájera had posed a threat to literature, became for Leduc a crucial first step in a literary and journalistic

career that spanned more than fifty decades.[20] Throughout his writing
life, Leduc playfully brought together popular referents with literary
forms, an aesthetic approach he attributed to his experience as a telegraphist for Pancho Villa's troops during the Mexican Revolution. As did
Leduc, many chroniclers of the avant-garde period overcame the perceived
impasse of technological progress by exploiting—rather than deploring—
the heterogeneous nature of the genre they practiced.

The chroniclers writing in the early twentieth century were part of a
generation that was more at ease with technology than were their predecessors. Many writers, like Leduc, saw the potential of newly commonplace
media and turned to them as metaphors to define their journalistic projects.
The Brazilian João do Rio, for instance, entitled his volume of articles on
Rio de Janeiro *Cinematógrafo* (1909). His compatriot Pedro Kilkerry named
his column on Bahía *Kodak* (1913). Instead of indicating a threat, these signs
of modernity came to symbolize an innovative and creative approach to
urban experience. Embracing new technologies was not a renunciation of
the literary quality of writing. Instead, it indicated a will to conceive of the
chronicle as a type of literary production that functioned best when open to
the influence of novelty.[21] Incorporating recently commonplace technologies into a renovated urban imaginary was also a means of presenting both
the reading and the writing of chronicles as intrinsic parts of daily life. If
chronicles were as readily available as films or radio programs, then there
was no reason for the genre ever to become obsolete.

For the chroniclers of the 1920s and 1930s, writing for the daily press
meant adapting to the needs of a diverse and not necessarily erudite audience.
It also meant developing a constant awareness of a mixed middle-class
reading public in which women played a growing role as cultural consumers,
and in which a single text had to appeal to readers with varying levels of
education. While this complicity with a broad readership had its pragmatic
reasons—selling texts—it also manifested an avant-garde stance regarding
the autonomy of art. In *Theory of the Avant-Garde*, Peter Bürger describes
the institution of art in bourgeois society in terms of its autonomy, or "its
(relative) independence in the face of demands that it be socially useful" (24).
European avant-garde movements would attack this definition by proposing
art as an expression that cannot be dissociated from "*the life praxis of men*"
(49, my emphasis). This association between art and praxis questions the
autonomy of art and implies that artistic creation and reception are no longer
perceived as individual processes but rather as collective happenings (51–54).
In a similar manner, the chroniclers I read here chose to intertwine the

process of writing with the flow of everyday life, challenging the distinction between a communal experience and the solitary gaze that characterized the bourgeois conceptualization of the artist.

While the creation and reception of art were certainly not perceived as a collective experience by all Latin American avant-garde writers—the Chilean Vicente Huidobro famously thought of the poet as "un pequeño Dios," a small god who operated alone—the daily practice of journalism and the shared process of reading and writing it implied did contribute, in the case of certain writers, to the shaping of their particular avant-garde posture. Journalism, in fact, fomented vanguardist literary aesthetics in early twentieth-century Latin America, as had been the case with *modernismo* in the late nineteenth century. This seems obvious if one thinks of avant-garde visual experiments with collage and typography, clearly reminiscent of the printed press and advertising. Yet the interpenetration of popular urban culture and the avant-gardes was not simply about borrowing ideas from mass media and taking them to a "literary" realm. Journalism was central not only to the gestation of many vanguardist literary projects but also to their publication and reception. A cursory glance at the original publications of many Latin American vanguardist writers reveals a remarkable intimacy between avant-garde aesthetics and an incipient mass media. Many works of the period that are now considered canonical were published alongside mundane articles on fashion or frivolous social happenings, and there is no doubt that they also had to respond to the editorial criteria of the newspaper or magazine that originally published them. Emblematic figures within these literary and artistic movements also contributed regularly to the urban popular as journalists. To give just two examples, the Estridentista Arqueles Vela wrote chronicles on fashion for *El Universal Ilustrado* in Mexico City while Borges published weekly columns in the women's magazine *El Hogar* during the 1930s in Buenos Aires.

In great part because it was considered an ephemeral genre intrinsically tied to the rhythm of modern life, the chronicle became a site for the development of an avant-garde sensibility that went beyond boundaries of genre. Despite its obligatory referentiality, it was not always easy to separate the chronicle from other avant-garde literary projects. The generic ambivalence of Novo's "El joven," to return to our opening example, is hardly coincidental. It has been alternatively described as a chronicle, a short story, and an essay. This ambiguity confirms that chronicles written during the avant-garde period of the 1920s could not necessarily be dissociated from a literary project they enabled elsewhere. Rather, chronicles were themselves sites of innovation where literary prestige could be developed, even if they circulated surrounded by markers of popular media such as photographs, advertisements, or caricatures. My reading of the chronicle therefore differs from the notion of commodity culture as a homogenizing force through which "literature ceases to be an instrument of emancipation and becomes one of subjection" (Bürger, *Theory*, 54). The chroniclers who wrote during avant-garde times negotiated with commercial culture to express idiosyncratic experiences, to make room for creative engagement, and to draw in consumers as active participants in the formation of modern urban cultures.

Reading the chronicle as a transparent expression of vanguardist thought, however, has its pitfalls. Vicky Unruh has aptly pointed out that the Latin American vanguards rarely critiqued the institution of art with the intensity of their European counterparts: "Institutionalizing literary traditions was a relatively recent phenomenon in Latin American cultural life, and, in some cases, the vanguardist movements themselves became enmeshed with the construction of national literatures, or canons" (*Vanguards*, 7). This was especially the case for Mário, who was committed to defining and fomenting a national culture that bridged urban modernity with autochthonous traditions.[22] In addition, the chronicle could not afford to be as contentious as other avant-garde expressions, such as manifestoes, for it had to respond to the added parameter of the market. Chroniclers could not overtly offend readers and risk alienating them; they had to both court and provoke their audience.

My optimistic reading of the chronicle does not intend to idealize what the daily practice of journalism meant for writers during the 1920s, nor does it wish to simplify the transition between *modernismo* and the avant-gardes by overemphasizing the idea of a drastic rupture between these movements.[23] The chroniclers who wrote during the avant-garde period continually crossed what Andreas Huyssen has called "the great divide" between art and mass culture, yet they did not necessarily put into question its existence.[24] While they might have flirted with the market, they did not resolve the tension between art and commerce that had caused so much concern for their predecessors, nor did they fully embrace the conditions that journalism imposed on their writing life. On the contrary, they often recalled the complaints of the *modernistas* by describing journalistic work in terms of quantity rather than quality and by measuring the worth of their articles in terms of kilos or kilometers.[25] But such complaints added an irreverent edge to the tension between art and markets, for surviving Gutiérrez Nájera's deadly telegraph meant finding a way for commerce and technology to work in favor of literature. Poking fun at texts "for sale" was a gimmick through which the chroniclers of the 1920s reinforced their presence in the public limelight, associating with a modern culture industry without sacrificing literary ambition. They needed to make do, and took liberties along the way.

During the 1920s and early 1930s the culture industry was still in an early period of growth in Latin America. Because its parameters were still taking shape, it maintained the flexibility and spontaneity necessary to enable a creative effervescence that would be unique to this period. During this window of opportunity, the urban chronicle would become a site for a productive negotiation between avant-garde ideas and a growing culture industry.[26] The writers studied in this book worked from the chronicle as a third space that unsettled the dichotomy between art and commerce, too often defined as straightforward. They exemplified a shift between perceiving mass culture as an enemy and seeing its potential as an ally, a change that coincided with the rising visibility of commerce and advertising in the printed press.[27] The chroniclers of the avant-garde period did not define themselves as private men of letters who invested the newspaper with a moralizing or educating function.[28] They considered themselves part of a broad system that produced consumer-oriented media, and as such, they used journalism as a means to promote and reinforce a public status.

In the 1920s, chroniclers became journalistic celebrities who conspicuously displayed their texts as one of the new necessities of a modernizing lifestyle, thus fashioning themselves as public figures that city dwellers could recognize and follow. Each article served as an advertisement for its author, cultivating readers of newspapers and magazines who might potentially be interested in a chronicler's forays into other genres, such as poetry or fiction. If these writers constantly recalled the influence of commerce and portrayed writing as a business more than as an artistic endeavor, this admitted disadvantage served as a means for them to gain public visibility and remain relevant.

The Rhetoric of Accessibility

The chroniclers of the avant-garde period consolidated their writing personas through an acute awareness of their readership, responding to— and encouraging—an urban public's growing taste for leisure reading. By working from the condition of the genre as a mix of art and markets, the chroniclers of this period presented themselves as *accessible intellectuals*. I will here expand on the ramifications of this oxymoronic term, for it can suggest broad conceptual guidelines through which to conceive of the chronicler as a particular type of public figure. The notion of *accessibility*, in particular, provides a useful concept through which to theorize the relationship between the chronicler, the written text, and urban culture.

By virtue of their profession, chroniclers are easy to access. They are recognizable figures that frequent public spaces and attend important social or political happenings. They appear approachable and interested in listening. Their public availability extends to the texts they write: their articles can be bought in newsstands and kiosks or lie discarded on streetcars and park benches waiting to be picked up by an inquisitive passerby. Chronicles thus coexist with the flow of urban public life. They are brief and can be read while waiting at the barbershop, at a café, or on the way to work. They are regularly exchanged in the cultural market of the city, and many can buy them, for "accessible" also means they are affordable, unlike books, whose production and distribution in Latin America lagged far behind that of newspapers in the early twentieth century and whose purchase often demanded a significant investment from readers.[29]

Accessibility makes the chronicler vulnerable to the unforeseen happenings of public life. He or she must be willing to comment on the unexpected with originality and speed. This vulnerability extends to the contested space of the chronicle in cultural production. As Brazilian critic Antonio Cândido has noted, the chronicle "fica perto de nos"; it remains close to us, its readers (*A crônica*, 13). Near the streets and daily life, the chronicle remains open to philosophical and political discourses, serving as a liaison between erudite ideas and a diverse public when it isn't simply aiming to amuse. Accessibility thus works in contrast to what is not accessible, that which requires training or specialization to be understood. The chronicler does not have the time to become a specialist through study; he or she needs to become one on the spot, delving in—and promptly leaving—discourses such as literature, anthropology, sociology, history, art, or film criticism. The same flexibility is expected of the reader, who must also be open to novelties, willing to be amenable in tastes and preferences. The experience of writing chronicles, like that of reading them, is thus conditioned by the fragmented nature of the modern urban experience. Journeying through the city is analogous to leafing through the heterogeneous pages of the popular press, in which diverse tones, subject matters, and aesthetics coexist and interact. The chronicler, like the reader, must be receptive to interruptions, disjunctions, and contaminations.

The chronicle, in my reading, is more than a genre.[30] It is also a *practice* whose double function encompasses both the writing and the reading of texts, be they journalistic, literary, or even urban.[31] In *The Practice of Everyday Life*, Michel de Certeau uses the term "practice" to describe, as active, acts of consumption that are often considered passive. A practice is an "art of making"; like the daily activities of walking, reading, or shopping, it is an action that produces without appearing to do so. De Certeau refers to a practice as a silent production, one that "produces without capitalizing, that is, without taking control over time" (xx). These words could almost be describing the chronicle itself. In its original, newspaper-based form, the chronicle closely followed daily events, describing them without the benefits of hindsight and without aiming to outlast the day. Like all dwellers, urban chroniclers were some of the many "users" who consumed the culture of the city and shared its public space while following rules that they had not established. Even if for a chronicler the practice of the city overlapped into another, that of writing, the similarities of these activities were notable. Working as a chronicler was a daily occupation that responded to a system of production—journalism—that was mediated by commercial rules that an individual chronicler could not bypass. The chronicler's relationship to the newspaper was thus similar to his or her relationship to the city, a fact that encourages us to consider urban practices and the practice of the chronicle as mutually enriching, and inevitably intertwined, activities.

Thinking of the chronicle as a practice brings to the forefront the civic potential of a genre intrinsically meshed with the minutiae of urban life. The writers studied here were well aware of their agency as chroniclers and worked it to their advantage, even if they would not necessarily use the genre as a platform for political intervention, as would a subsequent generation who began writing during the 1960s and 1970s.[32] Instead, the chronicle of the 1920s functioned in a less targeted manner, working to place culture— and more specifically reading—at the center of an urban collectivity. For many city dwellers of the early twentieth century, reading newspapers or magazines was a normal part of the day. For this reason, the chronicle involved a practice of writing that imagined, and even generated, a communal practice of reading. Through these journalistic articles, city dwellers could access texts that in turn influenced ways of being in, or reading, their societies. But also, as a light genre that above all aimed to cultivate an audience by entertaining consumers, the chronicle helped keep the machinery of cultural production well-oiled. It was not simply about introducing an audience to the offerings of their city but also about inserting the chronicle as an indispensable part of this shared culture. The point of contact between chroniclers and anonymous readers, what brought them together, was the broadest common denominator: everyday urban life, shared public spaces, and the daily paper.

The chronicle's improvisational quality reflects its tactical nature, for the genre functions through what de Certeau has called "the art of the weak." A maneuver that cannot be autonomous, a tactic improvises, seizing "the chance offerings of the moment" that are fleeting and need to be constantly reappropriated (*Practice*, 37).[33] Similarly, the chronicle needs to be spontaneous and to respond to the unexpected. As Mexican chronicler Luis Urbina once put it, "a chronicler is at the mercy of events" (quoted in Monsiváis, *A ustedes*, 39). What a chronicle describes one day might be obsolete the next, prompting the writer to improvise and, in turn, encouraging readers in search of novelties to come back for more.

The tactical nature of the chronicle as an "art of the weak" plays out most notably in the case of women writers. Women in the 1920s and 1930s were becoming established as regular readers and independent cultural consumers, but very few had become public figures as writers. Those who published chronicles, such as Alfonsina Storni in Buenos Aires and Cube Bonifant in Mexico City, underhandedly included avant-garde themes and aesthetics within supposedly sentimental writing that was explicitly directed to female readers. At the time, the participation of women in writing was distinctly linked to performance culture and, hence, to the creation of a public persona that depended on the theatrical manipulation of an image.[34] The press of the period was still uncertain as to how "feminine" texts should be presented, and thus women chroniclers had to find ways to negotiate their writing personas and stake a place on the newspaper page from the out-skirts of both literary and journalistic authority. While male chroniclers had to learn to target a growing audience of women—this was often difficult for Arlt, who took pleasure in riling the many middle-aged housewives who assiduously read his column—women chroniclers had to work alone in a male-dominated profession and, if they wanted to be read beyond the "feminine" page, had to learn to downplay any conspicuous gender markers in their voice.

Yet the tactical negotiations of the chronicle, especially in regard to gen-der, did not apply only to the works of women writers. The chronicle's ambivalent location between the seriousness of literature and the frivolity of mass media was often reflected in the gendered terms used to define the genre, as was already apparent in the kind and feminine aunt who for Gutiérrez Nájera represented the chronicle. In fact, Gutiérrez Nájera had addressed a specifically female audience when sharing his fear for the future of the genre, as was the norm in his column *Crónicas de Puck*. While this female addressee is revealing of the nature of his audience, which presumably included bourgeois women of the Porfirian elite, the chronicler's choice also highlights the perceived displacement of literature in favor of industrial "easy" writing, which was frequently associated with the feminine.[35] These feminine attributes were occasionally extended to the male chroniclers themselves. While this was certainly the case with Gutiérrez Nájera—the dandy *modernista* who frequented the elegant Jockey Club and was invited to the parties of the elite—the most relevant example is that of the openly homosexual Salvador Novo, as we will see in chapter 4.

If chroniclers were often perceived as operating from a "weak" position due to their dependence on journalism, this disadvantage also extended to their restricted access to the markers of cultural prestige. None of the chroniclers studied here came from a privileged background. In many ways, they were autodidacts, formed in Latin America without the luxury of travel or a university education. They acquired literary knowledge independently or informally with the help of mentors. While Arlt discovered European classics in cheap translations, Mário de Andrade always cringed at exclamations from fellow artists: "You never went to Europe!" or "You say this because you've never been to Paris!" (*Vida literária*, 170).[36] In Mexico City, Novo was a self-proclaimed local expert on magazines published abroad, discovering international trends by leafing through old copies of the *Saturday Evening Post,* the *Literary Digest*, or the *Country Gentleman*. In 1921, Cube Bonifant lamented never having reached even Veracruz, the port of departure for Europe, and Alfonsina Storni was faced with the harsh reality of having to earn her living, only entering the literary sphere through the middlebrow activity of poetry declamation. These chroniclers formed part of a middle class conscious of its identity outside the nation's elite. Like most chroniclers of the nineteenth century who also originated from the middle class (or from the lower class, in the case of Machado de Assis), they represented a type of intellectual striving to find self-definition outside expected artistic norms, such as high culture, a Parisian experience, and the disengagement from economic rewards. Because they could not afford to travel for amusement, their few trips were paid for by the publication they wrote for or, in the case of Novo, the government.[37] These experiences matched the condition of their readers, the city dwellers who relied on imported knowledge from abroad, often filtered by the individual tastes of hurried editors and haphazard translations.

Chroniclers were self-made intellectuals who worked from what was at hand, showcasing the potential of what their readers could also access: the heterogeneous life of their city. On many levels, chroniclers are comparable to Antonio Gramsci's model of the organic intellectual. Unlike traditional intellectuals who were historically considered autonomous (such as the clergy), organic intellectuals are, for Gramsci, minor figures who participate actively in practical life and cultivate strong roots in their local communities. They are organizers and educators who lead others, giving coherence and function to a social group by enabling critical awareness.[38] In *Representations of the Intellectual*, Edward Said points out that the Gramscian notion of the intellectual as a professional whose work is related to the production and distribution of knowledge can lead to overspecialization and hence to the anonymity of intellectual work (9). Said doesn't contradict Gramsci; rather, he highlights the personal element that makes each intellectual's voice particular. In Said's view, an intellectual must have the crucial ability to make himself or herself understood to a broad nonspecialized audience, a vocation that must be "publicly recognizable" and that, as such, hinges around the performative quality of an intellectual's interventions (13). Similarly, the impact of chroniclers in the everyday lives of their cities revolves around the cultivation of a recognizable public persona. By speaking to—and for—others in a subjective voice, chroniclers reveal their idiosyncratic humanity and establish an intimate relationship with their readers. Chroniclers might well be critical commentators, but their subjectivity ensures that they are not impartial ones. Their close involvement with the city and its commerce, like their desire to be read, gives them what Michel de Certeau has called the "blind spots" of the practitioner, who writes the urban text without being able to read it and who cannot see the big picture of city life (*Practice*, 91–110). It is precisely through the compelling individual contexts that shape—and invariably limit—their perspectives, that chroniclers are able to foment the potential for critical awareness among their readers, recalling Gramsci's notion of "integral" journalism: "one that seeks not only to satisfy all the needs (of a given category) of its public, but also to create and develop these needs, to arouse its public and progressively enlarge it" (*Reader*, 383).

Unlike Domingo Sarmiento in Argentina, Andrés Bello in Chile, or later José Vasconcelos in Mexico—intellectuals who wielded or aspired to political power—chroniclers often spoke from the margins of literary and political authority. This contrast between chroniclers and more traditional *letrados* can also be considered in light of the difference between the chronicle and the essay, perhaps the quintessential *letrado* genre, which usually presupposes a more structured distance between the intellectual and the national subject than the one at stake between the chronicler and his or her public. For instance, José Enrique Rodó's canonical essay *Ariel*, written in 1900, is structured around the figure of Prospero the teacher (a stand-in for the essayist himself), who lectures a group of students without engaging in any type of dialogical interaction. In the newspapers and magazines of the 1920s, however, the term "intellectual" did not have such clear-cut connotations. Instead, it was loosely used, and chroniclers occasionally chose to adopt the label, to visibly disregard it, or even to do both. Notably, the same fluidity that applied to the use of the term "intellectual" in the middlebrow publications where chroniclers wrote also applied to literature. In the writing culture of the time, the label of *literato* (literary writer) was used loosely, and it applied both to recognized writers and to those who aspired to recognition.

The chronicle's rhetoric of accessibility stems from what Walter Benjamin would call its lack of "aura." Benjamin uses the term "aura" to describe the authenticity of a work of art, which is endowed with "the unique phenomenon of distance, however close it may be" ("Work of Art," 222). Mechanical reproduction has the effect of reducing this distance. The original can "meet the beholder halfway" and be reactivated through the process of reception (220). Likewise, the chronicle works to attract readers, asking them to be active and sharing with them the credit for the encounter between text and public. Benjamin contended, with radical enthusiasm, that mechanical reproduction had the potential to eliminate the difference between author and public. He suggested that when newspapers permitted readers to send letters to the editor, they paved the way for a substantial transformation through which "at any moment the reader is ready to turn into a writer" (232). What instead happened in the 1920s was that the aura of the work of art, of the written word, was transferred to the writer, the literary and journalistic celebrity who was frequently photographed and interviewed in the press. In this manner, the aura of a work of art was extended to the few public figures who could access the mechanism of publication that enabled the construction of a broad readership. The growing industrial press of the 1920s, if used properly, was not only a means to forward a specific civic or cultural project; it was also a self-serving instrument to cultivate and achieve a form of cultural prestige.

Benjamin's optimistic view of the chronicle's potential lies at the base of the rhetoric of accessibility, but the equality and agency it promises have their limits. Oftentimes, the rhetoric of accessibility can be tricky and provocative, even unsettling. A lighthearted tone can be slippery and elusive. Easy access can also be a promise that obscures something else beyond simple reach, a performance that playfully pitches together competing meanings and points to divisions in reading publics that were becoming more and more heterogeneous.[39] This elusiveness kept the chronicle's latent literariness just beyond the reach of a broad audience, but always in view, slyly hinting at the very exclusivity that these chroniclers publicly minimized. The chronicle might well invite identification from its readers, but the celebrity of the chronicler who penned it was hard to come by, a distinction that was frequently—if underhandedly—reinstated.

The Chronicle and Literary Modernity

The underlying argument of this book is that that the urban chronicle played a crucial role in the configuration of Latin American literary modernity during the early twentieth century, in ways that would have long-term consequences for the genre. As an institution, literature has often been considered inherently at odds with modernity. A literary work is often defined by its permanence; it possesses that unique quality which makes it timeless.[40] Modernity, on the contrary, is defined instead by what is short-lived; it implies a continual process of renovation and reinvention. How, then, did the chronicle contribute to define the place of literature during the first decades of the twentieth century in Latin America, a time when rapid urbanization was shifting conversations on national identity from the countryside to the city, and when growing mass media were mediating encounters between literary writing and the public? Could the chronicle successfully combine the transience of modernity with the longevity of literature?

Let us think this through by returning to the opening example of Novo's chronicle "El joven." In more ways than one, this text captures the quintessential modern experience, for it is narrated through the perspective of a convalescent youth, and as Paul de Man has convincingly argued, modernity can be defined as a perpetual state of convalescence: everything is always fresh and novel and the immediate present is privileged over the past (*Blindness*, 157). But in Novo's chronicle, this experience of novelty is also inextricably liked to the familiar, the durable, the *literary*. The city is compared to a well-known book: "His city was like a book opened for a second time, which he noticed more today, and to which he had not paid much attention before" (*VE I*, 239). Novo shows us that returning to the familiar is also a process of discovery, that novelty can be found in tradition, and that literature can be apprehended in the same way as signs of modernity such as advertisements, new media, and the industrial press. Literature indicates not just a work of art and its recognized status; it designates *a way of seeing* mediated by both literary context and the very concrete manifestations of urban popular culture.

The chronicle, as Novo's text can show, contributes to literary modernity in two ways. First, it proposes an idea of literature that is not exclusively focused on the long-term value of a specific text. Literature, like modernity itself, is here considered part of a more diverse aesthetic experience. As such, it can be continually renewed and renovated through the constant publication and circulation of short-lived texts such as chronicles. Although each article can be ephemeral and hence risks being forgotten, the chronicler's aesthetic vision retains a continuous, yet always novel presence in the public eye. Second, by taking literary value beyond the status of a particular text (as a work of art), the chronicle broadens the scope of the lettered city to encompass both literary and urban popular culture. The chronicle, seen in this light, played an instrumental role in expanding—and even, to a certain extent, in *democratizing*—the lettered city in the early twentieth century. At the crossroads between discourses, the genre served as a bridge that inscribed the literary into other discursive fields, letting it speak through an incipient cultural industry that responded to pragmatic—and not simply aesthetic—referents. In an echo of Néstor García Canclini's argument that "consumption is good for thinking," the chronicle performed an exercise in citizenship that introduced literature into the public sphere informally.[41] Instead of making a grand entrance—as through a book—the chronicle ushered literature into the public sphere through the back door: the newspaper page.

The chronicle of the 1920s thus stretched the definition of literary culture to a point of discomfort, finding its locus precisely in this uneasy contact between contradictory impulses: that of fitting within a highly codified discourse—literature—while also defining itself through a continual process of renovation and reinvention conditioned by the rhythm of fast-paced cities. If the chronicle can embody the contradictory aspects of literary modernity, that is precisely because it is at once a genre and more than that, a tradition and a continually reimagined daily practice, an aesthetic way of seeing and a documentation of the present. Throughout the following chapters, my analysis purposefully slips back and forth between a focus on the chronicle and on the chronicler, text and author, for the genre's ambivalent location in cultural production overlaps into the public roles of the writers who practiced it. Being a chronicler did not simply imply being a writer; it also pointed to a way of acting in the public sphere, of participating in ongoing conversations, of intervening in the debates that were shaping Latin American modernity of the early twentieth century.[42] As Paul de Man points out, "the ambivalence of writing is such that it can be considered both an act and an interpretive process that follows after an act with which it cannot coincide" (*Blindness*, 152). This is perhaps all the more so for the chronicler, who needs to retain on a daily basis the enthusiasm of the convalescent who rediscovers a familiar city, while at the same time developing the critical distance needed to imagine and convoke a recurring reading public.

Chapter 2

A Common Citizen Writes Buenos Aires
Roberto Arlt's *Aguafuertes porteñas*

> I have the weakness of believing that the language of our streets, the language in which you and I converse in the café, in the office, in our intimate exchanges, is the real language. That I shouldn't employ such terms to talk about lofty subjects? And why not, my friend? I am no academic. I am a man of streets, of barrios, like yourself and so many others.
>
> —Roberto Arlt, "How Would You Like Me to Write for You?" *El Mundo*, September 3, 1929

Roberto Arlt did not consider himself an academic. Instead, he called himself a man of the streets, of neighborhoods and cafés, just another citizen among the many who lived Buenos Aires during the 1920's. In his numerous years as a chronicler, Arlt put this boast into practice, letting few areas of his city escape his sharp gaze and witty comments. Most of the works of this prolific journalist, novelist, and playwright, today recognized as one of Argentina's most influential writers, are set in the gritty reality of modern Buenos Aires. While Arlt's daily journeys through this city in search for topics for his chronicles clearly shaped his conception of urban life, journalism also framed his writing in a very literal way—many of his works, regardless of genre, were marked by the urgency of a deadline and written in the noisy confines of the newspaper room.

Arlt began writing chronicles for the newspaper *El Mundo* when it first came out in May 1928, and he continued publishing in it on an almost daily basis until his death on July 26, 1942. His column first appeared with the title *Aguafuertes porteñas* and his signature in August 1928, but he would alter its name various times throughout the following years. After the fall of President Hipólito Yrigoyen and with the military dictatorship of the 1930's, Arlt became highly critical of the government's abandonment of the working classes. He used his chronicles, now entitled *Buenos Aires se queja* (Buenos Aires Complains), to denounce social problems such as urban planning, hospital hygiene, and the poor conditions of schools.[1] When he traveled as a correspondent for *El Mundo* in 1935–1936, his titles varied according to location: *Aguafuertes africanas*, *Aguafuertes asturianas*, *Aguafuertes madrileñas*, and so on. With his return to Buenos Aires, the column changed from *Tiempos presentes* (Present Times) to *Al margen del cable* (On the Margins of the Newswire), where he privileged international issues such as World War II.

Arlt's first articles are firmly grounded in the everyday life of Buenos Aires and, more specifically, in the practice of specific cultural cartography of the city. They portray the middle and lower working classes, describing anecdotes set in bustling streets such as Corrientes and Florida, newly developed neighborhoods, cafés, cinemas, and parks. They bear witness to the social and political conditions of the time by depicting urban characters and their changing lifestyles: the photographers of public plazas who were losing their clientele due to the new popularity of portable Kodak cameras, the unemployed who frequented cinemas during the day to postpone returning home empty-handed, middle-class families and their attitudes toward marriage, would-be movie stars and the promoters of the new acting schools that preyed on their Hollywood ambitions. Arlt's Buenos Aires was a diverse space where the traditional middle class coexisted with newly settled immigrants and where a variety of accents and expressions could be heard on the streets.

"Aguafuertes porteñas," the title of Arlt's first column in *El Mundo*, already evokes the complex cultural status of the chronicle. An *aguafuerte* is an etching, a painstaking and original rendering of, in this case, Buenos Aires street life.[2] But etchings are also prints, which links them to the press and to the possibility of their mechanical reproduction and distribution. By the 1920's, etchings were hardly innovative in comparison with the increasingly popular medium of photography. Instead, they suggested a slightly archaic stylization that photography did not connote by combining traditional techniques of representation with the novelty of serial reproduction. An etching, or *aguafuerte*, thus pinpointed the duality inherent to the genre of the chronicle. As a literary text, the chronicle is unique and crafted, but it is also intended for reproduction and distribution to a broad public. The dual connotations suggested by the term *aguafuerte* also applied to Arlt's writing persona. As one of the prominent figures of the rising newspaper industry, he negotiated his access to established literary circles as well as to the popular world of Buenos Aires. Working from a contradiction that juxtaposed *agua* (fluidity, movement) with *fuerte* (intellectual rigor, reliability), accessibility with intellect, this chronicler offered himself as a mediator who synchronized literature and culture with the daily flow of city life.

In the epigraph to this chapter, taken from the chronicle "How Would You Like Me to Write for You?" Arlt addresses his readers in the first person, with a personal tone that sets up his column as a stage for the creation and affirmation of a writing persona. He claims to believe in the authenticity of street language, yet the forcefulness of his declaration indicates a tension between the vernacular and a language that circulates in contained erudite circles rather than in the streets. In a gesture characteristic of many avant-garde tracts, Arlt establishes a dialectical relationship with formal knowledge that contrasts the spontaneity of the Buenos Aires vernacular, or *lunfardo*, with a structured and stagnant cultural sphere.[3] Through this contentious choice, Arlt pointedly acknowledges his notorious lack of formal education—he often claimed to have studied only until the third grade—but reformulates this limitation into an asset that confirms his capacity to express himself for a general public without sacrificing his innate ability to broach lofty subjects.[4]

Arlt imagines his audience as an urban collectivity to which he himself belongs, a sweeping gesture that recalls Benedict Anderson's description of the "deep, horizontal comradeship" that accompanies an imagined community such as a nation or, in this case, a city (*Communities*, 7). The chronicler and his readers are defined through their urban belonging: a crowded cityscape becomes a means for mutual recognition, an indication of a specific cultural identity. But this claim to a shared citizenship, in fact, indicates Arlt's belonging to a specific social group: the lower- and middle-class newcomers to Buenos Aires who were occupying the city's outskirts, the barrios—neighborhoods where *lunfardo* was the street language of choice. This localized bond adds a twist to Anderson's cultural paradigm, in that the city rather than the nation mediates communal identification.

A far cry from the rural gaucho that was making a comeback as the emblematic national subject in the works of Ricardo Güiraldes and Jorge Luis Borges, the characters that populate Arlt's chronicles are representative of a cultural citizenship defined by the street culture of the capital instead of the Argentine pampas.[5] There is thus a counterintuitive exclusivity to the imagined community that this chronicler appeals to. Through a calibrated gesture, he singles out a new population that was seldom represented and appeals to a localized urban citizenship. The "friend" Arlt addresses is clearly not the traditional *letrado*, or intellectual, but instead a middle- or lower-class *porteño*—a resident of Buenos Aires—who, like the chronicler himself, did not identify with the cultural elite of the period.

The question Arlt asks of his readers, "How would you like me to write for you?" supposes a personal exchange between equals, as if a group of acquaintances rather than a variety of strangers were reading his articles. But this suggested closeness promptly reveals a distance between the chronicler and his readers. In this article, Arlt displays his public role more than he asks for advice, leaving no opening for true interaction and keeping intact his agency as a writer. He both sidesteps and invokes the binding "horizontal comradeship" that unites him with his imagined community of readers, alternating between a communal voice and an individual one. Arlt's query points to the difficulties of speaking to a broad and diverse public and confirms that a successful chronicler needed to develop a versatile persona, as his changing attitudes toward his readers, often ranging from solidarity to mockery in a single text, showed on a daily basis. But the question Arlt asks his readers leads us to others. How did he balance his singularity as a chronicler with his belonging to an urban community? Was it possible to write about and for the city and still remain a common citizen?

The following pages approach these questions by focusing on Arlt's *Aguafuertes porteñas*, written in the late 1920's and early 1930's.[6] At this time, he was beginning to establish his voice as a chronicler who commented on urban life for the city's own residents, constructing his writing persona through a rhetoric of accessibility that highlighted his continuous—if sometimes reluctant—presence in the public sphere. Arlt expressed his accessibility to the public by emphasizing his vulnerability to his city's events, his lack of economic autonomy, and his reliance on popular media to obtain the recognition of a broad audience. But revealing these discursive and material limitations also provided Arlt with a roundabout route toward literary and intellectual authority.

City of Strangers

As Arlt tells his readers, his daily journeys through a crowded Buenos Aires were hardly pleasant experiences. He had to survive pushes and shoves on the streetcar, had to make his way among hordes of pedestrians on the sidewalks, and could rarely find a quiet place in the city when he most desired it.[7] In many of his *aguafuertes*, Arlt complains about the omnipresence of crowds and the impossibility of finding solitude in his city, revealing how daily routines were affected by the enormous growth of this capital in the first half of the twentieth century. From the late nineteenth century to the 1950's, Buenos Aires received a large and diverse European population; Spaniards, Italians, Poles, and Czechs, among others, began to occupy new neighborhoods on the outskirts of the city.[8] In 1936, more than 36 percent of the residents were foreign; immigrants and children of immigrants reportedly contributed to around 75 percent of the city's growth. The city's population grew rapidly, going from 677,000 inhabitants in 1900 to close to two million in 1930 (J. L. Romero and Romero, *Buenos Aires*, 251).

New technologies responded to the city's expansion. In the 1920's the streetcar extended its routes to accommodate new neighborhoods, and electric lights replaced the gas and kerosene system.[9] The radio first appeared, and long-distance wireless communications were established.[10] As a result of the country's solid economic growth, more people began to participate in diverse aspects of the urban economy. New restaurants and cafés were opening, as were theaters, cabarets, and cinemas. Leisure sports, such as soccer, boxing, and golf, were also becoming increasingly fashionable among a population interested in keeping up with European and North American trends.

Another sign of change in Buenos Aires came with the multiplication of newspapers and magazines published on a broad scale. Bartolomé Mitre's newspaper *La Nación*, the most respected publication in the late nineteenth century, had seen competition rise in the form of magazines such as *Caras y Caretas*, *Mundo Argentino*, and *El Hogar* and popular sensationalist newspapers such as *Crítica*. *El Mundo*, where Arlt's column was regularly published, was a good example of the new mass publications that circulated in the city. It was Buenos Aires' first tabloid, a showy newspaper with large captions, flashy photographs, and catchy mottoes such as "Lo bueno, si breve, dos veces bueno" (What's good, if brief, is twice as good). The editors took pride in the simplicity and readability of a publication molded around reader response: "We want to create an agile, quick and synthetic daily that permits the reader to perceive, through direct images and chronicles that are brief and yet sufficient, everything that occurs and everything that can, in any manner, provoke the interest of the public" (quoted in Saítta, Introducción, 19). Easy to carry around and to read in the café or on the subway, *El Mundo* was ideal for the city dweller on the go, and it quickly became the third most-read of Buenos Aires' morning editions. In October 1928, a mere five months after the first issue was released, 40,000 copies circulated through the city. By October 1929 the number was already up to 127,000.[11]

Arlt's *Aguafuertes* quickly became a trademark of *El Mundo*, and the success of his column was so great that on the days it appeared, the newspaper sold significantly more issues. The editors quickly took advantage of this popularity and began publishing his articles on random days to encourage readers to purchase the newspaper regularly. Arlt ended up publishing his column almost daily on one of the first pages of the paper, surrounded by local news, advertisements, and usually above a comic strip. Although Arlt's column was never accompanied by etchings, it usually included caricatures illustrating the topic of the day. As the chronicler's prestige grew, so did the size of his name, which by 1930 was prominently featured above each article.

Buenos Aires' rapid growth clearly affected the cultural and social role of the newspaper, probably in a similar manner to Peter Fritzsche's reading of Berlin in 1900:

> With the daily influx of hundreds of newcomers, the break-down of older neighborhoods and turnover of residents in newer ones, and the widening physical separation of home and workplace, a great crowd traversed the city more frequently and for longer distances than ever before. These strangers found in newspapers indispensable guides to unfamiliar urban territory. Indeed, newspapers found a mass readership only with the emergence of big cities. (8)

If, like Berlin, Buenos Aires had become a city of strangers, the newspaper could function as a renewable guide to an ever-changing city and the chronicle as a personalized insight on everyday urban life. In articles such as "Demolitions Downtown," to give just one example, Arlt details the construction work that was dramatically altering the center of the city

Arlt's name rakishly displayed at
the top of his column. *El Mundo*,
September 3, 1930.

One of Arlt's first signed columns,
accompanied by a caricature.
El Mundo, September 1, 1928.

in the 1930's.[12] With a vocabulary tinged by imagery of violence, war, and destruction, Arlt documents an unsettling period of transition with both fascination and dismay. He describes a newly unfamiliar environment and the reactions of the workers, policemen, and housewives who wander the dusty streets. In this manner, Arlt attests to the irreversible nature of urban change and, at the same time, provides a reassuring continuity for his readers through his regular column.

Arlt's wanderings, as recounted in his chronicles, were frequently unpredictable. Many of his articles begin with an interruption, as if, surprised by unexpected events, the chronicler lost both the privacy of his walk and the thread of his narrative.[13] One can't help but wonder why Arlt includes such moments in his early chronicles instead of simply erasing them, especially as in the late 1920's he was invested in establishing a visible and confident presence in the journalistic scene. While this strategy astutely encouraged the empathy of Arlt's readers, it also signaled the chronicle's tense place in Buenos Aires' culture, giving us an insight into the sometimes risky discursive balancing act that the chronicler needed to accomplish on a daily basis.

In the chronicle "Youths Who Were Born Old," for instance, Arlt begins his narrative with a hiatus: "I was walking today along the streets Rivadavia and Membrillar, when I saw on the corner a young lad with the face of a *jovie* [old man], the bottom of his overcoat touching his shoes, his hands buried in his pocket" (*RA II*, 35). The chronicle's first sentence begins by promising a supposed journey along busy Rivadavia, but the itinerary does not hold its course. The article becomes instead a meditation on young men who look old before their time, as if a chance encounter had infiltrated Arlt's writing project.[14] The interruption in this chronicle is included within the textual frame of the narrative, but it is also framed within the city's geography, at the corner of Rivadavia and Membrillar, a referent rich with cultural connotations.[15] Rivadavia, one of Buenos Aires' main thoroughfares, links the center to the suburbs. It has been described by Ezequiel Martínez Estrada in *Radiografía de la pampa* as "long like a telescope" (145) and supposedly lacks the charms that make a city stroll tempting (Gorelik, *Barrio*, 58). In Borges' short story "Sur," this same street marks the threshold between the newer Buenos Aires and its older neighborhoods.[16] The street references in Arlt's article give his readers a means to follow his interrupted trajectory, but perhaps more importantly, they reconfigure the map of Buenos Aires by drawing the margins into the city's cultural panorama. It is no coincidence that Arlt stages a discursive interruption on a thoroughfare where the city's various sectors come into contact, as if the heterogeneity of the city had overflowed into that of his chronicle.

Arlt's narrative mapping of his encounters shares many characteristics with the gaze of the nineteenth-century Parisian flaneur, for whom the city symbolized all that was disorderly about modernity. When faced by the rapidly changing scenery of the city, many flaneurs reacted by textually organizing their surroundings, fragmenting the cityscape into more comprehensible areas. Walter Benjamin emphasizes the organizing purpose of the flaneur's gaze with the example of Delveau, who "claimed that he could divide the Parisian public according to its various strata as easily as a geologist distinguished the layers in rocks" (*A Lyric Poet*, 39).

Delveau traversed the city while "botanizing on the asphalt," transferring an empirical observation of nature to the urban realm without putting his structuring system into question. Writing about the city implied recognizing the unknown and cataloguing it. In a similar manner, Latin American chroniclers at the end of the nineteenth century also saw the city as a space that condensed problems of representation. For many Spanish American modernists, describing the city was an exercise in control, a means of imposing a narrative order on a space in constant fluctuation: "Representing the city was one mode of superseding it, reterritorializing it," comments Julio Ramos (*Divergent Modernities*, 123). Seen in this light, writing is much like an instrument of panoptic surveillance that can impose a symbolic—and perhaps even literal—order on urban space.[17] Strolling through the city, in what Ramos has termed "the rhetoric of strolling," permitted the modernist chronicler to establish narrative junctures between disarticulated and unsettling fragments of the cityscape.

By clearly mapping out the location of his interruptions from the start of his chronicles, Arlt appears to continue the tradition of the flaneur, as many of his predecessors writing in the nineteenth century had done. Arlt's articles often create archetypes of people that can be found in specific neighborhoods, much like the *physiologies* that were popular in the Paris of the 1840's, and he frequently wrote about forgotten or ignored urban areas, registering the changes and losses that accompanied modernization.[18] For these reasons, his *aguafuertes* are often likened to the genre of *costumbrismo*, a tradition related to the chronicle that designates texts describing popular customs and lifestyles in a light, picturesque, and satirical manner.[19] This tradition gained recognition in the nineteenth century, with contributors such as Mariano José de Larra in Spain, and in Buenos Aires the modernist Enrique Gómez Carrillo and José S. Alvarez, who wrote in the weekly *Caras y Caretas* under the pseudonym of Fray Mocho.[20] When describing cities, *costumbristas* took note of the changes affecting them, documenting traditions at risk of being obliterated by a changing cityscape, proposing through their archetypes an often moralizing representation of a country and its customs (Rama, *Lettered City*, 62–63).

Even though Arlt shares many characteristics with Latin American modernist chroniclers, his writing nonetheless differs in important aspects of the flaneur's relationship to public space. The Spanish American modernist flaneur, especially as analyzed by Ramos, surveyed the city with a gaze that tended toward the authoritative. Arlt, however, stages a vulnerable belonging to the city. Writing emphasizes, more than mitigates, the discomforts inherent to his experience.[21] Rather than smoothing out unsettling urban change through an organizing "rhetoric of strolling," Arlt's walks hinge around moments in which *the city* interrupts the chronicler and appears to take over the narrative. Such unbalancing interferences signal, in Arlt's writing, a pivotal part of urban belonging and serve to establish his chronicles as part of a daily practice of Buenos Aires street life. Surprises and interruptions might be disorienting and anxiety-provoking, but Arlt does not react by retreating to a familiar urban past. On the contrary, he embraces the unsettling. Buenos Aires is home precisely because it has become an unrecognizable city of strangers.

Arlt's chronicles do not translate a popular world for an erudite audience, as had many nineteenth-century *costumbrista* texts. Instead, Arlt writes for the very same characters that populate his articles. The middle- and working-class citizens that appear in his column are also his readers; the culture he describes is thriving rather than endangered. The chronicler's diverse reading public was made possible by Buenos Aires' high literacy rates: by 1930, only 6.64 percent of the city's residents could not read (Sarlo, *Modernidad*, 18). This shift away from a picturesque form of *costumbrismo* also confirms the changing intellectual geography of Buenos Aires. Rather than a center writing about its margins, Arlt's *aguafuertes* consolidate working-class neighborhoods as new spaces from which representation and writing could originate (Gorelik, *Barrio*, 43). Such dramatic changes affected the already debated cultural space allotted to the chronicle. No longer a vehicle for nostalgia, as it often was for Spanish American modernists, the chronicle, in Arlt's practice, both witnessed and fomented urban change.

Arlt's depiction of Buenos Aires was one that consistently looked toward the future. In great part, Beatriz Sarlo has argued, this was because Arlt was a new Argentine for whom "the value of the present eliminated all concern about betraying a history in which [he] had no part" (*Imagination*, 39). The chronicler was himself an emblem of the newcomers he wrote about—and for. His father was born in the Prussian province of Posen, his mother in a small Italian village, and neither had Spanish as a native tongue. Arlt's name was notoriously difficult to pronounce: "It is not pleasant to demonstrate to people that a vowel and three consonants can be a last name," he laments jokingly in a chronicle titled "It Is Not My Fault" (*RA II*, 42). The dissonance of his name points to both his foreign origin and his belonging to the lower end of the social strata.

In the 1920's the elites and the traditional middle class were increasingly fixated on last names, drawing a line between "decent" families—those with a criollo name—and the families of recent immigrants, such as Arlt's. But *la gente decente*, the mainstream majority who could not pronounce the chronicler's last name, was itself becoming a minority in the greater picture of the Argentine capital. And the chronicle, a genre bound by its journalistic ties to privilege the minutiae of the present over a grand narrative of the past, was proving remarkably apt as a means to coalesce the experiences of a diverse population that was reinventing itself on new soil—or, perhaps more accurately, on new asphalt.

A Flaneur with a Salary

Many nineteenth-century modernist chronicles had served as guides to the luxurious excesses provided by city life, mitigating the unsettling aspects of modernization by recalling the glamorous lifestyles of European and North American cities. José Martí's chronicles from New York, for instance, were directed toward cultivated readers of *La Nación* in Buenos Aires who were interested in discovering the novelties of life abroad. They provided his readers with a showcase that displayed the seemingly endless extravagances of modern life (Ramos, *Divergent Modernities*, 90). In Arlt's chronicles, however, luxurious goods are stale more than they are tempting, for the consciousness of being a salaried worker makes this journalist feel uncomfortable in the spaces destined for luxury. If the Baudelairean flaneur feels at home in the Parisian arcades, protected from the multitudes in what Susan Buck-Morss has called a flaneur's "reservation" (*Dialectics*, 344), Arlt feels alienated by the "terror of the electric light" in Buenos Aires' elegant Pasaje Güemes and bored with the endless display of commodities beyond his reach: "It has been forever since I've set foot in the Pasaje Güemes. I don't know if due to boredom or lack of cash," he admits (*RA II*, 207). Arlt feels marginalized from the purchasing power symbolized by the Pasaje Güemes, as probably did many of his readers. Inaugurated in 1915 as Buenos Aires' first arcade, the Pasaje Güemes, located off the chic Florida Street, was modeled on European arcades and housed some of the city's most expensive boutiques. Arlt compares this arcade to New York, a city that he frequently associated with modern commercial extravagance.

The Spanish American *modernistas* had often made the metonymical slip between luxury—or excess—and literature, so as to distance themselves from the utilitarian requirements of journalism. If one follows a similar logic, Arlt's feeling of exclusion from high commerce might extend to the sphere of writing, as if literary recognition were as unattainable as the goods this chronicler could not afford. Arlt himself equated literature to luxury numerous times, the most striking example being found in his somewhat bitter prologue to *Los lanzallamas* (The Flamethrowers), where he describes the difficult task of writing the novel while also publishing a daily newspaper column: "I proudly affirm that writing, for me, constitutes a luxury. I don't dispose, as do other writers, of income, time, or sedating government employment. Earning a living by writing is laborious and hard. Even more so if when one works, one thinks that there are people for whom the preoccupation of finding amusement produces strain" (189).

Comparing literature to luxury, and hence linking it to commerce, signals the alternative route taken by this writer to further his literary ambitions through his journalistic practice. In many of his articles, as in the above-mentioned novel *Los lanzallamas*, Arlt privileges the informal transactions that are left out of a regulated economic system.[22] Thieves, scammers, and petty delinquents constantly surface in his writing, an interest that can be traced back to his professional experience on the crime beat for the sensationalist daily *Crítica* in 1927. *Aguafuertes* such as "Philosophy of the Man Who Needs Bricks," "The Jovial Parasite," and "Conversations between Robbers," to name just a few examples from Arlt's early articles, all describe characters that improvise and reach their objectives through indirect and unethical means, bypassing the formal economy represented by locations such as the Pasaje Güemes. Much like the petty delinquents who operate outside the formal economy and often appear in his texts, Arlt circumvented the literary establishment through unorthodox maneuvers. A scavenger of eclectic knowledge, his indiscriminate taste led him to devour technical manuals and cheap translations of books ranging from Dostoyevsky's novels to Ponson du Terrail's series on the adventurer Rocambole, all while building his cultural prestige through the alternative route of journalism.

The daily toil of writing a newspaper column might have been a hardship that limited Arlt's freedom to explore other genres, but this salaried labor was not without potential rewards. In his *aguafuerte* "Cómo se escribe una novela" (How a Novel Is Written), Arlt reveals the very literal interconnectedness of literature and journalism in his daily life. He writes both his fiction and his articles in the same space: the newspaper office. As he works on *Los lanzallamas* late one night, his editor stops by and asks him to write a chronicle about writing a novel. Arlt responds, "With pleasure (it doubles as publicity)" (*Aguafuertes*, 325), and proceeds to showcase his own literary endeavors through this chronicle. This pragmatic alliance between journalism and literature confirms that the motor of commerce drives both, even if to varying extents: the chronicle here works as a bridge that reduces the distance between mass publications, such as the newspaper, and literary works that circulate on a reduced scale. Instead of being a display window through which to discover a distant modernity, the chronicle lets Arlt unveil his own "merchandise": his forthcoming novel.[23]

Money was a constant worry for Arlt, and the recognition he craved as a writer was not divorced from the expectation of economic rewards. He cared about selling his books and regularly entered local writing competitions that carried a monetary prize.[24] A successful novel was an almost magical promise of a financial boost out of poverty, an optimistic objective that recalled the chronicler's fascination with inventions. In the 1920's and 1930's new technologies had initiated a subculture of self-taught scientists and inventors in Buenos Aires. Arlt, who spent years trying to perfect and patent a formula to create a pair of unbreakable stockings for women, prominently figured among them. Mastering new technologies promised an unlimited potential for discovery, knowledge, and, of course, the tempting possibility of making money fast.[25] Unfortunately for Arlt, his stockings were never successful—he was unable to reconcile practicality with aesthetics, at least in the scientific realm—and he had to continue to rely on his meager but dependable income as a columnist.

Aguafuertes such as "How a Novel Is Written" offer the chronicler's readers the privilege of going behind the scenes of writing. Although Arlt frequently chose to present himself as a rebel who was dismissed by a literary elite that considered him a "bad" writer with no knowledge of spelling or grammar, this did not mean that he did not write from an advantageous position.[26] Arlt often overstated the hardships of his condition as a salaried chronicler. He was, in fact, quite comfortable in the journalistic establishment. He was one of the newspaper's star writers, and his high visibility in the paper's front sections meant that he often got his way with his editors and had substantial freedom in his assignments. Furthermore, *El Mundo* often heralded Arlt's accomplishments in other genres by regularly announcing the appearance of his new novels and the staging of his plays. Few other writers in Buenos Aires could count on such a mechanism to promote their works, but even this could probably not erase the painful fact, for Arlt, that few literary critics complimented or even acknowledged his work.[27]

Arlt's description of the street Florida in a February 1929 chronicle underscores, perhaps even more so than his piece on Pasaje Güemes, his unease with the literary establishment. This luxurious street, according to Arlt, does not have much to offer: "its only virtue is that of being the channel for our urban boredom" (*Aguafuertes*, 223).[28] This harsh dismissal is all the bolder given Florida's significance during the Argentine vanguards. During the 1920's this elegant street in the city's center had given its name to the avant-garde *grupo Florida*, recognized for its aesthetic interests. Arlt's choice to privilege a material description of Florida

Advertisement for *El lanzallamas*. *El Mundo*, November 3, 1931.

without acknowledging its literary significance highlights the chronicler's relationship to Buenos Aires as one mediated by the daily practice of the city, which he shared with the broad spectrum of readers who followed his column. The importance of being intimate with the streets of his city was such for Arlt that he reportedly ceased speaking to Borges when the latter admitted he was unaware of the location of the popular neighborhood Villa Luro.[29] Along with Villa Pueyrredón and Saavedra, Villa Luro was one of the far western neighborhoods located away from the city center that marked the edge between urban and rural worlds (Walter, *Politics*, 84). Regardless of whether this anecdote is accurate, it gives us an insight into how the cartography of Buenos Aires connoted a distinct hierarchy that was social, cultural, and even literary. It also indicates that Arlt's familiarity with the city's marginal neighborhoods was for him both a source of pride and a glancing reminder of his position as an outsider to the capital's intellectual circles.

Even if Arlt distanced himself from the Florida avant-garde, this did not mean that he associated whole-heartedly with the rival Boedo group, which was more socially and politically engaged.[30] While both these vanguardist groups had a notable urban focus, the relationship they imagined between the city and artistic discourse was radically different, and the very locations that gave name to the movements—a commercial street for the former, a working-class neighborhood for the latter—testify as to how literary positions were codified in the city's geography. Arlt remained peripheral, yet connected, to both the Florida and Boedo factions. Before writing for *El Mundo*, he had worked as a secretary for Florida's Ricardo Güiraldes, and a fragment of his novel *El juguete rabioso* (Mad Toy) was published in the journal *Proa* in 1925. At the same time, he remained closely linked to the Boedo group through his social commitment and his closeness to figures such as Elías Castelnuovo and the brothers Raúl and Enrique González Tuñón, who were journalists for the daily *Crítica*. Perhaps more importantly, Arlt was also close to Antonio Zamora, founder of the publishing house Claridad; located on the street Boedo, it published many of Arlt's novels during the 1930's.

Arlt's aloofness from both the Florida and Boedo literary terrains, like his dismissal of fashionable Pasaje Güemes, helps explain why this chronicler identified with one of Buenos Aires' most idiosyncratic streets: Corrientes. In the Buenos Aires of the 1920's, "Corrientes was one of the neutral territories where the culture of the center and marginal cultures crossed paths and worked together without conflicts" (J. L. Romero and

Romero, *Buenos Aires*, 17). Corrientes was a street populated with bars, such as the Bar Domínguez, and cabarets and cafés, such as La Helvetica and Los Inmortales, landmarks for the creation and diffusion of the tango.[31] This street was an in-between space where the canonical *Martín Fierro* and pornographic books were sold side by side, where writers, actors, musicians, prostitutes and dandies could cross paths at all times. Florida might be sterile, rigid, and boring, but for Arlt, Corrientes burst with sensuality and life:

> Fallen among the grand cubical buildings, featuring panora-mas of chicken "on the spit" and golden halls and cocaine stands and theater lobbies, how delightfully brazen is by night Corrientes street! How lovely and how idle! More than a street it seems a living thing, a creation that oozes warmth through all of its pores; our street, the only street with a soul in this city; the only one that is welcoming, truly welcoming, like a trivial woman and prettier for that. (Appendix 1)

In this glowing description, Corrientes is compared to a thriving body, welcoming and even flirtatious. This street is exciting because it permits both literal and conceptual freedom without demanding much expense from this salaried chronicler. Corrientes was a street that Arlt could afford to frequent regularly, each time discovering new knowledge and creative stimulation. This is also where his articles and his novels circulated freely and where, throughout the 1930's, his plays were staged at the Teatro del Pueblo.[32] It is not coincidental that Arlt identified with Corrientes, for this street's eclectic commercial life represented a hybrid third space where literature and popular culture circulated as equals. This diverse space was the ideal home for the chronicle, not only because it brought together disparate cultural elements, but also because it promoted the circulation and accessibility of diverse texts to a broad audience. The implications of this street's name could hardly have escaped Arlt. Even though the street was named after the capital of the Argentine province of the same name, the term "Corrientes" connotes both something common (as opposed to exclusive) and a current that flows and circulates continually. Both inter-pretations imply multiple meanings, while recalling the flow and move-ment promised by the title of Arlt's column *Aguafuertes*.

By comparing the street Corrientes to "a trivial woman," Arlt links the experience of popular culture to the sensuality of superficial, short-lived encounters. The street has erotic potential only insofar as it is separated from the traditional mores of the middle class and the responsibilities connoted by family, marriage, and bourgeois standards of feminine behavior. This imagined sexual freedom also connotes conceptual flexibility. Locations such as Florida and Pasaje Güemes do not engage Arlt, precisely because, unlike Corrientes, they do not permit the discursive slippage from which he chooses to write. While Arlt reinstates the stereotypical equation between the feminine and popular culture in his description of Corrientes, what is most notable here is his implicit assumption that his imagined community of readers would, like him, be seduced by the advances of a "trivial woman." I will return to Arlt's conceptualization of gender later in this chapter, but I briefly wish to point out how Arlt imagines a homosocial bond with his readers, implicitly obscuring the importance of women in his regular reading public. This evocation of a male community recalls Arlt's description of himself as "a man of the streets, of barrios, like yourself and so many others" (quoted in the epigraph), in which Arlt identifies with the masculine street culture of Buenos Aires' new neighborhoods. For this chronicler, flaunting his masculinity was a means of revendicating popular, as opposed to elite, culture, and his references to the feminine, like the female characters that occasionally surface in his chronicles, are often simplistic and stereotypical.[33] Unlike Salvador Novo, who, as we will see in chapter 4, played with gender ambivalence as a means to question cultural hierarchies in postrevolutionary Mexican culture, Arlt chose on the contrary to reinstate—and even overwrite—his masculinity in order to defend the vigor and relevance of the popular.

Despite the vagabond quality that Arlt admires in Corrientes, the chronicler's journeys through Buenos Aires were never expressions of idleness. Arlt's walks through the city were instead a part of his daily professional routine, even if he took to the streets with no predetermined schedule or direction. This chronicler was a flaneur with a salary, exemplifying Benjamin's conception of the flaneur as someone whose experience of the city was intrinsically linked to journalism and the literary marketplace (*Arcades*, 446). For these reasons, there is a significant difference between Arlt's city walks and the idle meandering that Borges, a writer who has become emblematic of the Argentine literary establishment, described in works such as *Fervor de Buenos Aires*.[34] In many of Borges' poems on the city, such as "Buenos Aires" or "Límites," the poetic subject wanders quiet streets alone in search of remnants of traditional Argentine lifestyles. The suburban Palermo neighborhood becomes a point of departure for self-reflection, a backdrop for a nostalgic journey that never interferes with the poet's meditations, remaining instead a well-behaved mirror in which he searches for an epiphany. In Arlt's *Aguafuertes*, however, the city—and the professional responsibilities it is a constant reminder of—enables no escapism. Arlt's Buenos Aires is not that of quiet, leafy Palermo; it is that of the intense, bohemian nightlife of Corrientes, where unexpected happenings continually draw the chronicler into the rhythm of the city.

Arlt's vulnerability to the streets recalls the writing of another of his contemporaries, Oliverio Girondo. In *Veinte poemas para leer en el tranvía* (Twenty Poems to Read on the Streetcar), this poet expresses a sensual abandonment to the hallucinating experience of the modern city. In many ways, Girondo's poetry radicalizes the exuberant sensuality that Arlt finds in Corrientes. This collection has as its protagonist a "hands-on" poet who opens his senses to the erotic experience of Buenos Aires. He walks it, smells it, touches it, and even absorbs it: in "Apunte callejero" (Street Sketch) he muses, "I wonder where I will keep the kiosks, the streetlamps, the passersby who enter my pupils." The poet's city strolls, like the chronicler's, leave him exposed to urban surprises. But while Girondo fuses erotically with the cityscape in an intimate exchange that leaves no room for other participants, Arlt describes his encounter with Buenos Aires as a group experience shared by an infinite number of dwellers, even if they are, implicitly, a male group seduced by a flirtatiously feminine city.[35] Arlt is not *the* observer of the city; he is an observer simply by virtue of being a resident. Instead of defining him exclusively, this condition helps him lose particularity among the crowds. Girondo's abandonment to the city is a sensual expression of leisure. A flaneur by choice and for pleasure, he was independently wealthy and never needed to publish chronicles to make a living.[36] Arlt's journeys were instead part of his journalistic work. For this professional wanderer, the city became a routine as well as an adventure, a condition that brought him closer to his readers, salaried workers like himself, for whom an urban journey marked the beginning and the end of the working day.

Despite their differences, the city is, for both poet and chronicler, a place where reading takes place. Girondo's "Twenty Poems to Read on the Streetcar" suggests that traveling the streets is an experience analogous to the reading of poetry. Girondo's poetic gaze is conditioned by movement, and in Arlt's chronicles, the act of reading, like that of writing, also follows the rhythm of the city. But in a calibrated play between the conceptual and the literal, Arlt's chronicles displace the poet's metaphor. His articles truly circulate in the streets and could easily be read by anyone riding a streetcar to work.

Streetcar Spectacles

Every public experience of Buenos Aires, however banal, was for Arlt a spectacle in the making. Any passerby could potentially become an observer and even, unwillingly or unknowingly, part of a show. The comparison of the city with a spectacle is hardly new to the tradition of the flaneur, for it was frequently used to describe the contradictory feeling of alienation and recognition provoked by urban modernity. When considered in the context of mass media, the concept of the "spectacle" has generally been read critically. In *La société du spectacle* (The Society of the Spectacle), Guy Debord proposes the spectacle as an alienating system of mass media where a passive audience lacks control over its means of production. Arlt, however, wrote some forty years before Debord and had not reached the latter's pessimism. On the contrary, Arlt's chronicles frequently proposed the incipient mass media of the period as an engaging experience that contributed to a modern way of perceiving the city, while also enabling the formation of an active community of citizens.

Like many of his contemporaries, Arlt was at ease with media such as film, already a commonplace presence in Latin American cities in the early twentieth century. By the 1920's a growing segment of urban populations could afford the cinema regularly. In 1923, Buenos Aires had around 137 cinemas, and though most films shown were from Hollywood, a few local productions made their way to the screen (Walter, *Politics*, 95–96). Popular media such as film, radio, and, of course, the press were beginning to shape city dwellers' interpersonal relationships. Most city dwellers mutually recognized each other as consumers of popular culture. They frequented theaters, saw the latest films, listened to radio programs, read the morning and evening papers, and were exposed to the same cosmopolitan fashions. Arlt was himself an admirer of the cinema who occasionally wrote film criticism for *El Mundo* and even considered taking over that section of the paper in the early 1930's.[37]

Conceiving of the city in terms of a modern spectacle such as the cinema enabled Arlt to invoke an audience of readers who could recognize themselves through his column.[38] A look at his February 1930 article

"The Cross-eyed Lover" can help elucidate this process. In this chronicle, Arlt is riding through Buenos Aires in a streetcar when he becomes mesmerized by an odd-looking couple: "I was sitting on the streetcar today when my gaze tripped on a couple composed of a robust cross-eyed man, with tortoiseshell-framed glasses, and a blondish young woman, with the face of a pseudo movie star" (*RA II*, 61). The streetcar suddenly becomes a parody of a theater or cinema, with the passengers doubling as public. The parallel between public transportation and the cinema is remarkably apt. Unlike the space of the streets, where encounters can be chaotic, the streetcar is organized and protected. It implies a mode of apprehending the city defined by speed, regulated stops, and having to view other passengers in a confined space for long periods of time.[39] Viewing the city through the windows of a moving vehicle implies a cinematographic way of seeing the city, conditioned and defined by fleeting images. A ride in a streetcar also implies a temporal marker, a beginning and an end. Like a film playing to an audience in a cinema, a ride necessitates a public contract, tickets must be purchased, and certain rules of behavior are expectedly maintained. As a service that in the late 1920's could be purchased for ten cents, the streetcar provided a group experience affordable for the majority of Buenos Aires' working- and middle-class population.[40]

The oddly mismatched couple described by Arlt is so absurd that it attracts the gaze of all the streetcar's passengers, who find themselves accomplices in observing a grotesque seduction:

> The cross-eyed man did his seducing work with his damaged eye[;] with the other, he watched over the passengers who were biting their lip so as not to smile, and no one could escape the curious emotion provoked by this *fulano* [guy], well combed, well bathed, who wielded his "cross-eyedness" like a tremendous combat weapon destined to soften the heart of the blonde. (*RA II*, 62)

As with a film or a theater performance, there appears to be an obvious distinction between the show and its public. The passengers who observe this couple are normal observers; they are neither cross-eyed nor ridiculous. This process of definition by exclusion has often been highlighted as one of Arlt's strategies to homogenize Buenos Aires society following the standardizing impulse of *costumbrismo*. Once again, we find a group's identity sealed through the exclusion of undesirable elements, whether they be academics (as with the "I am no academic" cited in the epigraph) or, in this case, a cross-eyed seducer. The comic scene transforms all the streetcar's passengers into voyeurs who appear hypnotized by this unlikely show, an apparent homogeneity that might suggest, if one were to read this scene in the light of Debord's arguments, that the spectacle is the only point of contact between the passengers, the only factor that defines them. But the *bizco* (cross-eyed man) undermines the apparently passive homogeneity of his audience, which is composed of passengers like himself. He works to seduce his companion with one eye, and with the other he looks back at his public. He participates in the same act of observation that defines the standardized normalcy of his audience, but at the same time, his askew gaze unbalances the dynamics of the spectacle by drawing others into the melodrama of which he is a protagonist. The *bizco* thus symbolizes both an act of exclusion and the impossibility of fulfilling such an act, just as Arlt's dismissal of academics in "How Would You Like Me to Write for You?"—another apparently clear-cut marker of difference— signals a tension between discourses that remains unresolved. Although the passengers of the streetcar are never described in the chronicle and thus remain homogeneous and impersonal, they mirror the spectacle that gazes back at them, participating in a grotesque exchange where one is at once subject and object of the gaze of others.

The reciprocal gaze between the *bizco* and his spectators reproduces the "mise en abîme" of observers that Beatriz Sarlo associates with the crowd-ed Buenos Aires of the 1920's and 1930's: "The flaneur is a voyeur sunken in the urban scene of which, at the same time, he forms a part: in the abysm, the flaneur is observed by another flaneur who at the same time is seen by a third one" (*Modernidad*, 16). This type of duality between performer and public, observer and observed, is full of possibilities for a chronicler like Arlt, and not only because it enables the temporary anonymity so desired by the professional observer. A mise en abîme implies a loss of referential-ity, an endless possibility of similarities and simultaneities reminiscent of Anderson's imagined communities. It suggests at once intimacy and an endless possibility of participation, and it also implies that intervening in a spectacle, as in any system of commercial exchange, is a condition intrin-sic to urban belonging. In "The Cross-eyed Lover," the audience, like the spectacle itself, shifts constantly. Whether it is composed of the streetcar's regular passengers, of the couple being mocked, of an observing chronicler, of the readers of *El Mundo*, or of some juxtaposition of all of the above, the spectacle is shared and experienced on multiple levels.

Árlt uses the imagery of the spectacle to conceive of a public sphere in which popular culture engages and coalesces an active audience. Chroniclers are observers of their society, and they relate to other city dwellers as fellow spectators. I here use the term "spectator" as explained by Hannah Arendt, who in her *Lectures on Kant's Political Philosophy* develops the idea of a critical spectatorship:

> The public realm is constituted by the critics and the spectators, not by the actors or the makers. And this critic and spectator sits in every actor and fabricator; without this critical, judging faculty, the doer or maker would be so isolated from the spectator that he would not even be perceived. (63)

Arendt insists on the importance of spectatorship in the constitution of a public sphere, for this critical capacity enables a dynamic interaction between those doing and those watching. The slippage between the actor and the spectator, such as the one performed in Arlt's chronicle, is crucial for Kant's conception of an active public sphere. In "The Cross-eyed Lover," being a spectator becomes an expression of agency that is rhetorically extended to all the passengers who share the same streetcar and, by extension, to the readers of this chronicle in the pages of *El Mundo*.

Mass culture, therefore, works in this chronicle as a parody of alienation rather than a symptom. Arlt uses humor to draw his reading public into the creative dynamics of the spectacle, a tactic that broadens the scope of his imagined audience. Within the frame of the chronicle, the laughter of the streetcar passengers is exclusive and directed against a grotesque other, the way an audience laughs at the mishaps of a stage clown. The readers of the chronicle, however, laugh at Arlt's description of the interaction between the *bizco* and his public, between spectator and spectacle. The strange couple might be funny, but the reaction of the passengers, including that of Arlt himself, is even more absurd: all are absorbed by this scene as though they were watching a silent film or reading a popular serial novel. This saga, however, stars not only a cross-eyed leading man but also a blonde who looks like a "pseudo film star." The readers might feel momentarily superior to the passengers taken in by this parody of a spectacle, but they could also find themselves, streetcar riders and cinema aficionados, portrayed in this anecdote. Arlt draws the readers of his chronicles into this absurd scene through pointed references to urban popular culture. The monstrosity of the cross-eyed seducer transforms: "the romantic aspect of the situation in something like a serial melodrama" (62). The passengers are compared, not with the spectators of a bad film, but with consumers of the popular press to which this very same chronicle belongs. This displacement of the recipient of mockery has been described by Freud as one of the recurring techniques of jokes (*Joke*, 154–173). In this case, displacement and omission work to broaden Arlt's imagined audience by leaving unclear who is the butt of his mockery. With his use of humor, Arlt gives an unmeasurable reading public the cohesiveness of spectators physically united in the face of a show. The streetcar functions as a microcosm of Arlt's reading public; it becomes a reflective space where city dwellers reciprocate in mutual recognition, performing on a measurable scale the process that Arlt aims to recreate between his chronicles and his readers.

Arlt's description of this comic romance is worth contrasting with another memorable streetcar ride, described in Manuel Gutiérrez Nájera's "La novela del tranvía" ("The Novel of the Streetcar"). This chronicle, set in Mexico City of the 1880's, has as its protagonist a more traditional flaneur, who rides for the pleasure of anthropological observation. This flaneur, like a visitor in a museum of live culture, conceives the city as an exhibit: "nothing is more amusing nor more curious than the series of tableaux vivants that can be examined on a streetcar." His personal space remains unaffected by his observations: "I spend the hours pleasantly boxed in this miniature Noah's ark, poking my head out the window" (*Cuentos*, 109). Gutiérrez Nájera's flaneur remains protected and isolated from the scenery he describes. His confident tone overflows into the text's form, to the extent that this chronicle calls itself a novel, extending a singular experience into a coherent narrative of the city. Like Noah's ark in the midst of an urban deluge, Gutiérrez Nájera's ordering narrative provides a haven from the uncertainty of the streets.

The chronicler who narrates "The Novel of the Streetcar" keeps his distance from the crowds. He never imagines an unspoken, intimate bond with the individuals surrounding him, as Arlt does in "The Cross-eyed Lover." He prefers instead to speculate, like a detective, on their ordinary lives. The narrator projects sinister outcomes to their journeys, suggesting, for instance, that the well-dressed lady sitting next to him has a meeting with a lover—why else would a woman travel alone during the day? He visualizes bringing her to justice by informing her husband and paints the bloody drama that ensues. Yet, as soon as she leaves the streetcar, his imagination comes to a halt and all returns to normal: "A cold sweat bathed my face. Fortunately, we had arrived at Loreto square, and my neighbor descended from the car. I saw her dress: there was no bloodstain. Nothing had happened" (*Cuentos*, 114). The simple fact that he rides the streetcar renders this chronicler participant in a communal system of transportation, but his ethnographic gaze establishes him as an outside observer whose readers can afford to travel through other means. In Gutiérrez Nájera's schema, the space of reading does not coincide with the practice of the city.

Arlt's journey by streetcar, a vehicle much analyzed as a marker of urban modernity, is instead a normal ritual of daily life included nonchalantly in many of his articles. Arlt follows in "The Cross-eyed Lover" a model similar to that of the ethnographic participant observer, an oxymoronic condition that enables a discursive flexibility similar to the one he associates with the street Corrientes. For James Clifford, "'participant observation' stands as a shorthand for continuous tacking between the 'inside' and the 'outside' of events" (*Predicament*, 34). For another anthropologist, Marc Augé, riding the metro in his own city sheds light on the dual condition of the participant observer: "Nothing is so individual, so irremediably subjective, as a single trip in the subway [. . .] and yet nothing is so social as one such trip" (*Metro*, 36). The dual condition of the participant observer—or, in this case, of the actor-spectator—enabled the chronicler to simultaneously engage with daily city life and with his regular readers. The importance Arlt gave his public—even if through irreverent mockery—was essential to his rhetoric of accessibility. Because his chronicles needed to appeal to a variety of readers from Buenos Aires' growing working and middle class, he had to leave room for their differences while creating a bond that spoke to all. Like the cross-eyed seducer who draws the streetcar passengers into his melodrama, Arlt was a unique protagonist whose own askew gaze aimed to enthrall a broad reading audience.

Through this duality between practice and observation, Arlt transforms the characteristics that define the consumption of urban popular culture—whether it be of a filmlike episode on a streetcar or of a chronicle read in *El Mundo*—into a form of creative agency. It is possible to be enthralled by a spectacle, Arlt shows us, and still express individuality through observation and interpretation. Yet, in the mise en abîme of city dwellers and consumers of popular culture, what distinguishes the chronicler from other citizens is the act of writing and the possibility of publishing. This appears a simple, almost accidental distinction but instead forms part of an authorizing gesture obscured by the simultaneity of the ephemeral chronicle. The turnaround of writing and publishing chronicles in *El Mundo* is so fast that Arlt could share the streets with his own texts.[41] This enabled him to establish an empathic relationship with his readers, while implicitly reinforcing his possession of an advantage that others did not share—that of writing, publishing, and being read.

Although he frequently reinstated his persona as a common citizen, presenting himself as a practitioner of Buenos Aires like the thousands of others who crossed the city daily, Arlt also took advantage of the often humorous side effects of his journalistic celebrity. He starred, after all, in the daily installments of his own column. His name was well known, even if his physique was not as recognizable as that of a famous screen star. In "Dos ancianas y el autor" (Two Elderly Ladies and the Author), another chronicle set in public transportation, Arlt transcribes a conversation that he supposedly overhears between two respectable ladies with whom he boards the subway at the Plaza de Mayo and who then, coincidentally, sit facing him. While he travels "bearded and unrecognizable, looking more like an unemployed man than anything else," the two ladies criticize his recent articles on marriage, deploring the effect they might have on potential sons-in-law. They repeatedly refer to him as "Ar" and dismiss him with this: "He has a foreign last name. Go figure what a commoner he must be!" (*RA II*, 345). The chronicle was published in *El Mundo* alongside a caricature that represents two respectably dressed older ladies, with a notable embonpoint, animatedly waving their hands around as they converse. The woman on the right has an abnormally large hand pointed upwards in an accusatory manner: the emblem, perhaps, of public opinion. Behind them, discreetly hiding behind an open newspaper and a hat, we can supposedly discern the chronicler. Both the chronicle and the caricature stage the deceiving anonymity of a large city in which multitudes make it difficult for any one person to stand out—lest he or she be, of course, as absurd as a cross-eyed lover. Arlt's self-deprecating tone in this scene works as an inside joke shared with his readers, one that explicitly excludes the two ladies whose conversation he claims to have overheard and who never find out the real identity of the man who sat facing them—unless they continue to read his column in the days that follow. The ladies might have been mocking the chronicler and critiquing his articles, but from the pages of *El Mundo*, Arlt certainly had the last word.

This eavesdropped dialogue exemplifies the doubling of Arlt's persona that had already been suggested in "The Cross-eyed Lover." Arlt becomes a public figure whose articles are debated by random citizens, but he achieves this prominence by constructing a writing persona that hinges around the portrayal of himself as a common city dweller. The chronicler slyly shows that he is well known enough to be recognized by his public by mentioning that he traveled incognito. Chronicles such as "Two Elderly Ladies and the Author" create a mise en abîme similar to the one described in "The Cross-eyed Lover." This one, however, reflects the act of reading and discussing a chronicle rather than the observation of an urban spectacle. The *aguafuertes* and Arlt, their recurrent protagonist, are endlessly reflected as the meeting point between citizens, the element that transforms a group of strangers into an active community of readers. As Michael Warner has shown, a public is "the social space created by

"Two Elderly Ladies and the Author." *El Mundo*, August 29, 1931.

the reflexive circulation of discourse" (*Publics*, 90). Following this argument, it is productive to think of the two gossiping ladies on the Buenos Aires subway as participating precisely in the type of activity that constitutes a public. Particularly in the case of a reading public united by a temporally structured circulation, such as that of the daily paper, the chronicle invites conversations and enables readers—unbeknownst to themselves in the case of these two ladies—to participate in the renovation and circulation of ideas (Warner, *Publics*, 94–95).

It is hardly surprising that the readers discussing Arlt's chronicles are two elderly women. Despite the homosocial imagined community he often appealed to, Arlt was conscious of his female readership, and *El Mundo* often included advertisements for Arlt's new works that directly targeted women. The chronicler both courted and provoked this specific demographic through some of his articles on "feminine" themes such as marriage, which succeeded in creating an impact by shocking the middle-class standards of morality shared by many of *El Mundo*'s readers. In "Two Elderly Ladies and the Author," the anonymous public that discusses and thus reinstates the importance of Arlt's column is clearly female, even if the feminized image of public opinion that the chronicler creates is petty and conservative rather than creatively critical. The public figure who becomes the center of attention of these discussions, however, is "bearded," as if implicitly flaunting his masculinity. Reinstating the act of writing as a male privilege was almost a cliché during the 1920's, in the artistic avant-gardes as well as in the popular press. Even chroniclers such as Mexico's Salvador Novo, who played with the gender of the chronicle, never questioned the maleness of writing, as we will see in chapter 4. The democratization of reading, an activity that was drawing in more and more women as cultural consumers, did not imply the disappearance of a gendered hierarchy in perceptions of readership. Women, Arlt implies through this evocation of the two gossiping elderly women discussing his articles, were far from being complex, sophisticated readers.[42]

The authority of writing is not reflected in the mise en abîme created by Arlt in "Two Elderly Ladies and the Author"; instead, it is both obscured and enhanced by the chronicler's public persona. While Hans Magnus Enzensberger has argued that media are more than a means of consumption—they are also a socializing means of production with democratizing potential—he also highlights the difference between a producer and an amateur. This distinction is maintained through a "protective formulation" used by professionals of the media, such as

Señoras:

ROBERTO ARLT ha escrito la novela corta

"UNA NOCHE TERRIBLE"

que publica "MUNDO ARGENTINO".

No dejen de leerla, pues la originalidad de su argu-
mento y su extraño protagonista son de los que
apasionan, sobre todo a las lectoras de novelas
inspiradas en la vida real.

LEA "MUNDO ARGENTINO" DE HOY

Advertisement targeting women. *El Mundo*, August 26, 1931.

Arlt.[43] The chronicler advertises the egalitarian potential of media such as popular newspapers while at the same time shielding his particularity as a professional. Arlt thus astutely takes advantage of the contradictions between his apparent accessibility and his privileged place in the pages of *El Mundo*.

The Chronicle as Uncollectable Commodity

By presenting reading as an experience that is endlessly reflected and repeated, Arlt places this practice at the center of an urban collectivity that is synchronized with the speed of modern life. Newspapers such as *El Mundo* and the chronicles they published are similar to a spectacle, to a radio program, or to a film, in that they are consumed as experiences of reading rather than as objects to be kept or exchanged. The person who finishes watching a film walks out of the cinema empty-handed. Likewise, the person who finishes reading a newspaper can leave it in a park, on a streetcar, or in a café for the next passerby to experience.

Like film, the chronicle—in its original, newspaper-based form—is not meant to be collected as a commodity. Christian Metz considers film difficult to characterize as a fetish, for "it is too big, it lasts too long, and it addresses too many sensorial channels at the same time to offer a credible unconscious equivalent of a lacking part-object." Perhaps more significantly, film cannot be fetishized, because it "cannot be *touched*, cannot be carried and handled" (quoted in Jay, *Downcast Eyes*, 485). This is obviously not the case of the chronicle. As a text published in a newspaper, it has a very concrete physical presence. Like a film, however, the chronicle does not have a concrete, measurable *value* as an object to be collected. The chronicle read one day will be out of date the next and replaced by a new one. More than the specificity of a single article, the process of continual renovation determines its cultural worth. In this sense, chronicles differ from *folletíns*, the serial novels that were published in the penny press and were meant to be collected and eventually bound into volumes. The chronicle's lack of value as a collectable cultural object works as an asset for Arlt's rhetoric of accessibility. The newspaper, and hence the chronicle, can be found everywhere in the city: it possesses little exclusivity. Most citizens can be consumers without necessarily becoming collectors or accumulating cultural capital. One can experience Arlt's *Aguafuertes* as one experiences the spectacle of the streets, just by virtue of living in the city. The habitual practice of consumption—more than the end result, the accumulation of goods—is the element around which hinges the definition of a community of readers.

While neither a chronicle nor a film session has a value that can be accumulated, cultural artifacts such as books function differently. As they are not ephemeral, they have exchange value and can be treasured as commodities. A book can become a fetish, an object to be collected that has, for James Clifford, "the power to fixate rather than simply the capacity to edify or inform" ("On Collecting," 65). According to Marx, commodity fetishism implies that the different conditions of the owner and the producer of an object are obscured and that the social conditions under which the object is created are hidden: social and cultural relations are replaced by relations among objects mediated by the market economy. The chronicle, however, continually reenacts the conditions leading to its production. It is an expression both of the chronicler's interaction with the city and of his or her working relationship with the newspaper industry. And, as seen in Arlt's "How a Novel Is Written," the chronicle can also shed light on the hidden side of writing a book, even if this glimpse works to reinstate, rather than question, the status of a literary object such as a published novel.

One could, however, also argue that, like a book, the newspaper can become a fetish. The dwellers of Buenos Aires recognized and identified each other by what they read in public. The newspaper itself, as an object of a particular brand (*El Mundo, Crítica*, or *La Nación*, for instance), would then become an ephemeral fetish of a day, mediating the relationships between individuals who defined themselves through their choice as consumers. The value of this short-lived fetish would lie in that, although it provoked desire, it could also be discarded and replaced, permitting city dwellers to recognize each other through the renewable signs of modernity. One cannot imply, therefore, that the chronicle undermines the fetishism that a literary object such as a book can provoke. Rather, it modernizes fetishism in the light of the renewing impulse of a culture fascinated with change: the value of the book-object is replaced by the value of novelty.

In many of Arlt's chronicles, collecting or accumulating objects is portrayed as shameful, even monstrous. In the *aguafuerte* "Taller de composturas de muñecas" (Doll Repair Shop), for example, Arlt accidentally comes across a business dedicated to repairing old and broken dolls. So surprising is this encounter that he repeatedly compares this sighting to a nightmare. When he tries to move on, he finds that he cannot escape the grotesque dolls that are being repaired:

> Between the elbowings of the concierges, who were going shopping, and the shoves of the passersby, I walked away, but it was clear that I couldn't avoid the subject, for when I reached Uruguay street, in an even more dilapidated display window than the one on Talcahuano, I saw another strangled doll, and below it, the usual sign: "We fix dolls." (*RA II*, 38)

The strangled doll hangs on display behind a store window, but instead of tempting the viewer to come in for a purchase, it resembles a dead body or an object of witchcraft. This uncanny doll marks, not the expected display of a new commodity, but rather the specter of an aging fetish that halts the city's constantly renovating impulse of commerce, enacting the phantasmagorical appearance of an object whose conditions of creation remain occult. The fact that a doll is to be repaired, and not simply given away or replaced, indicates that it is intended not for use but rather for display: "Since the doll was so pretty and had cost quite a few pesos, the girl was never able to play with it" (38).[44] This disturbing image reveals, perhaps, the afterlife of the desirable but inaccessible objects sold in the Pasaje Güemes or the street Florida.

The monstrosity of the repaired dolls lies in that their display value overrules the possibility of their use. In the same manner, collecting books as objects makes it impossible for the written text to be put to use, to circulate and reach a broad audience. One of the most memorable scenes of Arlt's first novel, *El juguete rabioso*, describes the theft of books from the protective pedagogical space of a school library to be sold through the informal economy of the city streets. Silvio Astier, the protagonist, steals the books with other members of his anarchist youth group and then proceeds to classify them according to their street value, considering above all which will sell and which won't.[45] Through the regular publication of chronicles, Arlt puts into practice Silvio Astier's symbolic theft of books from the school library. For what the chronicler does, essentially, is to put writing into circulation. He replaces a collectable fetish with a fetish for the day and becomes the go-between who takes the grotesque doll, or the "mad toy" that stands for literature, to the streets. Even if a library is meant as a place for reading, where a general public can gain access to books that might be unaffordable, the contact between book and reader in this institutional space is regimented and structured, as opposed to the free-flowing circulation of information in the unregulated space of the street. This is where another of Arlt's underhanded contradictions comes into play. He presents massive circulation as a rebellion against a regulated system of knowledge, even though it forms part of another very tightly controlled system of production and distribution: that of industrial journalism. Similarly, Arlt's dismissal of luxurious collectable objects—and hence, in my reading, of the legitimizing framework of literary value—is hardly straightforward. Arlt's distaste for places such as the Pasaje Güemes is so vehement as to be almost defensive, just as his disgust for the mended dolls in "Doll Repair Shop" expresses a feeling of revulsion under which a strong fascination is undeniable.

Without a doubt, the chronicle's ephemeral nature enabled Arlt to create an audience where books might have failed. In the case of Berlin, Peter Fritzsche mentions that "in a time when Berliners hurry along in streetcars and steal glances at newspapers there is simply no place left for books or booksellers" (*Berlin*, 24). In Buenos Aires, a city undergoing a similar growth process, tabloids such as *El Mundo* could take over, permitting city dwellers to take texts from their display cases and into the streets.

In this sense, the chronicle evokes de Certeau's description of the practice of reading, which he describes in terms of movement: "readers are travelers; they move across lands belonging to someone else, like nomads poaching their way across fields they did not write" (*Practice*, 174). In Arlt's *Aguafuertes*, the activity of reading is also presented as a process of constant movement, at once literal (reading newspapers while circulating through city streets) and conceptual (acquiring an aesthetic way of interpreting urban life through a heterogeneous genre that shifts between the informative and the literary). By synchronizing his column with the flow of public life, Arlt modified the cultural cartography of Buenos Aires. Not only did his chronicles reaffirm the aesthetic value of street culture, but they also drew attention to lower- and middle-class neighborhoods and streets, redefining them as sources of literary knowledge.

Arlt's early chronicles on Buenos Aires thus offered an experience that promised belonging while purportedly bypassing hierarchical distinctions based on economic status, social class, or intellectual prestige. At the same time, they enabled their author to cultivate his distinct status as a writer and to create a visible enclave for himself within his city's cultural milieus. Arlt's persona as a chronicler, in this manner, embodies the duality between circulating and staying put, distributing and amassing cultural capital, remaining accessible and cultivating exclusive cultural prestige. Arlt might well have been a man of the streets, but he was also a *porteño* unlike any other, for his unobtrusiveness was at the base of the aesthetic gaze that singled him out.

Chapter 3

Taking Readers for a Ride
Mário de Andrade's *Táxi*

> The moments that aren't free are to write *Táxi*, or other
> silly things that don't improve me at all. Pure breadwinning
> that isn't even pure, because I write these things without
> any interest, between one classroom and another, between
> pleasure and monotony.
>
> —Mário de Andrade to Manuel Bandeira,
> December 27, 1929

When reflecting on his work as a chronicler, Mário de Andrade often
expressed himself disparagingly. In the letter to Manuel Bandeira
quoted above, he dismisses his column *Táxi* as an uninteresting exercise
that permits him to earn an income but does not become an intellectually edifying endeavor.[1] Mário's complaints echo those of many Latin
American chroniclers from the late nineteenth and early twentieth centuries. As seen in chapter 1, Rubén Darío, José Martí, and Manuel Gutiérrez
Nájera, along with Brazil's Olavo Bilac, also lamented the lack of creative
freedom that a regular column entailed.[2] Most of these critics differentiated the autonomy of literature from a journalistic enterprise contaminated by its commercial nature. Mário's description of his work as "pure
breadwinning that isn't even pure" also highlights the unattainability of
purity through journalism. In this sense, Mário's conceptualization of the

chronicle seems hardly innovative. He questions neither the division between literature and journalism that concerned many chroniclers of the late nineteenth century, nor the lower status of the chronicle in the hierarchy of cultural production.

Unlike the other writers in this book, whose importance as public figures was intrinsically linked to their practice of the chronicle, Mário had become known as a leader of the Brazilian modernist movement with early works such as *Paulicéia desvairada* (Hallucinated City). He recited from this homage to São Paulo during the Modern Art Week in February 1922, the multifaceted artistic celebration that coincided with the centennial of Brazil's independence and expressed the modernists' interest in forging a national cultural identity. Clearly, Mário did not need the chronicle to establish himself as one of Brazil's leading modernist intellectuals. In the epigraph to this chapter, Mário describes how he wrote the articles for his column *Táxi*, reinstating through his complaint the undefined cultural location he assigns to the chronicle. He writes between one classroom and another, between pleasure and monotony. In his view, the chronicle exists only outside normative spaces: it is separate from didactic or edifying purposes and provokes no definite reaction, only vague emotions that hover between pleasure and monotony, identification and disengagement. It comes as no surprise, then, that in the preface to *Os filhos da Candinha* (The Children of Candinha, 1942), the only collection of Mário's chronicles to be published in his lifetime, he declares that the genre was not instrumental to his intellectual projects. "I never made of the chronicle a way of life, and when I did I frequently was wrong or mistaken." The chronicle was, for Mário, "a true escape valve through which I rested from myself" (9); it was a diverting release from the more earnest endeavors he drew from to construct his intellectual persona.

Mário's dismissal of his work as a chronicler, however, brings to the fore the most relevant characteristics of his column *Táxi*, highlighting the continuous state of movement, becoming, and transformation that guides each of his articles. This conceptual movement points to the conditions that define writing and reading in a modernizing city such as São Paulo, where speed and a structured time frame are imposed on any creative activity; at the same time, it enables discursive flexibility and promotes a dynamic relationship between the chronicler and his readers. Mário's column *Táxi* is imagined as a moveable locus where the chronicler engages in intimate conversations with his readers, setting up a dialogical space from which a modern urban identity can be debated and renewed.

The chronicle, in this manner, becomes a site from which the modernist intellectual intervenes in daily life, incessantly negotiating his engagement with his city and with his public, with art and accessibility.

Chronicler, Taxi Driver, Agent of Movement

The titles of Mário's only two regular columns in São Paulo's *Diário Nacional* mirror the indeterminate cultural location that this chronicler attributed to the genre. Both *O turista aprendiz* (The Apprentice Tourist, 1928–1929) and *Táxi* (1929–1930) connote movement and travel, within and beyond the city. While *Táxi*, with its obvious urban referent, was written in São Paulo, *O turista aprendiz* documents the urban intellectual's journey beyond the city to the Northeast of Brazil, where he traveled as a correspondent.[3] Each of these columns also reflects a particular aspect of Brazilian modernism. While the title *Táxi* is suggestive of modernism's interest in technology, vehicles, and speed in the panorama of the city, *O turista aprendiz* responds to the flip side of modernism, which calls for a rediscovery of autochthonous Brazilian culture. In these chronicles, described as "a viagem etnográfica" (an ethnographic journey), Mário documents for São Paulo readers his exploration of Brazil's national cultural identity through its indigenous traditions. This interest also permeated some of his other works from the late 1920s, such as the collection of poems *Clã do jabuti* (1927) and the novel *Macunaíma* (1928). Mário's focus on Brazil's autochthonous roots was not considered antimodern. On the contrary, it marked a desire for cultural autonomy that moved away from the parameters established by European culture, and aspired to consolidate an authentically Brazilian way of life that drew from both cosmopolitan and autochthonous elements (Sevcenko, *Orfeu*, 237).

As his comment to Manuel Bandeira reveals, Mário had to juggle various occupations to earn a stable income. Like many intellectuals of his generation, he expressed himself through a diversity of forms: poetry, photography, music, essays on folklore and musicology, art criticism, the novel, and of course the chronicle. Instead of receiving an allowance from rich landowners and patrons of São Paulo arts, as did other leaders of Brazil's modernist movement, this intellectual preferred to earn his living independently.[4] He taught history and aesthetics of music at São Paulo's conservatory, gave numerous lectures on musicology, and worked to document his country's musical patrimony. As well as writing regular chronicles, such as the early column *Crônicas de Malazarte* in *América*

Brasileira (1923–1924), he also published art criticism in *A Manhã*, the modernist publication *Klaxon*, and the *Diário Nacional*. In the 1930s he worked as a civil servant in São Paulo's department of culture and was one of the founders of the Serviço do Patrimônio Histórico e Artístico Nacional, an institution that catalogued architectural and artistic works that were representative of Brazilian cultural history (Resende, "Brazilian Modernism," 212).

At first glance, the chronicle seems to contradict this versatile intellectual's description of art, mostly because of the genre's commercial nature. In a series of three articles from *Táxi*, Mário defines art through disinterest, which functions as a "precarious mesh" that delicately envelops art by defining it in contradiction to the practice of daily life: "[Disinterest] reveals the practice of life and does this with such an irking insistence that truly it cannot exist but through the principle of contradiction" (*T*, 117). The aloof, unengaged nature of true art guarantees that, unlike a mercantile endeavor such as chronicle writing, it becomes neither a "ganha vaidade" (vanity winner) nor a "ganha pão" (breadwinner) (*T*, 118). If disinterested art implies patience, time, and pleasure in creation, then the daily obligation of writing chronicles under time constraints excludes it all the more from the relaxed pace of artistic creativity. This conception of journalistic work was closely attuned to the views of the period, as shown in an anonymous article in the *Diário Nacional* from January 22, 1928. Entitled "O homen sanguinario: Indiscripções sobre a vida de um reporter" (The Sanguinary Man: Indiscretions from the Life of a Reporter), it dwelled on the morbid fascination of reporters with violent crimes, who, rather than consider the tragic aspect of any such event or reflect on its social consequences, saw in them only the opportunity to make a quick penny by selling the story.

At first, Mário's notion of art appears to leave no room for social or political engagement, nor for the chronicle, whose closeness to daily life links it to the very notion of practice contradicted by disinterest. However, as Vivian Schelling has aptly pointed out, most of this writer's declarations in favor of art for art's sake are accompanied by contradictions, for he also advocated the humanizing power of art and the humanizing purpose of his work (*Presença do povo*, 150). This defense brings to the fore Mário's belief in art's public responsibility, thus opening a window for the chronicle to be included within his porous conceptualization of art. Conceiving of art as a humanizing force implies engaging art with experience, making it available to an audience by facilitating creative appreciation.[5] It also

O homem sanguinario
Indiscrições sobre a vida de um reporter

Chronicle about a bloodthirsty
reporter. *Diário Nacional,*
January 22, 1928.

highlights the importance of accessibility: humanizing means engaging
art with experience, making it public by opening a path for an audience's
creative appreciation. One way to reconcile the distance between disinterested art and a genre engaged with the practice of daily life, such as the
chronicle, would be cultural criticism. Mário once declared that "criticism
is a work of art" (*Vida literária,* 14), broadening the notion of art defined
by disinterest, and putting into question the expected distance separating
criticism from art, or reception from production. Critical thinking, in this
sense, is a bridge that brings together disinterest and practice. It functions
as the humanizing vehicle that renders art, and the faculty of judgment
necessary to engage with it, accessible to a public.

When looking back on his work, Mário once described himself as an
"agent of movement," a destiny that was "perhaps less 'divine than that
of creating the repose, the pleasure, the evasion of this world that Beauty
gives,' but more human" (quoted in Schelling, *Presença do povo,* 145). The
label "agent of movement" designates Mário's self-appointed role as a
critic and promoter of cultural change. He is one who instigates and gives
continuity to the evolution of a cultural scene more than simply being
one of its actors. In this sense, he is the ideal chronicler: a learned observer
who participates in cultural creativity by sharing his personal impressions
with other city dwellers. He catalyzes cultural production, promoting

and humanizing artistic expressions by combining criticism with a close-up of daily life.

Mário indirectly confirmed the chronicle's potential as a vehicle for critical thought when he divided his chronicles into two categories: "as crônicas propiamente crônicas" (chronicles properly chronicles) and "as crônicas críticas" (critical chronicles) (Lopez, "A crônica," 168). He originally planned to edit two volumes divided along these lines, but he finally opted to publish only the first, lighthearted collection, which became *Os filhos da Candinha*. Tellingly, the articles included in this volume, "as crônicas propiamente crônicas," are described by their lack of definition, as if the genre was so amorphous as to defy any paradigmatic description. This absence of definition is significant, for it recalls the lack of a precise objective, or intentionality, that Mário perceives in this practice. Nonetheless, these "crônicas propiamente crônicas," many of which are taken from the column *Táxi*, do have a clearly critical perspective, albeit one that works indirectly. They provide readers with a personal and often playful description of a city and its customs. Stepping away from abstractions, they humanize criticism through their colloquial and intimate tone, staging the chronicler's thinking process rather than a specific argument. To borrow from Hannah Arendt's description of critical thinking, these chronicles "recommend themselves by their modesty" (*Lectures*, 33). Their lighthearted nature, usually associated with commercial motivations, could paradoxically be considered a form of disinterest, in that these chronicles do not strive for the longevity of genres such as the novel or poetry. Mário's practice of the chronicle thus brought together the daily routine of writing "without any interest" with the disinterested nature of art, enabling a productive cooperation between practice and critical distance.

Like many intellectuals of his time, Mário was greatly concerned with promoting a dynamic Brazilian culture that encompassed both urban and rural areas. But in contrast to the many traditions that the modernists up-held as symbols of Brazilian culture, such as popular dances and music, the chronicle does not seem an ideal medium to promote a national identity. Because of its urban nature, the genre maintains a commercial malleabil-ity that takes into account the interests of readers and the fluctuations of the cultural market, referents that can interfere with the broad and often didactic conceptualization of national culture proposed by the Brazilian avant-gardes. This urban specificity was precisely what made the chroni-cle such a productive tool for Roberto Arlt in Buenos Aires, a writer who did not fit in well with his city's avant-garde, felt disengaged with Argentine national symbols, and chose to privilege a popular *porteño* imaginary in his writing. For Mário, leader and founder of Brazilian modernism and great admirer of the Argentine Ricardo Güiraldes' revival of the gaucho genre, Arlt's choice of the city over the nation was not an option. Nonetheless, when read in the light of Mário's reflections on rural popular culture and the Brazilian vernacular, his column *Táxi* indicates ways in which popular traditions can invigorate the practice of the chronicle and mitigate some of the conditions that restrict its production and reception. With these distinctions in mind, an analysis of *Táxi* can help us explore both the potential and the limits of the chronicle for Mário, a thinker whose yearning to define national culture underscores the difficulties faced by early twentieth-century writers in representing an uneven Brazilian modernity.

Zooming through the Cityscape

Táxi, Mário's first regular column to be written in the daily newspaper *Diário Nacional* and directed to its São Paulo readers, was short-lived; it circulated only from April 1929 to January 1930.[6] The title itself tells the reader that this chronicler conceptualized his column as a vehicle ready to take any willing reader for a ride through the city. While the term "taxi" ubiquitously designates a chauffer-driven vehicle that transports passengers within a city to the destination of their choice, the name's origin is significant. "Taxi" comes from "taximeter," an instrument invented in 1891 to measure the distance traveled by a vehicle, and consequently the rate charged, or "taxed." This way of measuring the worth of a ride echoes the business of journalism. If the taxi driver is paid for traveling short but frequent distances, the chronicler is paid for writing articles on a regular basis and oftentimes according to the length of the article. Mário's *Táxi* suggests the enticing possibility of a readily available journey through the city. A speedy motorized vehicle that can travel ample distances highlights the broad distribution of newspapers and their accessibility, for a price, to a diverse readership. Picking up a copy of this column is as easy, the chronicler implies, as flagging down an available taxi circulating through the city streets.

By naming his column *Táxi*, this chronicler situates it in the current of many Latin American vanguards of the 1920s that affirmed the vehicle as a motif of modern life. The magazine *Klaxon* (Brazil), named after the trademarked electric horn; the column *Sidecar*, by Salvador Novo (Mexico City); the magazine *Motocicleta* (Ecuador); and collections of poems such as the Argentine Oliverio Girondo's *Veinte poemas para leer en el tranvía* (Twenty Poems to Read on the Streetcar)—all seek to textually recreate the effects of modernity on the urban landscape.[7] In the 1920s a car symbolized more than a utilitarian object; it was consistently advertised as part of a novel way of life. Vehicles and speed were recurring figures in the works of many Brazilian modernists. In *The Modernist Idea*, Wilson Martins cites many examples of poems referring to speed and the sensorial transformation it enabled. Luís Aranha dedicated a poem to the airplane; influenced by Jean Cocteau, Sérgio Milliet spoke of "the automobile century"; Oswald de Andrade "had one of his characters come down the Santos road at two hundred kilometers an hour"; and Guilherme de Almeida "wrote a poem at the more modest speed of ninety-six kilometers an hour" (Martins, *Modernist Idea*, 30–39). Mário also appropriated the language of speed and technology, describing in *Hallucinated City* his fellow modernist Oswald de Andrade zooming by in a Cadillac.[8] A man of his time, Mário shared the fever for cars that had gripped São Paulo, and was a member of his city's automobile club, even though he probably lacked the means to acquire a car of his own. With his column *Táxi*, however, he made his chronicles as omnipresent in the city as these symbols of urban modernity and included the chronicle alongside other newly commonplace indicators of progress, such as radios, cameras, telephones, typewriters, and cinemas.

By the 1920s, São Paulo had become an emblem of Brazilian modernity. The city's economic expansion as the commercial center of the country's coffee exports had attracted a large number of immigrants. The city had almost 300,000 inhabitants in 1905, and by 1920 the number had reached 579,000 and would grow to 1,060,120 in 1934.[9] Such growth brought about dramatic changes in the cityscape. The city's expanding population also led to greater transportation needs. Electric streetcars had been in use since 1900. By 1921 the city had 407 streetcars that transported thousands of passengers daily. In 1925 approximately 3,500 automobiles were circulating in the city, 2,275 of which were commercial vehicles for hire.[10] Mário's vehicle of choice was thus a ubiquitous sight in the streets of his city.

While a taxi brings to mind the busy traffic of a growing São Paulo, a taxi ride can also offer repose from the pace of the city. The interior of the taxi permits a private moment of tranquility within the public space through which the taxi circulates. Unlike the streetcar—a reference common to many Brazilian modernists and a frequent mode of transportation for Roberto Arlt in Buenos Aires—a taxi cannot be crowded.[11] It also follows no predetermined journey, giving a moment of individual creativity to both the rider, who chooses the destination, and the driver, who chooses the route. In the same manner, the space occupied by *Táxi* in the newspaper gives Mário room to improvise his chronicles, imposing no predetermined direction to his texts. With his articles, the chronicler drives many citizens and consumers through their city's cultural offerings, discussing visits to São Paulo by the cubist poet Blaise Cendrars and the architect Le Corbusier, along with miscellaneous events such as the competition for Miss Brazil or the selection of the "queen" of Brazilian flowers. The column also offers meditations on the reforms of orthography and language that were being debated by Brazilian academics. With this diversity, *Táxi* becomes a vehicle in the service of many while preserving the intimate nature of a private exchange at close quarters, within the cozy confines of an automobile.

The creation of *Táxi*, like its reception, is imagined as a process in constant transition, spontaneously reproducing movement and responding to improvised routes.[12] The chronicles that make up this column are brief cultural lessons conceived on the go. Didactic without being exhaustive, they are critiques of the moment and susceptible to the unexpected flow of the city. According to critic Antonio Cândido, the Brazilian chronicle is a genre that exists "ao rés do chão," on the ground floor (*A crônica*, 13–22), a description that coincides with the guiding image of Mário's *Táxi* and confirms the genre's intimacy with city life. In a similar manner, Michel de Certeau describes the practitioner of the city as one who lives and operates "down below," in the midst of its activity, writing the urban text while lacking the distance necessary to read it as a whole (91–110). *Táxi* reproduces this closeness to urban life in that it offers numerous rides through São Paulo's culture, giving its readers close-ups of specific cultural occurrences rather than a big picture of the city's cultural life.

By locating the chronicle "on the ground floor," Antonio Cândido speaks not only of the genre's intimacy with the urban scene and its grounding in daily life. He also indicates its lower position vis-à-vis literature in the hierarchy of cultural production. "Ao rés do chão" describes the chronicle's original location in the newspaper. The feuilleton, or *folhetim*, to which the chronicle is related, was in many nineteenth-century newspapers located at the bottom of the first page, which was considered "an empty space destined for entertainment" (Meyer, "Voláteis," 96). This location was allocated to the light news of the day, knowledge that dwellers of the same city were likely to share and talk about. As an undefined space, the "ground floor" of the newspaper page possesses no permanence; it is continually filled and emptied by the city's latest events. This movement of texts and information reiterates Mário's *Táxi* as a column that is driven by the continuously renovating impulse of commerce and bound to the changing interests of its readers.

The chronicle's mobility throughout the city recalls a distinction Mário proposed between two types of traditions: "There are mobile traditions and immobile traditions. The first are useful, they have an enormous importance, people must preserve them as they are[,] for they transform themselves through the simple fact of their mobility. As for example the cantiga, poetry and popular dances" (*TA*, 254). Mário developed this notion of mobile traditions during his travels to the Amazon and the Northeast of Brazil and would later reaffirm them in other reflections on folklore, such as *Aspectos das artes plásticas no Brasil* (Aspects of Plastic Art in Brazil). He attributed the label of "mobile traditions" to performance-based cultural expressions, such as dance and music (for instance, the traditions of "A Ciranda" and "Bumba meu boi").[13] Mobile traditions are cultural expressions that are not frozen in time but instead undergo a constant process of reinvention through practice. Although their particularities might change, these traditions survive by adapting to the cultural needs of their practitioners. They provide a flexible means for cultural identification that can be continually renewed and reaffirmed, maintaining the specificity of a tradition while dynamically incorporating it within a changing lifestyle. In contrast to these practices are immobile traditions, which cannot evolve to reflect the changing needs of a community: "Immobile traditions do not evolve on their own. In the infinite majority of cases they are prejudicial. Some are perfectly ridiculous, like the carriage of the king of England" (*TA*, 254). Immobile traditions are superfluous, decorative, and artificial. They are frozen cultural symbols, such as the anachronistic horse-drawn carriage that is paraded in the twentieth century to reaffirm an identity that has already been left behind. Chronicles such as those grouped in *Táxi* possess an adaptability that replaces the horse-drawn carriage emblematic of immobile traditions with the contemporary speed of a motorized vehicle. Although Mário never included the genre in his list of cultural expressions that qualified as "mobile traditions," his observations on popular culture collected in *O turista aprendiz* (1928) might well have influenced him a year later in his writing of *Táxi*. The chronicles published as part of this column arguably extend to the cultural economy of the city the flexibility attributed to folkloric mobile traditions. In this manner, Mário's work as a chronicler would enable him to become an "agent of movement" who puts into practice a mobile tradition within the realm of urban culture, offering, if only metaphorically, a means to bridge the gap between rural traditions and urban modernity.

While the title *Táxi* obviously connotes a literal displacement through São Paulo, it also implies a way of perceiving urban culture conditioned by speed. For sociologist Georg Simmel, who wrote around two decades before Mário's column was published, "the rapid crowding of changing images, the sharp discontinuity in the grasp of a single glance, and the unexpectedness of onrushing impressions" that characterize the speed of life in a metropolis causes the "intensification of nervous stimulation" in the individual dweller (*Culture*, 175).[14] According to Mário, speed reveals how language, as a vehicle for communication, can fail to catch up with urban experience and thus can lose its effectiveness along the way of the taxi ride: "And now it is easy to recognize the expressive precariousness of language in relation to the life of the senses. *In the taxi zooming by*, wanting to express the state of sensibility in which I find myself when I see an elephant, I fatally ended up with illogicality . . . and called this thing 'a synesthetic state'" (*T*, 96, my emphasis). In this chronicle, "A linguagem III" (Language III), Mário describes how the image of an elephant provokes a reaction that he erroneously defines as a synesthetic state. This article explores an instance when language fails to build a bridge between a sensorial experience and a linguistic expression. The chronicler acknowledges the inability to put into words his perception of an elephant, significantly, when he is "no táxi passando," zooming by in a taxi. This observation might literally refer to the act of circulating through the city in a motorized vehicle, in which case the speed of city life and of modernity makes it difficult to use language effectively to communicate a particular sensibility. Speed would in this case be a condition that impedes the city dweller from developing the critical distance necessary to communicate his or her experience accurately to others. The greatest problem with a taxi ride in São Paulo, Mário suggests, is that it is faster than language. The same could be said of his column *Táxi*: "no táxi passando" can also refer to the text of the chronicle that speedily passes through the hands of its readers only to become obsolete the next day. If any written text is unable to catch up with lived experience, this is all the more so for the chronicle. With its strained conditions of production that call for a rapid turnover, the chronicle does not give Mário the time to build a solid argument for his readers or to lend a clear-cut intentionality to his texts.

Yet the speed that shapes the existence of Mário's *Táxi*—on both conceptual and practical levels—is arguably the condition that makes it possible to transmit the sensorial experience of being in the modern city, of feeling vulnerable to the multitude of impressions that flee by but cannot be comprehended. Speed infuses many of *Táxi*'s chronicles with the accelerated rhythm of public life in São Paulo, making the resulting texts seem imperfect and improvised. While these supposed shortcomings are an inherent part of the style of the chronicle, which critic Susana Rotker has described as "literature under pressure" (*Martí*, 43), they also work to provide a more accurate picture of urban life. The chronicle captures the experience of modernity precisely by revealing the impossibility of condensing it within a comprehensive representation.

If public space in the modern city can be defined as "a derivative of movement," as Richard Sennet has argued in *The Fall of Public Man*, the taxi—like the chronicle—is the ideal vehicle to counter the erosion of public expression associated with such a constant flow of people and vehicles (14). And in São Paulo during the late 1920s and 1930s, when a growing population was crossing the city daily, movement was certainly the definitive characteristic of public space. In his chronicle "The Cult of Statues," Mário refers to public statues to describe the street as a shared space: "Every public statue has to represent a public cult. The street is for all, and everything that is on the street is for all" (appendix 2). The street is communal, argues Mário, not because it is a place where strangers can meet, bond, or form a public identity, but because all citizens have the privilege of circulating through it by exercising their freedom of movement. As street monuments, he considers statues useless memorials, simply because city dwellers get used to their presence as they routinely walk by, no longer noticing them. Instead of becoming a significant landmark where historical memory is articulated, statues are normalized as objects on the sidelines of a busy street. They do not fit in with the rhythm of the city; rather, they are (literally) "immobile traditions," surviving only to become "*um bibelô*" (*T*, 150), a decorative object that loses its aesthetic value with time. Mário's concept of public statues thus recalls, in a manner that is more kitsch than uncanny, the phantasmagoric dolls that haunted

Roberto Arlt's journeys throughout Buenos Aires. For Mário, a statue can become memorable only by provoking discomfort or by obstructing traffic, as did the advertisements that were appearing throughout the city, such as those for Castelões cigarettes and the Marmon automobile (appendix 2). Unlike statues, advertisements can halt city dwellers by provoking curiosity. The ads are constantly renovated to display new products, and no one has the time to get used to their continuous presence. More than an object in itself, an advertisement is a vehicle that entices a city dweller to approach the object for sale. The chronicle, in a similar manner, renovates itself constantly and encourages the reader to find new ways of engaging with the city and its culture. The chronicler's function as an agent of movement here coincides with advertising in that he entices readers and consumers by proposing culture as an object of desire. Paradoxically, given Mário's reluctance to identify with commercial culture, the continually renovating mechanism of advertisement coincides with the flexibility he so admired in popular mobile traditions.

The growing importance of advertising in the early twentieth century was, in fact, instrumental to the formation of a class of professional intellectuals in Brazil, many of whom worked as chroniclers (Süssekind, *Cinematograph*, 46). While some, such as João do Rio, embraced the influence of commerce and technology on urban culture, others, like Olavo Bilac, resented it. Mário's relationship to the chronicle's commercial nature remains hesitant, yet the parallel he creates between a chronicler and a taxi driver smoothly includes his articles within the commercial give-and-take of a modern city, something that was emphasized by the editorial layout that framed his chronicles. The typeface chosen by the *Diário Nacional* for the title of Mário's column is bold, uppercase, slightly edgy, and telling of the influence of advertising. The pages of this newspaper often included ads of varying sizes that shared the page with his chronicles. Toward the edges of the pages, one could find small illustrated ads—for example, for the men's fashion store Casa Kosmos, which offered wedding suits for grooms. One ad for a medicine called Eurythimine announced a cure for both colds and rheumatism, and another, for a remedy called Vigogenio, promised to relieve weakness of the muscles, lungs, or nerves. Large advertisements were few, but occasionally one would take up almost a quarter of the page, as did the one for the Fiat 525 that sprung up alongside Mário's *Táxi* column on May 22, 1929, boasting, "The architectural harmony of ancient Rome lives again in the lines of this prodigy of modern motoring that is the 525." This quote, attributed to none other than Pope Pius XI, announced an exhibit of new Fiat models in São Paulo. While this advertisement confirms the commercial and social importance of automobiles in São Paulo of the 1920s, its presence next to the column *Táxi* also highlights the parallels between both vehicles. A taxi might well find itself next to a Fiat, as could conceivably happen at any street corner, but in this case, the two vehicles that coincide on the same newspaper page are a commercial advertisement and a chronicle, each of which serve to guide the reader toward a particular way of engaging with urban modernity.

Táxi column next to a Fiat advertisement. *Diário Nacional*, May 22, 1929.

Instead of halting the city's flow or of being left behind, the taxi, like the chronicle, follows its drift. The chronicle is thus defined by its circulation through the city, but also by its shifts between registers, be they literature, journalism, history, advertising, or criticism. Thinking of Mário's *Táxi* as an example of a mobile tradition reveals multiple angles through which the cultural roles of the chronicle can be negotiated and renewed. Such a conceptualization is not without its caveats, for the column's fixed—and hence privileged—space on the newspaper page can arguably be read as a form of immobility. Furthermore, the guiding image of the moving taxi is itself rarely exploited in this column, and references to the physical experience of riding through the city in a motorized vehicle are few and far between. Such apparent contradictions, however, work to magnify the creative role of the public. It is up to each reader to individually interpret the guiding image of the column, to decide in which direction he or she wants to take the suggested symbolism of its title.

Conversations in a *Táxi*

Taxi rides are good conversation starters. One can discuss the topics of the day, knowing the ride will be quick and the encounter brief. Fittingly, traces of dialogue surface throughout Mário's column, particularly in references that establish continuity between his articles. Expressions such as "I will say in a next *táxi* . . ." (*T*, 148) and "I was saying the other day . . ." (*T*, 167) give his chronicles the feel of a daily talk. He also includes letters from his readers and exchanges with friends or acquaintances in his articles, as, for example, in "The Devil," "Conversation at the Edge of the Wharf," and "Mrs. Stevens," chronicles that juxtapose many voices and points of view into a single text.[15] The spoken quality of the chronicle has already been noted in the works of nineteenth-century writers such as José Martí. It was, however, linked to oratory more than dialogue, as though the chronicler was delivering an elaborate speech to his readers.[16] In the case of the Brazilian chronicle, critic Antonio Cândido has defined the genre's oral quality as *conversational* (*A crônica*, 14). The chronicle's sensibility is in tune with daily experience, and its language reproduces the act of speaking and communicating in its most natural form. The chronicler obtains the information he will communicate to his public by dialoguing with his fellow citizens and, in turn, shares this information with his readers in a chatty, accessible manner.

A dialogue is based on the interaction between two or more perspectives and evolves through the mutual influence of one voice over another. In a dialogical situation, explains M. M. Bakhtin, the speaker expects a reciprocal interaction with the listener: "The word in living conversation is directly, blatantly, oriented toward a future answer-word: it provokes an answer, anticipates it, and structures itself in the answer's direction" (*Dialogic Imagination*, 280). As opposed to a monological expression, whereby the listener merely mirrors the speaker, in a dialogical relationship the listener plays an active role that molds the discourse at hand. Through its conversational, and hence dialogical nature, the chronicle enables readers and writers to mutually influence each other. The intimacy of a private vehicle suggests the possibility of a spontaneous dialogue between driver and passenger. Mário's column enables him to guide his audience, who in turn have the possibility to read creatively, communicate with him through letters to the editor, and perhaps even influence his choice of subject matter.

The dialogical nature of the chronicle, however, must not be overemphasized. As a taxi driver, or agent of movement, Mário shares his knowledge with his readers, yet he never gives up the privilege of knowing more than his passengers. His chronicles become journeys, which sometimes come to an end before the conversation between driver and passenger has ended, as happened in the chronicle "Decorativismo II": "Let's see if today I say what yesterday my taxi came to an end without my having said" (*T*, 141). The interruption performed here indicates that the chronicler has no control over the length of his articles, presumably determined by an editor. But the metaphor of the chronicle as a taxi ride also confirms the authority of the driver: he offers a ride, but he never relinquishes his vehicle. The chronicler's readers and passengers are transient visitors to a space he has appropriated. Mário facilitates public access to culture, but the dialogical agency he imagines for his readers does not edge him out of the driver's seat—nor eliminate his protected position as an intellectual. This clearly differs from many of Roberto Arlt's *aguafuertes*, such as "The Cross-eyed Lover," in which the chronicler is one of the many travelers on the streetcar, purposefully obscuring the barrier between himself and the potential readers of his articles, his fellow citizens. In *Táxi*, Mário doesn't obscure his authority in the manner of Arlt. He has no need to take an indirect route to achieve cultural prestige, for he has already established his public persona through his highly visible participation in the modernist movement. While Arlt worked from the outskirts of the lettered elite in Buenos Aires, Mário's confidence in navigating through his city indicates his comfortable status as an established mediator between art and its potential public.

Machado de Assis, arguably the most recognized and studied Brazilian chronicler of the nineteenth century, had already affirmed in 1877 that the chronicle was born from conversation: "I can't positively say in what year the chronicle was born, but in all probability it can be believed that it was contemporary of the first two *vizinhas* [female neighbors]" (*Crônicas escolhidas*, 14). By linking the chronicle to the birth of community living and to an urban setting where neighbors can meet regularly, Machado de Assis gives the chronicle a fablelike beginning before the existence of writing. The chronicle's closeness to daily life would be intrinsic to the formation of a community, instead of being a practice invented a posteriori to document it. The two neighbors Machado de Assis places at the origin of the chronicle are women (the feminine *vizinhas*), a detail that can't help but remind us of Arlt's gossiping women in "Two Elderly Ladies and the Author." This reference to female conversation highlights the informal nature of a genre that circulated outside official (male) cultural circles, and it points to the importance of a female readership for Machado de Assis' chronicles.[17] The question of the "gender" of the chronicle has often surfaced in later considerations of the genre, as is discussed in the following two chapters, but it must be noted here that the two women credited with the origin of the chronicle did so through oral means— as if writing were to come later, with the intervention of an implicitly *male* chronicler. Such a distinction confirms that although women were often considered the consumers of popular press, rarely were they seen as authors or creators.

As would Mário a few decades later, Machado de Assis paid much attention to how new modes of transportation altered the face of the city he wrote about, Rio de Janeiro, and shaped close encounters between citizens. *Bondes*, or streetcars, are frequently mentioned in his articles. The chronicler, who both witnesses and participates in urban modernity by riding the streetcar, listens to and transcribes the many conversations he purportedly overhears during his journey. In a chronicle from October 2, 1892, for instance, Machado de Assis describes how the first electric streetcar to arrive in Rio coincided with a presentation of an opera by Wagner. He asks himself: "Will the donkey and Verdi fall at the same time?" wondering if the demise of the donkeys that had pulled the old streetcars would coincide with that of Verdi (*Crônicas de bond*, 21). A couple of weeks later, on October 16, Machado de Assis takes the conversational element of the chronicle to an even more humorous level by transcribing an imaginary dialogue between two soon-to-be unemployed donkeys: "All of a sudden I heard strange voices; it seemed to me that it was the donkeys conversing; I leaned forward (I was on the front bench); it was they" (*Crônicas escolhidas*, 64). More than a voyeur who fantasizes about what he sees—as does his Mexican contemporary Manuel Gutiérrez Nájera in another famous streetcar chronicle, "La novela del tranvía"—Machado de Assis is an inventive eavesdropper who molds his texts around the voices he hears or imagines. The conversational quality of his chronicles speaks of a less structured relationship to the city than the one apparent in Gutiérrez Nájera's work.[18] While the latter observes and textually organizes the city from the monological and protected enclave of the streetcar, the former sidesteps this authoritative gaze by staging in his chronicles a playful dialogue with his surroundings. The chronicle, here, proposes a way of *listening* to the city—not just of seeing it—and thus makes it impossible to remain aloof from the dialogical give-and-take of urban life.

If the chronicle is a representation of an urban community as described through the many voices that shape it, the chronicler's role would therefore be one of pulling together these disparate utterances, of translating orality into a written form. More than simply being an author, the chronicler also functions as a mediator who participates in a collective process of listening and speaking, reading and writing. Mário reinstates Machado de Assis' portrayal of the chronicle as a gossipy genre in his collection *Os filhos da Candinha*. According to Telê Porto Ancona Lopez, "*Os filhos da Candinha*, in the language of our days, are the gossipers, those who know of everything and comment on events in their own manner; they are, better yet, those who work with invention, reinvention, starting with reality, with the true fact" ("A crônica," 169). The plural expression "os filhos da Candinha" suggests that the experience of telling, receiving, and circulating news is a communal activity. It also reflects the short-lived nature of a conversation that dies down quickly but that, through gossip, is recreated and reinvented on a daily basis. With the conversations it might provoke, the chronicle can continue to occupy the cultural imaginary of the city, even if the original article has been forgotten and the newspaper that published it thrown away. The chronicler can thus intervene in public opinion and in the formation of a modern urban imaginary far beyond the repercussions of a single article. The conversational nature of the chronicle suggests the formation of a community that evolves and reinvents itself constantly. The many individuals, or the "filhos da Candinha" who gossip, possess the autonomy to imagine and reimagine their community by reading the paper on a daily basis. Reading functions here as a starting point; it provides a daily conversation topic that enables the dwellers of São Paulo to participate in a form of public discourse.[19]

The conversational quality of Mário's chronicles takes on greater significance when linked to the Brazilian vanguards' interest in the vernacular. Many modernists, among them Mário and Oswald de Andrade, placed spoken Brazilian Portuguese at the core of their desire to artistically represent Brazilian culture. Infusing their works with oral expressions was a means to question their nation's dependence on European and North American cultural influences and to cultivate a national sense of self. The manifestoes of Brazilian modernism—such as Oswald de Andrade's Cannibalist Manifesto and in particular his Brazilwood Manifesto, which was also titled "Falação" (Chat)— expressed this desire to recover the county's autochthonous origins.

The Brazilian modernist movement has often been divided into two periods (Schelling, Presença do povo, 75). The first "heroic" period at the start of the 1920s created polemics around official art and culture and was overtly critical of the bourgeois establishment. Characteristic of this period were artistic innovation, experimentalism, and the search for an aesthetic language that would actualize art according to the new spirit induced by the modernization of the country. The second period of Brazilian modernism was more ideological than aesthetic. Elaborating a national culture, rather than a regional one, was seen as a means to attain a certain universalism. Here, the modernists differed from the line of thought defended in Gilberto Freyre's Regionalist Manifesto of 1926 (Oliven, "Brazil," 59), where regionalism rather than nationalism was considered the key for cultural definition.[20] The column Táxi arguably coincides with the transition period between these two aspects of Brazilian modernism. It addresses questions of language and aesthetics but also reveals a growing concern with the role of art and culture in shaping a national identity, and with the ways a writer can intervene to enhance the public's dynamic relation to national culture. That this column was published in the Diário Nacional—the newspaper of the newly founded Democratic Party, which attracted many intellectuals—also confirms Mário's commitment to the political potential of his writing.[21]

Mário's novel *Macunaíma*, described by Vicky Unruh as a "major linguistic achievement" that "incorporates elements of regional language, idioms, and proverbs into a hybridized amalgam" (*Vanguards*, 225), exemplifies the author's intention of creatively drawing oral and popular cultures into a conceptualization of Brazilian national identity.[22] The focus on orality was not a means for Mário to "decorate" his style but rather an organic way to reconfigure the idea of Brazil through its vernacular (Schelling, *Presença do povo*, 123–126). This work was conceived as a project that brings together all kinds of linguistic regionalisms into a collage that allegorizes Brazilian national identity. The national culture at the center of this allegory is curiously absent: the hero, Macunaíma, combines idioms to form a language that no one speaks. He is also conceived as having no character; like Brazilian culture and language, which are "mobile traditions," this protagonist is in a constant state of becoming. The linguistic project developed in *Macunaíma* can also be discerned in the oral quality of Mário's chronicles. Likewise, the novel's protagonist, who lacks a defined and specific character, recalls the chronicle's indeterminate nature (exemplified by Mário's reference to "as crônicas propiamente crônicas"). But while *Macunaíma* brings together linguistic regionalisms in a calculated and crafted manner to allegorize a national identity, the chronicle only echoes the speech of São Paulo, one of the many localities represented in the novel. The chronicle's conversational aspect, therefore, both demarcates its urban belonging and signals the limitations of its reach.[23]

According to Mário, Brazilian language does not represent a static entity; it is instead "a live organism, dynamic, that received, through the participation of the people, constant modifications" (*Mariodeandradeando*, 58). Brazilian modernists aimed to incorporate folkloric traditions into their movement dynamically and creatively. In the same way, they strove for a "sentimental, intellectual, ironic and ingenuous" sensibility that permitted an active absorption of European influences (Schelling, *Presença do povo*, 93).[24] Using the vernacular is a means to engage language and folkloric traditions with contemporary conditions, much in the same manner that Mário's "mobile traditions" adapt to the needs of their practitioners. Mário's reflections on how to develop a Brazilian language that conserved its particularity from Portugal became the subject of many *Táxi* chronicles, and he even intended to work on a *Gramatiquinha da fala brasileira* (A Little Grammar of Spoken Brazilian Portuguese), a project that he never completed.[25] In the *Táxi* article "Fala brasileira" (Brazilian Speech), he expresses his opinion on some of the intellectual debates regarding the differences between Peninsular and Brazilian Portuguese. He defends the latter as a manifestation of the historical and social particularities of its culture: "It is a language affirmed gradually and unconsciously in the national man. It is a language that represents Brazil intellectually in the universal communion" (*T*, 111). As opposed to a fixed written language protected by institutions such as the Academia Brasileira de Letras, vernacular language is an instrument meant to evolve with use and reflect the realities of its speakers.[26] Language is thus conceived as a social phenomenon more than as a scientific or linguistic subject of debate for academics. Mário here distances himself from an academic perspective by articulating his thought from outside institutional locations and in the realm of popular practices. Language foments national identity, not only because it permits a mutual recognition of Brazilian citizens through dialogue, but also because it permits its users to actively participate in the creation and evolution of the language that defines their cultural identity.

Mário's position coincides here with that of Roberto Arlt, who boasted that he was "no academic" and, in his chronicle "El idioma de los argentinos" (The Language of Argentines), compared the language of grammarians to the art of boxing meant for display only. For Arlt, perfect grammar resembles "a type of boxing that works perfectly for exhibitions, but that for fighting is absolutely useless, at least when faced with our antigrammatical young boxers" (*Aguafuertes*, 177). He prefers to defend the language that evolves through use and circulates outside the bounds set by grammarians, outside the boxing ring. By comparing grammar with boxing, Arlt pits different cultural categories against each other: boxing was a popular sport that was often discussed in the press of his day and was considered a working-class pastime more than an aristocratic one, while grammar was, of course, an interest of the intellectual elite. But Arlt's parallel also indicates a play between a theory of language and a language that exists as a practice.[27] In a remarkably similar manner, Mário critiques the fixed nature of a written language sanctified by the academy. Just as Arlt wants to take language outside the protected arena of boxing exhibitions and into the streets, Mário defends a language that is culturally significant because it evolves through use. Both chroniclers conceive of language as a continually evolving entity that, much like their articles, is shaped by a dialogical give-and-take between members of a broad and active public.

Just as the popular *lunfardo* of Buenos Aires often surfaces in Arlt's *Aguafuertes*, many of the chronicles in *Táxi* are written in a language that purposefully reproduces the conversational tones of spoken Brazilian Portuguese. Mário identified himself as a writer who expressed himself in the vernacular: "In Brazilian speech wrote Euclides, Machado de Assis, João Ribeiro, etc. And I" (*T*, 113). With this inclusive statement, Mário links his use of the vernacular to literary tradition. In this sense, his choice would not be a transgression of tradition but rather a mark of its continuity. This move would also seamlessly include the chronicle within Brazilian literary production. In the preface to *Os filhos da Candinha*, he reveals that his articles were often corrected by editors: "Sometimes newspapers and editors still pull out my foul-mouthed grammar, they correct me, and from there result numerous Portuguese sayings slipped throughout my writings" (10). He describes his grammar as *desbocada*, foul, wild, out of control. It has transgressed the bounds set by the Academy of Language, left the boxing ring for back alleys. This chronicler claims to have purposefully relinquished the reins that keep his grammar together. His self-deprecating comment, however, does not imply a loss of control but rather a calculated gesture to include the spontaneity of orality in his written texts.[28]

Perceiving the chronicle as a cultural expression linked to the vernacular suggests continuity with other Brazilian traditions that are based not on writing but on performance, such as music, dance, and oral traditions— in short, practices that function outside the realm of urban modernity, outside the lettered city. The similarity between Mário's defense of mobile traditions and his appreciation for the vernacular suggests a potential link between the chronicle and oral or performative culture. But even if the column *Táxi* represents a mobile tradition put into practice in the urban setting of São Paulo, the gap between the mobile traditions that for Mário manifest a national consciousness, and the chronicle, whose conditions presuppose an urban locality, is difficult to overcome. The chronicle responds to urban referents that were absent from the popular traditions Mário defined as mobile. In Brazil, low literacy levels limited the potential readers of chronicles, even in cities such as São Paulo and Rio de Janeiro. In 1890, only 18.5 percent of the country's total population could read, and the figure had reached 33.1 percent in 1900 (Süssekind 49). The reading audience was also relatively limited in urban areas. *O Estado de*

São Paulo, one of the city's most important newspapers, had in 1913 a circulation of thirty-five thousand (reaching less than 10 percent of the city's population). One can venture that the circulation of Mário's *Táxi* in the *Diário Nacional* was in the tens of thousands, consequently also reaching significantly less than 10 percent of the city's population.[29]

The possibility of a mass audience for Mário's *Táxi* is thus difficult to confirm. In fact, the guiding metaphor of this column already indicates the restrictions of its readership. Not all city dwellers, after all, can afford the privacy of a taxi. The citizens on the lower tiers of São Paulo's population are implicitly excluded, unlike in highly literate Buenos Aires, where Arlt's middle- and lower-class readers traveled by streetcar alongside the chronicler. The metaphor of the motorized taxi further restricts the circulation of chronicles to an urban setting, confirming that modern media was still beyond the grasp of the nation's majority: "In the Brazil of the 1930s and 1940s, there was no 'mass' culture which could compete with the legitimacy of traditional popular culture. At this time, in spite of the advent of radio and the press, one still cannot speak of the presence of 'culture industries', and there was no system for the nation-wide dissemination of cultural goods" (Ortiz, "Popular Culture," 134). The chronicle could thus hardly keep up with the popular expressions that were practiced in rural Brazil. Rural culture had long been documented and incorporated into literary traditions, but such influence was unidirectional. Brazil's uneven modernization made it difficult to take writing, even in an accessible and seemingly lighthearted form, outside the lettered city.[30]

Defining the chronicle as part of a conversational practice is a way to broaden its imagined audience. In this manner, the chronicle can, at least metaphorically, speak where reading is out of reach. Implicit in this line of thought, however, is that the chronicle remains tied to the written word and that its performative elements are still based on its condition as a text. If a performance aims to unite and congregate a public in a literal sense, the metaphor of the taxi indicates how the chronicle stops short of this objective by reproducing the ephemeral intimacy of a city where strangers relate through commercial exchanges on a small scale. The encounters between citizens in a taxi take place successively: one or a few individuals enter the vehicle, chat with the driver, and pay for their service, then leaving room for the next clients. The public congregated by the taxi ride, or by Mário's column, is united, not simultaneously, as Benedict Anderson has proposed in the case of an imagined community, but rather successively, with a time lag that signals both the limits of the chronicle's congregating reach and its long-term potential for renewal and regeneration. The very literal and physical audience of a performance can be created only rhetorically through the newspaper. This limitation might not have mattered as much to Roberto Arlt in Buenos Aires, for he privileged the city over the nation as a locus from which to articulate a cultural identity. For Mário, however, the limits of the chronicle made it difficult to ignore the fissures in his modernist impulse to promote a national Brazilian cultural identity that would speak to the entire country.

Being *Paulistamente* and the Limits of the Chronicle

Mário's work as a chronicler, like the intellectual persona he cultivated through his articles, cannot be dissociated from the location of his readers in the city of São Paulo. The column *Táxi* is intrinsically linked to an urban lifestyle, understood in a broad sense; it is also very much marked by the particular implications of writing from São Paulo during the 1920s. At the time that Mário was writing, the genre of the chronicle was associated with cosmopolitan Rio de Janeiro rather than with industrial São Paulo. From Machado de Assis to João do Rio, Lima Barreto, Benjamin Constallat, Álvaro Moreyra, and even later contributors such as Carlos Drummond de Andrade, Rubem Braga, and Clarice Lispector, Rio de Janeiro has been the location from which most recognized Brazilian chroniclers have written. As Beatriz Resende has pointed out:

> That the chronicle is a modality of urban literature, there is no doubt, but in the case of Brazil there is this peculiarity: it is in Rio de Janeiro that the genre was born, grew, became set. Making the exception of the multifaceted Mário de Andrade (especially of the series *Táxi*), we have to recognize that it is easier to have in our newspapers correspondents who speak of New York or Los Angeles than chroniclers who write of other cities in the country ("Cronistas," 35).

Rio de Janeiro was Brazil's cultural and political capital from 1763 to 1960. The architecture and layout of this city were comparable to those of European capitals such as Paris, inviting its chroniclers to stroll and document the streets in the tradition of the flaneur. Because of this, texts describing life in Rio were easily grouped with a Western literary tradition of urban writing, one that offered writers a vantage point from which not only to define urban locations but also to incorporate rural areas into a reflection that encompassed national culture. For many chroniclers, writing about Rio de Janeiro was a means to write about Brazil as a whole: "Chroniclers . . . reiterate a discursive slippage expressive of Rio de Janeiro's condition as capital, since, in their texts, many times 'Brazil' and 'Rio de Janeiro' are interchangeable terms" (Souza Neves, "História," 26–27). This slippage between city and nation was indicative of a lettered capital so confident of its discursive power that it imagined itself as a microcosm of Brazil.

The figurative leap between writing about a metropolis and writing about a predominantly rural nation was one that a chronicler such as Mário, who was profoundly engaged with Brazilian modernism, could not take so simply. He was too conscious of the hierarchical distance between a metropolitan center and its rural periphery, and even though he often spoke with the confidence of an established intellectual, he was unwilling to take this privilege for granted. In 1929 he reflected on the dissymmetry implicit in the modernist fascination with urban symbolism—a fascination that he obviously shared:

> [Cities] seek to synthesize a civilization and progress that do not correspond to the national reality. There is established, therefore, a disequilibrium between these centers and the rest of the country. . . . And when we remember that the fascination with cities is at the cost of that immense mass of Brazilians . . . we find a point for profound meditations. (Quoted in Gabara, *Errant Modernism*, 49)

Mário expressed the desire to define a modern cultural citizenship that went beyond the one shared by city dwellers, whose habitat familiarized them with the markers of urban progress. While Mário's sensitivity to the hierarchical unbalance between the urban and the rural can be traced back to the modernist interest in the recuperation of Brazil's folklore, another explanation lies in that he himself wrote from outside the privileged locus of the nation's capital. If texts written from and about Rio de Janeiro had the discursive reach to address broader issues such as national identity, São Paulo's condition as a newly expanding city in the 1920s did not provide this metonymical bridge. This particularity provides us with another angle to explain why Mário felt he could not fully address questions on Brazilian national culture through the chronicle. It was not simply that he was writing from an urban setting that excluded the rest of the nation's rural lifestyles; it was also that he was writing from São Paulo as opposed to Rio de Janeiro. Instead of provoking a nostalgic evocation of glamour and cosmopolitanism, such as Rio did, writing chronicles in São Paulo implied a turn to the future, a form of literary and journalistic innovation that indicated the city's potential as a new location from which the practice of chronicle writing could develop, even if it was still in its early stages. In this regard, we can draw another parallel between Mário and Arlt, his fellow chronicler in Buenos Aires. Despite the great differences in their standing with regard to the intellectual community of their respective locations, both used their writing as a means to include a new, previously underrepresented modernity in their nation's literary imaginaries.

São Paulo's growth and prosperity during the 1920s were a result of Brazil's sizeable coffee exports: "The city of São Paulo . . . became the keystone of the whole international coffee market, the place from where one could control production, stock, manipulation and export of about 70 per cent of all the coffee supplies available in the world from 1910 to the early 1920s" (Sevcenko, "Blaise Cendrars," 179). This industry concentrated an enormous amount of capital in São Paulo and provided the financial base for events such as 1922's Modern Art Week. Mário's *Táxi* evokes São Paulo's rapidly evolving cityscape by marking the transition between walking—the usual mode for a flaneur, who in Rio de Janeiro probably would have frequented the busy pedestrian Rua do Ouvidor—and riding in a motorized commercial vehicle such as a taxi.[31] Like walking, a taxi ride could take the reader through the midst of a city's activity, but it offered an accelerated means to experience a city that was being built with greater distances in mind. Being a taxi driver was one of the new jobs spurred by improving technologies that provided a respectful means to earn a living for a growing professional class of chauffeurs that in São Paulo, as in the rest of Latin America, quickly established itself in the first decades of the twentieth century. In Mexico City of the 1920s, for instance, Salvador Novo keenly noted the recent proliferation of uniformed chauffeurs, promptly anointing them as modern homoerotic symbols that promised endless opportunities for a sensual exploration of the city.[32]

Despite the drive toward modernity that characterized the growth of São Paulo in the 1920s, there was still a provincial and traditional side to the city (Ortiz, "Popular Culture," 140).[33] Although the Brazilian modernist movement sprang from here, this artistic surge was more indicative of an aspiration toward a modern future than a representation of contemporary reality. As Sevcenko has suggested, the very word "modern" became a fetish of the time: it advertised the desires of a population thirsty for a modernity that was not always consistent with daily reality (*Orfeu*, 228). Born into a traditional São Paulo family, Mário was himself extremely attached to his traditional local identity. In an early column, "De São Paulo," published in *Ilustração Brasileira* (1920–1921), he describes the city as an intimate accomplice: "I know of beautiful, singular things, that Paulicéia shows only to me, an incorrigible lover of hers" (quoted in Lopez, "A crônica," 173). In his collection of poems *Hallucinated City*, written during these same years, he exultantly dwells on the way São Paulo has shaped his identity. His oft-quoted line—"Oh! Este orgulho máximo de ser paulistamente!" (Oh! This greatest pride of being *paulistamente*! *Poesías*, 102)—describes belonging to this city, not simply as a way of seeing or relating, but as a more fundamental way of *being*. "Ser paulistamente" indicates not only identification but also a lack of distance to the point of fusion between the speaker and his city. Mário's identity as a *paulista* had manifold implications. On one hand, it established him as an ideal chronicler of São Paulo—like the other chroniclers in this book, Mário's evolution as writer was in sync with his city's rapid modernization and transformation. But on the other hand, this rooted identity seemed at odds with his self-imposed role as a cultural agent of movement. It contradicted the emphasis on flexibility and the lack of a definable "place" that a column such as *Táxi* entailed. It would seem as if the movement of the chronicle, like that of the chronicler, was fluid only as long as it remained within the city, having the oxymoronic quality of a *localized* mobility.

Perhaps because of his intimacy with his city, Mário was not much of a traveler. His ambivalent attitude toward "real" travel, as opposed to conceptual movement, is made all the more evident in his reluctant departures from São Paulo for his ethnographic trips to the Amazon and the Northeast. These excursions were documented in *O turista aprendiz*, which from its very title points to travel as an activity that did not come naturally for this chronicler. He felt divided between two identities, the local one and the one that would travel, as if caught between the pull of his urban persona as a chronicler and his ambitions as an ethnographer: "It has been already six days that I live as two men, and the new man, added now to me, is an unpleasant unknown capable of facing the enormous wave of the ocean" (*TA*, 201). This unenthusiastic traveler goes on to describe his departure from his city:

> What an unpleasant sensation! Good-bye, everyone!—Bon voyage, Mário!—Have fun!—Don't forget about us! . . . My impression is that everything is wrong. I had the urge to fling all those people into the train wagon, to stay on the eternally *paulistana* platform and to bellow happily to my departing friends: —Good-bye, everyone! Bon voyage! Have lots of fun! (*TA*, 201)

Mário's joking desire to stay on the platform as the train is about to leave São Paulo expresses a yearning for a stable identity, one that was precisely being eradicated from the very city he was reluctant to leave. São Paulo's rapid modernization was often compared to a train moving at full speed ahead—symbolically, the very train the chronicler now longs to abandon. São Paulo grew significantly in those early decades of the twentieth century, its population swelling to more than half that of Rio de Janeiro's by 1920.[34] Mário's desire to remain behind seems to indicate a paradoxical wish to halt the course of modernization, as if his choice to embrace a national cultural project entailed a renunciation of his localized identity. Once Mário was outside the city, movement seemed to recall the restrictions and the inconsistencies of a modernizing national project more than it suggested the potential of expressive freedom.[35]

This duality between traveling and staying put points to a deeper tension in the conception of cultural citizenship as well as in the role of the chronicler as an intellectual agent of movement. Mário appears divided between the familiar comforts of urban cultural belonging and the challenges of a sociopolitical citizenship that would entail the uneasiness of alterity. In his *Táxi* chronicle "Amazônia," he meditates on the authority of the "traveled man," whose practical experience of travel can put an end to any theoretical discussion, but he quickly undermines the authority of practice by insisting on its intellectual limitations: "The argument [of the traveled man] is powerful although intellectually it might oftentimes be a cowardice" (*T*, 164). This duality recalls Mário's contradictory desire for a "disinterested" art that he ambivalently juxtaposes with the defense of a humanizing practice. In this case, he desires the authority of travel but defends the advantages of learning from home. This dilemma points to the discursive double bind in which the chronicler from São Paulo finds himself. Travel does not come easily to him, but at the same time he feels the impulse to leave the city to speak for his nation, replacing with first-hand experience the problematic metonymical bridge that already existed between Rio de Janeiro and the rest of Brazil.

Being an agent of movement—an intellectual and a chronicler who makes cultural experiences accessible to a reading public—implies being in a constant state of dislocation and change, fostering engagement more than directly practicing it. In this sense, the chronicler would share with James Clifford's notion of the ethnographer the "perpetual condition of off-centeredness," of a citizen who "dwells in movement" (*Predicament*, 117–151). Departing São Paulo for an ethnographic experience implies exacerbating this lack of place, radicalizing the heteroglossia already performed by the urban chronicle. The chronicler, or taxi driver, would need to relinquish his confidence as a guide, surrendering both his authority as a driver and the protection of his vehicle. But in the 1920s and early 1930s, when Mário expressed the ethnographic penchant for discovering the "other" side of his Brazilian identity, São Paulo's own modernity promised more than was already at work. The chronicler couldn't afford to leave his city, or his vehicle, with the ease of European ethnographers who already felt alienated by the unfamiliar surroundings of their cities.[36] Mário's work in the city was not complete: he still needed to foment São Paulo's modernity through his practice of the chronicle, establishing his city's presence on the Brazilian literary map and promoting its cultural relevance for the Brazil of the future.

Chapter 4

The Chronicler as Streetwalker

Salvador Novo Performs Genre

> It is a spiritual bother not to know any respectable author who has uttered an immortal sentence on bathing, because epigraphs give strength and authority to speeches just like the opportune quotation of a legal article often gives freedom to prisoners, if the defense does it with tact and the jury believes them.
>
> —Salvador Novo, "Bathing Motifs,"
> *El Universal Ilustrado*, May 1924

In "Bathing Motifs," one of the first articles Salvador Novo published in the weekly magazine *El Universal Ilustrado*, the nineteen-year-old author dwells on the pleasures of bathing in the river or sea, discusses the urban experience of the public bath, and wittily teases his readers with the comforts of a bathtub of their own.[1] He writes on an admittedly frivolous subject yet claims to desire the serious consideration that an epigraph from a literary figure might solicit. This tongue-in-cheek lament reveals a willful mismatch of registers, a witty play with cultural hierarchies that would quickly become a hallmark of Novo's writing.

With an epigraph, Novo could establish cultural allies and anchor his ideas within a broader debate, suggesting to his readers ways to approach the text they were about to discover. An epigraph might also serve a purely aesthetic purpose, as Julio Torri, a contemporary of Novo's, once suggested: "[The epigraph] is a spiritual liberation from the ugliness and poverty of official literary forms, and it derives always from an almost musical impulse of the soul" (*Ensayos*, 17).[2] But if Torri elevated the epigraph by grandiosely equating it to a superior expression of the soul, Novo pragmatically brought it back down to earth by comparing it to a legal article quoted to a jury. In fact, Novo would eventually subvert the epigraph even further, using his own previously published words as a frame for his newer texts and astutely turning toward himself when in need of a figure of authority to corroborate his thoughts.[3] With this type of gesture, reminiscent of Mário de Andrade's self-dedication in his ode to São Paulo, *Hallucinated City* (1922), Novo cut short the dialogue promised by an epigraph, replacing an expected deference with a display of self-sufficiency.[4]

Why should an author who mocks epigraphs claim to need one for an essay on bathing? "I think of how well my bathing motifs would look, if their dome were ornamented by a phrase from, let's say, Shakespeare," confesses the impertinent Novo (*VE I*, 41).[5] His interest seemed purely decorative, but his aestheticism was not devoid of ulterior motives. A reference to Shakespeare indicated knowledge and status for a reading public educated enough to know this author's name but perhaps not erudite enough to grasp the superficiality of the reference. No longer limited to elite literary circles, Mexico City's growing print culture had made reading accessible to a middle-class public that was not fully versed in literature. Novo's reflection on epigraphs pointed to the ease with which a writer, through a few well-placed quotations, could pass as an intellectual. It also permitted Novo to link himself with high culture at the same time as he mocked cultural hierarchies.

The readers who leafed through the glossy pages of the *Ilustrado* in May 1924 and paused at "Bathing Motifs" were faced by a peculiar epigraph. Instead of a supposedly desirable quotation by Shakespeare, the sensual photograph of glamorous North American movie star Barbara La Marr, chatting on the telephone as she languidly reclines into a bubble bath, adorns the top of the page.[6] The *Ilustrado*'s blurb reads: "Barbara La Marr, the exquisite artist has, with this photograph, inspired Salvador Novo to write this present article." By replacing a respected literary figure with an attractive movie star in a risqué pose, the chronicler invited his readers to laugh at his unliterary source of inspiration. At the same time, in a calibrated gesture that enhanced his status as a public figure, Novo linked his public persona to the image of a female film star. Like this icon of cosmopolitan elegance, Novo seduced his audience through unconventional means: he flirted with his readers by creating a sensual and intimate atmosphere in his chronicles, all the while coyly keeping the distance needed to craft his own glamorous writing persona.

Including a photograph of La Marr in lieu of an epigraph displaced Shakespeare as a source of authority, much in the way that the Brazilian Oswald de Andrade's Cannibalist Manifesto, published a few years later, would substitute the well-known "to be or not to be" with "Tupi or not Tupi." But while Oswald de Andrade's play on words mocked a butchered—or "cannibalized"—pronunciation of the Western classic and replaced it with "Tupi," a reference to Brazilian indigenous culture, Novo instead rerouted the epigraph to stage a displacement of literature in favor of the urban popular.[7] In the 1920s, La Marr was a symbol of the cosmopolitan world of cinema, newspapers, and magazines, cultural forms that were less esteemed than literary sources but as familiar to an urban audience as Shakespeare was to literary critics. Novo knew his classics and could play the epigraph game, but he chose to forgo the authority

"Bathing Motifs," with a photograph of Barbara La Marr. *El Universal Ilustrado*, May 22, 1924.

of a literary quotation for a reference to a less sanctified artistic form, cinema. Likewise, his practice of the chronicle throughout his writing career constantly broke with expected conventions. As he did in "Bathing Motifs," Novo often *performed* literary codes in his journalistic work, not to conform to them, but rather to transgress them.[8] Novo's chronicles invited his readers to become voyeurs, to gaze into what was supposedly private, making them accomplices in his own textual—and sexual— transgressions. Doubling as a temptress or a prostitute, the chronicler made himself accessible to his readers by daringly displaying his sensuality and by playing with the conventions of gender as a way to provoke literary norms, all the while enhancing his own literary celebrity.

This brief close-up of Salvador Novo's play with epigraphs is, in itself, an epigraph of sorts. It is an emblematic example of how a young writer established his public presence in postrevolutionary Mexican culture. Novo was first known as an essayist and a poet, and as a member of the avant-garde "grupo sin grupo" (group without a group), later labeled Contemporáneos, along with fellow writers Xavier Villaurrutia, Jaime Torres Bodet, Carlos Pellicer, Jorge Cuesta, Gilberto Owen, Samuel Ramos, Elías Nandino, and José and Celestino Gorostiza. Novo began writing in the early 1920s and soon turned toward a career in journalism, regularly publishing chronicles and social columns in various dailies until his death in 1974. By the late 1920s and early 1930s he had already become a recognizable public figure. His name was associated with poetry, essays, journalism, and other forms of popular culture. He was frequently photographed in the press, and throughout the years, he could frequently be heard on the radio and also appeared regularly on television during the 1960s.[9]

Despite its contentious and occasionally outrageous elements, Novo's writing maintained a consistently conservative bent, and he clearly relished the public status that came with being affiliated to the literary canon. His chronicles often mingled details of urban daily life with pointed references to the genealogies of writers who portrayed life in Mexico City before him, such as Fernández de Lizardi, Gutiérrez Nájera, Luis Urbina, and Amado Nervo, among others. From the 1940s onward, Novo would be closely linked to Mexico's political and intellectual elite.[10] He was named official chronicler of Mexico City in 1965 by President Gustavo Díaz Ordaz, a title previously given to figures such as the esteemed Artemio de Valle Arizpe, an author and diplomat who wrote prolifically on Mexico's colonial period.[11] Novo's relationship to official circles was highly criticized in the late 1960s and early 1970s by a younger generation of intellectuals for his failure to speak out against the 1968 massacre at Tlatelolco. At this juncture, he supported the official version of events given by President Díaz Ordaz, a move that would lead critics to bypass his work for almost two decades after his death. It was only until the 1990s that his writing began to be revalued, in great part due to his unique perspective as a relatively outspoken gay writer in early twentieth-century Mexico.[12]

Because Novo was such a prolific chronicler, writing thousands of articles on Mexico City life in different columns and under various pseudonyms, this chapter focuses primarily on the metatextual aspects of his early chronicles and on his tense relationship with the national canon.[13] Novo began writing at a time when Mexican culture and literary authority were matters of constant debate, with private disputes often aired as public polemics. His contribution to the cultural negotiations of postrevolutionary Mexico, as well as to the long-term importance of the chronicle in his country's literary canon, can best be illuminated through a heated argument that took place in 1929 between the young chronicler and Rubén M. Campos, a well-known novelist and critic. Through the lens of this specific exchange, I will argue that Novo's turn to the chronicle, like his self-fashioning as a flirtatious accessible intellectual, stemmed primarily from his stance in the debates of the 1920s regarding the role of literature in the aftermath of the revolution. As a chronicler, Novo cultivated a provocative public persona, conspicuously exploring frivolous or banal themes precisely at a time when intellectuals were expected to act as solemn guides for a nation that was emerging from ten years of civil war. By humorously displaying his taste for the urban popular, Novo also pointed to the newfound cultural significance of commercial media, such as newspapers, magazines, radio, and cinema.

Transvestite Games

In the summer of 1929 a scathing polemic between a young Salvador Novo and Rubén M. Campos, an established composer, musician, novelist, scholar, and critic, appeared in the *Ilustrado*, the same magazine that had published "Bathing Motifs" five years before. The dispute began when Novo, in his article "Generación anecdótica" (Anecdotal Generation), published on June 13, 1929, dismissed the older thinker as part of a generation incapable of artistic creation. Campos, a leader of Mexican *modernismo*, had been a regular contributor to the *Revista Moderna* (1898–1911), along with Rafael López and Manuel José Othón. Around the time of the polemic with Novo, he had recently published two ethnographic studies, *El folklore y la música mexicana* (1928) and *El folklore literario de México* (1929). Despite Campos' accomplishments, Novo mockingly describes him as a survivor of the obsolete golden age of Mexican *modernismo*:

> [Rubén M. Campos] belongs to a generation for whom the dry law and the anti-alcoholism campaign were as strange as the trimotor; for whom the example of Alfred Jarry, of Verlaine, the misunderstood Baudelairean tradition, the legends of Poe's life, all made the artist of the nineties into a convert of inspiration, this equivocal term that in his case excludes culture and intelligence. (*VE II*, 399)

Novo depicts the *modernistas* as a group whose belief in artistic inspiration distances them from culture and intelligence and whose heavy-handed humor is ignited by drink rather than insight, an obvious reference to Campos' having, in the autobiographical evocation of *modernismo* entitled *El bar: La vida literaria de México en 1900*, located the center of literary life at the turn of the twentieth century in a bar.

Campos counterattacked on June 27 with "The '*Novísima*' Literary Foam" (a play on the similarities between "new" and "Novo"), in which he reproaches the chronicler for his homosexuality, criticizes his approach to literature as effeminate and banal, and makes public Novo's contributions to *El Chafirete*, a ludicrous magazine dedicated to chauffeurs in which Novo's writings had included a sexualized parody of Sor Juana Inés de la Cruz' poetry, published under the pseudonym "Radiador." When Novo responded to Campos on July 4, he called the final installment of this petty exchange "Carta atenagórica al 'ilustrado' sobre quien no lo es" (Athenagoric Letter for the '*Ilustrado*' on Who Isn't [Enlightened]). With this gesture, Novo purposefully recalled his previous parody of Sor Juana in *El Chafirete*, appropriating the title of the letter written by the Mexican nun more than two hundred years before. Sor Juana's original was a display of erudition, a carefully constructed argument coming from an unexpected source and directed to a male ecclesiastical authority, the Portuguese priest Antonio de Vieira. The letter was published in 1690 by the bishop of Puebla, Manuel Fernández de Santa Cruz, along with a reproach of Sor Juana's intellectual ambitions that he signed with the pseudonym "Sor Filotea de la Cruz." Sor Juana would then fire back with the famous "Respuesta de la poetisa a la muy ilustre Sor Filotea de la Cruz," in which she defended the right of a woman to pursue literary endeavors.

At the time of Novo's debate with Campos, Sor Juana's writings were making a comeback among literary critics. In "Estantería," as well as in "El cesto y la mesa"—two columns providing an overview of recent publications and cultural events that Novo wrote in 1929 for the *Ilustrado* and *Revista de Revistas*, respectively—he discussed recent academic publications on Sor Juana's writings, singling out his own mentor Pedro Henríquez Ureña and Ermilo Abreu Gómez, who had completed an edition of "Primero sueño" and was working on the "Carta atenagórica" (*VE II*, 213, 298). Sor Juana was certainly fresh in Novo's mind. His reference to her writings was a pointed means of demonstrating his current literary knowledge to Campos as well as to the *Ilustrado*'s mainstream readers, while advertising a lack of remorse at his own satire of her poetry. Like Sor Juana, Novo carefully displays his knowledge and defends his artistic stance when writing to a figure of cultural authority—in his case, an established member of a previous literary generation. Sor Juana's "Carta atenagórica," according to Octavio Paz, is a complex and polemic text which nonetheless includes inside jokes directed to her few select readers (*Sor Juana*, 512). Paz' remarks on the humorous undertone of Sor Juana's letter could very well be extended to Novo's article, which offered a flirtatious wink at the learned reader familiar with Sor Juana's work and his own.

By referring to Sor Juana, Novo affiliated himself not only with her gesture of self-defense but also with her durable presence in Mexican culture. This rebuked Campos' allegations, which had compared Novo's writing to "banalities blown away by the wind" (*VE II*, 401). Yet in his appropriation of the "Carta atenagórica," Novo never directly refers to Sor Juana, limiting himself to borrowing her title as though it were an epigraph. More than the particularities of the nun's letter, what matters here is the way Novo strategically links himself to a figure who needed to defend her right to write when critiqued by an established authority.[14] Novo replied to Campos through a figure recognized as doubly subaltern, both Mexican (vis-à-vis the Spanish crown) and female (vis-à-vis male ecclesiastical authority). This chosen ally can help shed light on Novo's turn to the chronicle, especially when put in the context of the heated conversations that took place among Mexico's leading intellectuals in the mid-1920s regarding the role of literature in postrevolutionary culture.

In the aftermath of the Mexican Revolution, the literary legacy of *modernismo*, which had been emblematic of Porfirio Díaz' era, was called into question by the intellectuals of the Ateneo de México, led by José Vasconcelos, Alfonso Reyes, and Pedro Henríquez Ureña. These figures were eager to leave behind the influence of positivism and the Francophile bent of literary aesthetics that were popular at the turn of the twentieth century. They now focused on the cultural heritage of the revolution and on creating a literature that embodied revolutionary ideals to help define a new national culture. Vasconcelos' work, in particular his messianic *The Cosmic Race*, strove toward a united Latin American political and cultural consciousness, developed through popular access to learned culture. As secretary of education, founder of the national university, and promoter of the nationalist muralist project that facilitated Diego Rivera's paintings, Vasconcelos exhibited a didactic militancy that advanced culture and education as tools for national progress.

During this period, the role projected for literature in a society reeling from conflict was often defined in sexually charged terms. Texts that expressed a nationalist concern with Mexico's political reality, its social struggle, and the potential of revolutionary change were labeled as robust and virile. Works with notable foreign influences and reminiscent of Mexican *modernismo* were dismissed as weak and effeminate. Obviously, these exchanges on the definition of literature were fundamentally misogynistic: "effeminacy" and "masculinity" were always adjectives defining a literature that was unquestionably male. Masculinity was associated with certain works, such as Mariano Azuela's novel of the revolution *The Underdogs*, while effeminacy was linked to texts with cosmopolitan interests that did not focus on the social and political impact of the Mexican Revolution.

On December 21, 1924, the essayist Julio Jiménez Rueda published in the daily *El Universal* his article "The Feminization of Mexican Literature." Here, he lamented the absence in Mexico of truly manly literature, establishing the parallel between virility and Mexican nationalism that Campos would later draw from in his article against Novo. Jiménez Rueda's article elicited a wealth of responses from other intellectuals, launching a debate that divided Mexico's literary world. On one hand, it set apart the group Contemporáneos, of cosmopolitan interests, from their avant-garde rivals, the Estridentistas, whose second manifesto pointedly declares: "To be *estridentista* is to be a man. Only the eunuchs are not with us."[15] On the other hand, Jiménez Rueda's article highlighted the rift between the Contemporáneos and the cultural politics of Vasconcelos' group, the Ateneo de México, for the debate on virile and effeminate literature had also reached Mexico's official cultural discourse.[16] Throughout these heated negotiations, a concern with the "orientation" of Mexican literature slipped into a debate on the sexuality of its writers.[17] If revolutionary change had been the fruit of aggressive masculinity and subsequent Mexican literature did not take note of such accomplishments, critics contended, then this discrepancy could be explained only by the uncertain sexuality of the new generation of Mexican writers.

Novo's literary orientation clearly placed him, along with his fellow Contemporáneos, in the effeminate, cosmopolitan camp. His growing dedication to the genre of the chronicle was not a means to give testimony of the social impact of a revolutionary struggle. Instead, he strove to document the interests of a bourgeois upper middle class who lived in Mexico City and stayed away from the nation's political upheavals. This choice represented a sort of literary treason to the intellectual mainstream, an affront both to Mexico by depicting urban lifestyles rather than a national reality, and to manhood by ignoring the rigors of social struggle. Much like Roberto Arlt, who in Buenos Aires identified with the culture of the capital rather than with a national community, Novo opted to privilege an urban form of cultural citizenship in his work. In the case of Mexico, however, a country whose sociopolitical structure was still frail as a result of the revolution, this choice reflected the lifestyle of a comfortable minority rather than the formation of new working-class communities. This difference might help explain why, in the case of Arlt, identifying with *porteño* street culture was considered a mark of virility, while, for Novo, the culture of the capital linked him intrinsically with dandy bourgeois comforts and hence the label of effeminacy. The frivolous tone and pointed, often aggressive humor characteristic of Novo's chronicles can thus partly be attributed to the contentious implications of his choice to write about comfortable lifestyles in the Mexican capital.

Novo was known to be an avid reader of André Gide and Oscar Wilde. He was considered an expert in all things foreign, to the extent that he was introduced by the editors of the *Ilustrado* as "a Yankee writer with solid English and French culture, who writes in Spanish" (May 8, 1924). The chronicler further confirmed this cosmopolitan image by publishing an article entitled "An Outline of American Magazines," in which he surveyed different American magazines, describing their focus, format, and price. This article was accompanied by photographs of an assortment of magazines: *Photoplay*, the *Country Gentleman*, *Liberty*, *Good Housekeeping*, *American Magazine*, *Scribner's Magazine*, the *Literary Digest*, the *World's Work*, *Hearst's International*, and the *Saturday Evening Post*. The editor's blurb reads:

> Nothing better than this summary, written especially for this issue, of the North American magazine. Its author, Salvador Novo, is one of the new literary figures who knows best the magazine movement in the neighboring nation, and from that he offers, in these pages, very juicy observations and very sensible ideas. (June 5, 1924, 24)

Articles such as this one highlight the interest of the *Ilustrado* in establishing a dialogue with American publications. Also notable is the presentation of Novo as a new writer whose importance stems, not from his knowledge of literary tradition, but rather from his acquaintance with contemporary North American serial publications. The U.S. magazine trade is curiously described as a "movement," a term that evokes literary innovation rather than the publishing business. In a subtle manner, this choice of words places journalism on equal standing with literature. As with "Bathing Motifs," Novo is presented as a respected writer who displays his intimacy with popular culture as well as with "high" literature and who is all the more admirable as a result.

Despite the support offered by the *Ilustrado*, Novo's interest in popular publications, added to his relatively open homosexuality, made him a ready target for the criticism that emanated from the literary debates of the mid-1920s. With such deep-seated concerns about masculinity in the air, it comes as no surprise that Novo's relationship with Pedro Henríquez Ureña reportedly soured when the latter heard of the young writer's homosexual promiscuity.[18] Henríquez Ureña cut Novo off from his intellectual patronage and suggested that he go "sweep snow in New York" to cultivate his manliness (Barrera, *Salvador Novo*, 104). Such attacks, however, did not imply that Novo was completely ostracized from institutional culture. Mexico City's intellectual world was small. Connections and collaborations were inevitable and are all too easy to ignore in hindsight. Novo worked as a public servant in the ministry

"An Outline of American Magazines." *El Universal Ilustrado*, June 5, 1924.

of public education (Secretaría de Educación Pública, or SEP) during the early 1920s and taught in English in the summer school of the National University. His fellow Contemporáneo Jaime Torres Bodet was Vasconcelos' private secretary when he was minister of education, and many of the members of this group worked either in the ministry of public education or that of health, under the protection of Bernardo Gastélum.

At the time of Novo's polemic with Campos, five years after Jiménez Rueda's initial article, the debate on the sexuality of Mexican literature had become more subdued, but it still influenced many publications dealing with national culture. In May 1929, for instance, an essay signed by Pablo Moreno and entitled "Los andróginos" (The Androgynous Ones) appeared in the *Ilustrado*, comparing the effeminacy of writers to a gangrene that weakened the national body. Novo's decision to speak through Sor Juana when defending his contribution to Mexican culture was thus all the more laden. By irreverently pairing the expected chastity of a nun with his own well-known homosexual promiscuity, Novo questioned both an intellectual's implicit obligation to produce a vigorous, manly literature and the idea that virility was inseparable from a Mexican national identity. This borrowing from Sor Juana also put into question the necessity of defining a national culture in absolute terms, as postrevolutionary nationalist discourse pretended. Novo thus shunned the intellectual and cultural responsibility held high by official discourse by playfully bringing together two categories that had been projected as mutually exclusive in the 1924 polemic: effeminacy and "Mexicanness."

When Novo responded to Campos' attacks under the cloak of Sor Juana's "Carta atenagórica," readers were faced not only with a young literary figure speaking through the voice of a canonized author but also with a male speaking through a female voice, creating a hybridity that borrows from both genders, just as the chronicle, which eventually was to become Novo's trademark genre, takes from the spheres of both literature and journalism, from both erudite and "nonserious" culture. Novo did not try to reconcile the oppositions highlighted by his appropriation of Sor Juana's letter (masculine versus feminine, chaste versus promiscuous, national versus foreign, "real" literature versus commercial journalism). Rather, he chose to speak *from* these differences, exercising a form of literary transvestism. A third space having the flexibility to question the validity of binary structures, transvestism, as Marjorie Garber argues, signals "the crisis of a category itself" (*Vested Interests*, 17). A transvestite does not try to pass as the "other" or become that which it imitates, but rather expresses his/her identity as its parody, making difference and artificiality visible. Like Novo's take on epigraphs, which renders visible the strategies at work behind them, his transvestism of Sor Juana is a means to destabilize the rigid definitions of sexuality, literature, and culture that were used in postrevolutionary Mexico to affirm paradigms of national identity. In this sense, Novo's use of Sor Juana claims a more versatile concept of the nation, one that leaves room for novelty and sexual difference. This doesn't, however, imply that Novo wished to annul cultural hierarchies. He still strove to link himself to the literary elite, albeit by dismantling conventional procedures to signal a crisis in the category of literature through which, as a chronicler interested in modern cosmopolitan culture, he could enunciate. Novo might well be irreverent and provocative, but he still cultivated his status within Mexico City's lettered culture.

That Campos brought up effeminacy yet again to critique Novo's writing in "The 'Novísima' Literary Foam" is hardly unexpected. Campos describes Novo as "a young master in the art of irony" who often turns toward the exquisite: "he wets his golden pen in rose ink." Novo is a "a blushing adolescent, who still has milk on his lips" and whose writings "burn with the fire of Sodom" (*VE II*, 401). This description of Novo as a dandy youth who has not reached puberty recalls reproaches often given to the Contemporáneos, characterizing them as a group who were too young to have felt the rigors of the revolution and therefore had never hardened into manhood. This description of Novo also explicitly echoes Jiménez Rueda's 1924 article, in which he had lamented: "But today, even the physique of the thinking man has degenerated. We are no longer gallant, haughty, rough. Now success is usually found, more than through the tip of our pens, through the complicated arts of the boudoir" (quoted in Díaz Arciniega, *Querella*, 58).

Campos' attack on Novo's sexuality, however, quickly backfired, for the chronicler replied through two seemingly contradictory strategies. On one hand, he conjured a female figure as his ally in his counterattack against Campos. On the other hand, he gave emphasis to the signs that made his masculinity visible by describing his body as manly and unfeminine: "And I realize the deplorable taste [of Rubén M. Campos], when, knowing my physique (one meter 85 tall, weighing 86 kilos), our domestic Rubén calls me an adolescent youth" (*VE II*, 401). Despite the attacks against his person, Novo fits within the very model of manliness desired by Jiménez Rueda. He truly *is* tall and vigorous, and yet he chooses to step beyond the supposed "masculine" requirements of Mexican literature. An intellectual stance is not about being, Novo suggests here, it is about *performing* or even about *posing*. It is as pragmatic as conveniently name-dropping Shakespeare to pass as an intellectual; it is subject to change on a whim. More importantly, posing indicates a contestatory cultural gesture that exposes the inconsistencies of his antagonist's argument, thus working to reinstate Novo's status as a provocateur whose intellectual persona is directly linked to his questioning of gender norms.[19]

By displaying his sexuality as an open secret, always obvious but never stated, Novo undermines the importance of "knowing."[20] Campos had backed up his references to Novo's sexuality with his supposed knowledge of his "secret" homosexual identity. But instead of contradicting Campos or proving his allegations correct, Novo shows that no one is immune from ambivalence. Novo familiarly calls him "our domestic Rubén," linking him to femininity and domesticity and to Rubén Darío, a poetic figure from the previous century no longer in vogue for Novo's contemporaries. At the same time, Novo suggests a parallel between Campos and the bishop of Puebla, the respondent to Sor Juana's "Carta atenagórica" who had written under the feminine pseudonym of Sor Filotea. If Sor Juana's interlocutor wrote under the disguise of a woman, Novo's adversary could not himself remain aloof from sexual ambiguity. Even the staunch defenders of a pure and "virile" Mexican literature, Novo shows us, couldn't help being contaminated by the frivolity of effeminacy.

Mexican Literature, a Fresh and Virile Girl

The underhanded humor with which Novo defines his cultural—and sexual—orientation goes hand in hand with his resistance to describe literature in absolute terms. In January 1925, Novo was interviewed by the *Ilustrado* for an article entitled "Does a Modern Mexican Literature Exist?" This survey, which drew from the opinions of many well-known writers, such as José Vasconcelos and the Estridentista Luis Quintanilla, was published alongside a drawing of an armed bandit on horseback: issues of masculinity, "Mexicanness," and popular culture were clearly at stake. Novo responded with purposeful ambiguity: "I suspect then, justifiably, that there exists a modern Mexican literature whose good reputation as a fresh and virile girl, the aching and moth-eaten tongues of those who discuss without creating have wished to opaque" (January 22, 1925). Just as he would later combine a description of his masculine body with his ventriloquism of Sor Juana, Novo here describes literature as a girl who is both feminine and strong. Instead of assigning a specific gender to literature, Novo chooses to present it as a hybrid figure that can play with its orientation.

Can the chronicle be the fresh and virile girl that Novo equates to literature? The notions of transvestism, hybridity, and excess discussed in the previous section can be helpful in broadening our reflection on the chronicle as a particular mode of cultural production. In many of Novo's chronicles, excess surfaces in his concern with the luxurious aspects of bourgeois life, in his willingness to move toward aesthetic interests and away from a functional notion of culture.[21] If the chronicle, like the transvestite, signifies a third space, it marks an unexpected excess that questions the simplicity of a binary system. Likewise, Novo's accessibility to his public is elusive rather than straightforward. His chronicles layer an abundance of meanings and possible interpretations, all of which promise to expose the chronicler's stance regarding the place of literature but always seem to fall short of revealing it.

Through his recurring references to sexuality when addressing cultural issues, Novo links his public persona to the literature he produces and appropriates the slippage between author and text that was brought

"Does a Modern Mexican Literature Exist?" *El Universal Ilustrado*, January 22, 1925.

forth by the debate on the feminization of literature. Novo's willfully "excessive" sexuality—that is, his physical manliness combined with his "effeminate" interests—paves the way for the polysemic nature of his writing. This heterogeneity plays out the chronicle's discursive transvestism, one that permits Novo to move in and out of different registers and to authorize himself through various discourses. In this manner, the chronicler accumulates ways of thinking literarily instead of replacing one literary model with another. Just as Roberto Arlt had transformed his "weakness"—his lack of formal education—into an asset, Novo's highly criticized sexuality becomes a means to render visible the chronicle's heterogeneous cultural discourse. Novo's "excessive" sexuality works to open a space in the Mexican literary canon for the chronicle, a complex genre that remains receptive to novelty, improvisation, and contradiction.

Novo's penchant for excess, particularly when documenting the superfluous aspects of city life, recalls the nineteenth-century chronicle's impulse to "decorate" the city by aestheticizing its utilitarian aspects and by proposing the chronicler as a guide to its offerings of luxurious goods.[22] In a chronicle titled "On the Advantages of Not Being Fashionable," for example, Novo describes life in the capital as an endless race to catch up with the latest novelties. Keeping up with the city's offerings is a full-time job, claims Novo, and one can escape from its excessive stimuli only if one is sick or in the countryside:

> Regardless of the branch of the social tree that you are attached to, if you live in the city, enjoying its well-known advantages—the roads, electric power, the telephone, French novels, public sector employment, Turkish baths—you must pay civilization a tribute by being up-to-date on its last cries and being able to discuss them uprightly. (Appendix 3)

In this seemingly haphazard list of urban luxuries, Novo includes examples that range from electric power to French novels, grouping together technological modernity with literary novelties. Likewise, the social responsibilities that come with being a city dweller are fully circumscribed to elite activities: keeping up with social gossip, wearing the latest fashions, and pretending to understand the latest "-ism." In an indirect manner, this satirical survival guide for the urban dilettante offers a humorous testimony of the richness of cultural life in Mexico City during the 1920s.

Novo's orientation toward a bourgeois chronicle of manners in pieces such as "On the Advantages of Not Being Fashionable" is reminiscent of the articles written by *modernistas* such as Gutiérrez Nájera, who had adopted a mundane, affectedly lighthearted tone. Monsiváis calls Gutiérrez Nájera "the chronicler by excellence of Porfirian society in its period of ascent," and adds that his love for French letters led him to describe a Mexico City that no longer existed: "He walks not through a city that will become more precise and real, but through a city that will remain for always inexistent. He invents a city to fit literary vocations within it" ("De la santa doctrina," 760). Even though Novo admired Gutiérrez Nájera's chronicles, he nonetheless distances himself from his predecessor in that he does not share his nostalgic need to remember a city of pleasures that was disappearing—if it had ever existed at all. Novo's emphasis on excess functions primarily as a means to write about a constantly changing reality that was being ignored and forgotten *in the present* by official cultural circles, which overlooked the effervescence of an urban middle class that was reveling in its newfound modernity.

The excess of cultural registers that permeates Novo's writing in the 1920s would come to distinguish some of his most important works. A closer look at Novo's *Nueva grandeza mexicana*, a book-length chronicle published almost twenty years after the polemic with Campos, can show the extent to which the tactics the chronicler used to establish himself as a flirtatious accessible intellectual at the start of his writing life would continue to shape his public persona throughout the years. In this work, Novo links himself both to a long literary tradition of writing about Mexico City and to vibrant aspects of contemporary modernity, defending his relevance in urban popular culture without relinquishing his link to high literature. He includes this work within a genealogy of texts going back to colonial literature, notably to Bernardo de Balbuena's epic poem, *Grandeza mexicana*, from which Novo takes his title, his structure, and also his epigraph.[23] Like Novo's borrowing of Sor Juana's letter, this emulation of Balbuena plays with different registers by bringing colonial texts into a modern setting. Here, Novo evokes a tradition of chroniclers that spans back to colonial times, completely erasing a fundamental difference between a modern journalistic genre that was published in newspapers and a genre that in colonial times responded to completely different political and aesthetic referents and, perhaps more significantly, usually addressed a single powerful figure rather than a broad, unknown, journalistic public. Associating himself with the colonial chronicle allows Novo to situate himself at the origin of the city's literary tradition by strategically linking his own text back to a foundational description of Mexico City.

Novo nonetheless combines the structure taken from Balbuena's text with constant references to modernity. More than a historian, the chronicler functions as a tour guide who translates urban life for a visitor from the northern city of Monterrey who is unacquainted with the pleasures of the capital. The chronicler interprets the cityscape as though it were a text open to many readings, a play on Balbuena's mention that "everything in this speech is encoded." This reference alludes to the multiple layers of meanings that can be discovered in the palimpsest that is the Mexican capital, but it also points to the homoerotic subtexts that surface in many of Novo's writings on public urban space. Despite his references to the clandestine nightlife of the capital, however, his eulogy of the city supports the official version of the progress that was touted by the government, ignoring the dark underbelly of poverty and corruption that also characterized the presidency of Miguel Alemán. In keeping with the vocabulary of modernity, the chronicle is tinted with references to technological progress. Novo makes frequent references to skyscrapers, cars, and, perhaps more notably, to the cinema, presenting his journey through Mexico City as a moving narrative that cinematographically links the city's past with its modern present: "Once again . . . . My memory has incurred in what in cinematographic jargon is called a *flashback*" (*VE I*, 178, original in English). Such references presume a reader familiar not only with the cinema but also with the English vocabulary that accompanies it. In this manner, Novo replaces the Francophile bent that characterized Gutiérrez Nájera's *modernista* vision of Mexico City with another cultural model, that of the United States and, more particularly, that of Hollywood.

Just as Novo successfully borrows from Sor Juana and Bernardo de Balbuena, he also portrays himself as a public figure comparable to Mexican movie star Dolores del Río. When he mentions Coyoacán, a neighborhood south of Mexico City, he notes: "There are only two notable Mexicans there, among them, Dolores del Río and Salvador Novo, owners of large gardens around Santa Rosalía street" (*VE I*, 225).[24] The chronicler refers to himself in the third person, becoming a character in his own description of the city. He links himself once again to femininity and more particularly to the cinema, a cultural form that in the Mexico of the 1940s had reached its golden age precisely through figures such as Dolores del Río, María Félix, and director Emilio Fernández, symbols of the country's new international cinematographic visibility. The chronicler here doubles not only as Balbuena, a colonial writer, but also as a movie star, imagining for himself a vast and unmeasurable audience. This self-aggrandizing gesture recalls the intimacy with Barbara La Marr that he flaunted in "Bathing Motifs," when at the end of his essay he designated himself as the privileged interlocutor of the sensual actress: "And for now, the girl in the illustration follows my advice and thanks me over the telephone" (*VE I*, 42).[25] While the continuity in the tactics Novo uses to fashion his public image is unquestionable, there is nonetheless a great difference in the implications of his status. By the 1940s he was no longer a young chronicler who aligned himself with a relatively new cultural form, such as the cinema. Rather, he was an established writer who linked his persona to one of Mexico's most important—and state-sponsored—cultural industries.

Throughout his writing life, Novo's association with glamorous icons of popular culture would be constantly reinstated by the theatricality of his public image. Starting in the mid-1920s, the *Ilustrado* frequently published photographs of him in poses emphasizing his dandyism—hair, plucked eyebrows, delicate hands. In an undated caricature strip published in *Excélsior* by Mariano Martínez under the title "People I Saw Today," Novo appears with his hair slicked back, arched eyebrows thinly plucked, and, more noticeably, slim hands with long fingernails and a large showy ring. The caption, "Un empleado de educación pública que tiene la facilidad de escribir e imitar a algunas personajes" (An employee of the ministry of public education who has a gift for writing and imitating certain [feminine] characters), insists on his androgynous characteristics and shows the extent to which his public persona was linked to imitation and parody.[26] Novo's penchant for performance would play out through his involvement in the experimental Teatro Ulises in the late 1920s, founded by the Contemporáneos under the patronage of Antonieta Rivas Mercado, and in the 1950s, in his own Teatro la Capilla, in Coyoacán. But theatricality was also a hallmark of his journalistic life. As a chronicler, Novo donned many masks and was known for using numerous pseudonyms, such as el Caballero Cartablanca, Cronos, Dip, Aureliano Mariátegui, Niño Fidencio, Radiador, Snov, and Carmen Reyes, among others. During the late 1930s and early 1940s, he often commented on his own articles from one pseudonym to another, to confuse some readers and joke with others in the know (Lomelí, "Salvador Novo," 217–223). In his diverse and often simultaneous columns, Novo would draw from a variety of sources, making artifice visible and layering an abundance of meanings and possible interpretations. In this manner, the chronicler extended to his own public persona the palimpsest quality that he attributed to Mexico City, a choice he emphasized in *Nueva grandeza mexicana* when he included "El joven"—the chronicle he wrote on Mexico City in the early 1920s—as an appendix to this more mature work.

The chronicler, like the transvestite, here undermines the simplicity of a binary system, be it high literature versus urban popular culture, nationalism versus cosmopolitanism, or masculinity versus femininity. Novo creates his public persona by superposing his visibility as a journalistic celebrity with his links to literary tradition. In this manner, he performs his own concept of literature by embodying both the "freshness" of urban popular culture and the "virility" of literary tradition. One can't help but wonder why in *Nueva grandeza mexicana* Novo didn't channel María Félix rather than Dolores del Río, given that the former, known as La Doña, was famous for her mix of masculine strength and feminine beauty.

Salvador Novo, the imitator. "Recortes de prensa," date unknown.

A Frivolous Intellectual

As seen above, Novo's vision of Mexican literature as "a fresh and virile girl" indirectly included the urban popular in a polemic that supposedly focused exclusively on literature. This slippage—between literature and popular media—is particularly relevant when considering the cultural place of the chronicle in the years following the Mexican Revolution. In the particular case of Novo, the chronicle sets the stage for a writer's incursion into the public sphere through a commercial press that dwelled on the frivolous aspects of daily life in the Mexican capital.

Not surprisingly, the tension between literature and the commercial press played a crucial role in Novo's 1929 polemic with Campos. Through the reference to "el ilustrado" in the title of his letter against Campos ("Carta atenagórica al 'ilustrado' sobre quien no lo es"), Novo describes as erudite a magazine whose original name, *Ilustrado*, ostensibly referred to the illustrations that adorned it rather than to its elevated contents. This purposeful slippage between two different registers—that of learned culture and that of a culture designed for entertainment—indicates, not a replacement of one category by another, but a doubling of two usually mutually exclusive categories. At the same time, this tongue-in-cheek reference to erudition describes Campos as someone who is precisely *not* erudite, presenting him as less knowledgeable than a publication that in the past had prided itself in being a "revista para peluquerías" (a magazine to be found at barbershops or salons), as an editorial note appearing in 1925 described the magazine.[27] It also mocks the concept of man of letters (*hombre ilustrado*), fundamental to the leading intellectuals of the time, whom historian Enrique Krauze dubbed the "cultural caudillos" of the Mexican Revolution (*Caudillos*, 16).

It would be too quick, however, to dismiss the *Ilustrado* as merely a "light" magazine without taking into account the complex condition of publications in Mexico City in the 1920s and 1930s. During the years following the revolution, there were few possibilities to publish outside of José Vasconcelos' messianic educational project. As secretary of education, Vasconcelos aimed to make culture accessible on a national level, not by vulgarizing it, but by elevating the educational level of the public so that it could reach a common appreciation for beauty that would unite the nation—and the American hemisphere—into a single "cosmic race."[28] While the publication and distribution of books was intrinsic to this project, the texts chosen were mostly limited to the Ateneo de México's Hellenic concept of high culture.

During these same years, the *Ilustrado* offered a radically different conception of reading and the circulation of texts. The publication defined itself as a "semanario artístico popular," an artistic popular weekly. "Frivolity" was a term associated with the mission of the magazine, not because it shunned serious matters, but because it presented important debates in a pleasurable and entertaining manner. When under the direction of Carlos Noriega Hope, a young journalist fascinated with Hollywood and closely associated with the Mexican avant-gardes, this publication followed the format of North American magazines and was oriented toward a middle- or upper-class readership.[29] It gave space to articles on food, fashion, and the lives of movie stars, as well as anthropological, historical, and literary essays, poetry by the Argentine Oliverio Girondo and the Chilean Gabriela Mistral among many others, and foreign articles translated mostly from English or French. This was one of the first Mexican publications to translate texts from the European avant-garde and to publish essays such as Ortega y Gasset's "The Dehumanization of Art" in 1923. Many contemporary Mexican thinkers, though associated with radically different intellectual currents and literary publications, coincided in this eclectic magazine that strove to build a broad readership. Mariano Azuela's *The Underdogs*, hailed as *the* novel of the Mexican Revolution, was published here in serial form, along with articles by Novo's close friend Xavier Villaurrutia, the Estridentista Arqueles Vela, Artemio de Valle Arizpe, and Federico Gamboa, among others.[30] During the 1920s, this magazine was one of the few means for young contemporary writers to be read.[31]

Novo's pun on erudite versus illustrated goes back to the criticism he had extended to Campos in his article "Anecdotal Generation," where Novo had described him as a collector of images devoid of creativity, a survivor of Mexico's intellectual golden age, "a friend of Tabladas, Valenzuelas and Nervos, Othones and Delgados; in whose brain, like in an album of photographic portraits, the covers of Julio Ruelas are kept."[32] According to Novo, Campos' thought represents a series of static illustrations. He would therefore be "illustrated," not as a man of letters, but as a figure whose imagelike thought process prevails over his intellectual ability. Campos, whom Novo describes as "this being, today denominated a folklorist, yesterday an erudite compiler," is a collector of sterile information, a transcriber who polishes the knowledge of others didactically and introduces it to a greater public: "He makes it his mission on earth to mend, as he would with shoes 'deformed by the use of uncultured people who neither feel nor think . . .' verse and prose, which he copies and at the same time transcribes for an ample public" (*VE II*, 398). According to Novo, Campos intends to protect popular art from the ravages of daily use; he struggles to erase the evidence of public consumption in order to guarantee that art remain in its intact, original form.

Campos' interest in popular art echoes Vasconcelos' drive to rescue and incorporate popular indigenous traditions to strengthen Mexico's national identity. Compiling folklore into a volume reveals a respect for the book as a cultural expression capable of educating a public, promoting the preservation of culture, and fomenting a national identity. Krauze reflects on the importance of the book in Vasconcelos' campaign: "Founding a library in an isolated and small village seemed to have as much significance as building a church and putting on its dome brilliant mosaics that announced to the passerby the proximity of a place to rest and recuperate" (*Caudillos*, 105). If founding a library and distributing books represents a labor of messianic fervor for Vasconcelos, Novo counterpoints this faith in his article "On the Utilization of Books," where he dismisses the book as an object that exists primarily through commercial exchange:

> Life is, on top of everything that those who tend to sentence it say, an infinite chain of acquisitions in which enter in a principal manner some objects called books, visibly different from suits and furniture, and that do not keep but a pretended spiritual relationship with the food that usually nourishes our stomach—interminable candies that do not disdain from sucking, at the same time or successively, the brains of people. (*VE I*, 125)

Far from being a sacred object to be revered in the churchlike space of the library, the book is stripped of its cultural value and defined by Novo through its function as a commodity that can be used and traded in an exchange economy. This concept of use, however, does not dwell on the explicit act of reading and its cultural and symbolic implications. For Novo, the book-object is meant to circulate rather than be accumulated. Instead of representing a protected form of knowledge that remains isolated from a daily economy, books cannot be separated from their commercial condition. Novo's stance recalls Roberto Arlt's defense of the chronicle's ephemeral nature, a gesture that, in his case, replaced the fetish of the collectible object (the book) with the fetish of the day (the newspaper). But while Arlt critiqued the act of collecting culture because it was associated with luxury rather than pragmatic street culture, Novo's defense of circulation hinges precisely on the importance of luxury. For Novo, the consumption of books, like that of candy, is driven by the promise of pleasure.

Novo offered a radically different concept of art from the one espoused by Campos. According to the chronicler, Campos defended a form of popular art that portrayed Mexico's social inequalities as picturesque and primitive, freezing the popular into a rigid and anachronistic conceptualization of national identity. Campos' focus on national culture's indigenous elements remained out of sync with the contemporary reality of urban spaces such as the capital, where cinema, photography, magazines, chronicles, and other expressions of cosmopolitan culture were on the rise. Campos' endeavor was all the more fruitless, in the eyes of the young writer, given that Mexico's nationalistic impulse reflected European influences more than it did local needs.[33] Novo, on the contrary, believed that art should be valued through its ability to keep up with the fast-paced rhythm of modern urban commerce. In a previous article, "Radio Conference on the Radio," where he had gone so far as to suggest that radios should replace libraries, Novo had affirmed: "Today's art is worn through its use because it has practical applications and this produces the advantage of its constant renovation, the abolition of museums and of archeological investigations" (*VE I*, 39).[34] On one hand, the combination of art and science embodied by media such as cinema and photography represented what was living and contemporary. On the other hand, institutions such as museums were obsolete signs of a culture that was no longer relevant, precisely because it was not put to use in daily life. To the figure of the intellectual as a collector and guardian of obsolete culture, Novo counterpointed that of an intellectual defined by accessibility. He informed the public on the ever-changing nature of modern art, via the chronicle, an ephemeral medium that was also defined through its condition as a commodity to be read and exchanged. The chronicler therefore functioned as a distributor of the new, a guide for readers and potential cultural consumers who looked for entertainment rather than instruction.

Novo's concept of accessible art is devoid of the didactic purposes that accompanied Vasconcelos' mission and that had also guided Mário de Andrade's interest in fomenting Brazilian national culture. Rather than aiming to educate a given public, Novo instead focuses on the repercussions of accessibility on art itself and on the experience of the consumer. In his view, knowledge and culture must reach a public through immediacy in order to be vibrant and relevant—a conception that, in turn, serves to reinstate the importance of the chronicle. As an expression characterized by its rapid turnover, the chronicle becomes both a form of accessible art and a medium through which readers can be informed of other artistic productions. Like the other chroniclers in this book, Novo defines art primarily through the public's experience, echoing many critiques of the European vanguards against the existence of art as an institution in bourgeois society.[35] But while both Arlt and Mário take the concept of use to address social and political matters, Novo eschews this possibility. He uses the chronicle as an intermediary to demarcate a bourgeois exclusivity that avoids any potentially "serious" cultural project.

From the start of his writing life, Novo was notorious for his purposeful frivolity. He preferred to shy away from a definable cultural objective and consciously avoided didactic projects, as we saw in his satirical rendering of urban modernity in his chronicle "On the Advantages of Not Being Fashionable."[36] Similarly, the titles of some of Novo's early chronicles confirm the banality of the themes he privileged; "Meditation on Eyeglasses," "Speech on Beds," "About Beards," and "On the Infinite Pleasure of Killing Many Flies" are just a few of the more memorable examples. Novo's humor, like his penchant for double entendres, distanced him from the expected labor of the intellectual in postrevolutionary Mexico. As Miguel Capistrán points out, in the 1920s "it seemed as if the basic ingredient to be considered a writer was solemnity, and consequently, humor was a motive for reproof, for it equaled not only something bothersome for the national character but also something similar to the superfluous" ("Notas," 346). During the same years, Alfonso Reyes had voiced his concern for Novo in a letter to Xavier Villaurrutia, expressing his hope that the young writer was distancing himself from unedifying work such as the writing of chronicles: "What does he do? I don't like seeing him tied to the hard bench of the chronicle. Has he already emancipated himself from this? Has he let his wine repose a bit?" wonders Reyes, suggesting that the rapid production rate of the chronicle prevents Novo's writing from slowly maturing into more serious matters, such as "real" literature (Capistrán, "Notas," 352).

In "The '*Novísima*' Literary Foam," Campos, like Reyes, had picked up on Novo's preference for banal themes:

> Fortunately, in today's youth there are distinguished writers who do not boast of being geniuses nor hammer away advertising their merchandise; but that instead labor to produce a work of art that is nobly human, and not banalities blown away by the wind, false naiveties that don't add anything to literature. (*VE II*, 401)

By describing Novo's texts as merchandise advertised for sale, Campos reinstates the dichotomy between a "real" art that exists autonomously and a superficial art that forms part of a commercial enterprise. He argues that Novo's writing is not even worth quoting, as it lacks creativity and originality: "it is reduced to clichés of other literatures, to childish stupidities of ridiculous ingenuity, to lamentable glosses of common places, to themes with the variation of a ventriloquist, that were aborted by a failed intellect" (*VE II*, 400). Campos accurately pinpoints many of Novo's strategies: parody, artifice, use of clichés, childishness, ventriloquism. Also worth noting is Campos' reference to "aborted" intellectual thought, a failure of productive intellect linked to Novo's "defective" reproductive biological capacities, namely, his homosexuality. Once again, Novo's intellectual orientation is compared to a choice in sexuality, his lack of manliness a sign of the ephemeral nature of his work. Here, Campos dismisses the performative aspects of Novo's work as indicative of intellectual shallowness, while they arguably form an intrinsic part of the latter's tactics to establish himself in a public sphere that was beginning to reflect the growth of the culture industry.

Novo's audience consisted of those citizens who could afford entertainment. They went to the cinema, purchased newspapers and magazines, were interested in the latest international trends in culture and fashion. In other words, they were remarkably similar to the dilettante portrayed in "On the Advantages of Not Being Fashionable." In a chronicle published in his column, *Consultorio a cargo del Niño Fidencio* (loosely translatable as "Niño Fidencio's Medical Advice"), Novo jokingly describes Mexico City as a modern paradise where Eve is a bourgeois housewife who stays at home reading the newspapers, while Petra, her maid, goes out to the market: "Eve finds today her substitute in Petra, who goes to the market while she stays looking at the newspaper pages, and Adam leaves to board the streetcar—eight cents a ride, in closed car—and goes to face a Remington and not a plough" (*VE II*, 246). In this column, Novo takes on the voice of the popular *curandero* Niño Fidencio, who at the time was performing miracles and healing the sick in the northern state of Nuevo León. The chronicler reroutes the skills of this mystical figure to cure the absurd aliments that affect a bourgeois dweller of the capital.[37] In "Nueva patología externa" (New External Pathology), for instance, he provides his readers with suggestions to cure diseases such as *contractio pantalunae*, the shrinking of pants; and *inflatio genu*, the stretching of the pants' knee area after prolonged sitting (*VE II*, 267).

To define his readers, Novo turns to the *Ilustrado*'s frequent self-description as a magazine to be found at barbershops:

> If this magazine can be found in *peluquerías*, it will still be found there, for many weeks, because all civilized people cut their hair and clean their footwear. On the contrary, other ephemeral magazines from Guadalajara, as they are made with softer paper, can be found in other places where everyone goes, civilized or not. (*VE II*, 113)

Novo selectively addresses a public that participates in the bourgeois rituals of cleanliness and is interested in articles such as "Bathing Motifs." In the early twentieth century, a *peluquería* was generally associated with men, and the term would loosely be translated as "barbershop." But when women began to cut their hair as a result of the influence of American "flapper" fashion in the 1920s, the gender specificity of the term *peluquería* started to fade.[38] Novo's focus on the patrons of barbershops or beauty salons, although inclusive of both genders, completely erased the rest of the nation as potential readers. This choice is not unexpected, as Novo made many problematic statements about racial and social divisions in Mexico throughout his writing life. In his essay "Meditation on Eyeglasses," for instance, he explains that eyeglasses are an accessory of civilization necessary to apprehend both literature and the city and that they would consequently be out of place in indigenous environments: "Ignorant of glass, Indians had never used eyeglasses. Perhaps they understood that a dark face looks, with them on, like an adobe house with very fine crystals" (*VE I*, 39). Since an indigenous gaze would not blend in with the aesthetics of the city, Novo opts to simply erase this unlikely rural audience from his community of readers and identifies instead with well-established city dwellers for whom reading, like a regular visit to the *peluquería*, is an activity inseparable from daily life.

Habermas observed, in the case of Europe, that the rise of mass media accompanied the formation of an elite audience for popular culture that differentiated itself through its consumption from the rural population (*Transformation*, 173). In the particular case of Mexico in the 1920s, a country still reeling from the conflict of the revolution, the accessibility of popular culture through magazines, periodicals, radio, and cinema was even more restricted to middle- and upper-middle-class city dwellers.[39] This is undoubtedly a very different setting from Roberto Arlt's Buenos Aires, where a highly literate community enabled the practice of reading to cross class boundaries. Novo's elitism, however problematic, can be considered a pragmatic response to Mexico's precarious publishing industry. The chronicler responds to the reality of the capital's existing reading public, stepping away from an activist notion of art as a vehicle for social change and indirectly pointing out the limits of Vasconcelos' idealistic cultural project. Novo's choice suggests that if art lives through its consumption, targeting an existing audience can guarantee its constant renovation. Art and culture become defined by their exchange value; they become that which can be consumed by the middle class.

The *Ilustrado*'s readers, according to Novo, participate in the very same "complicated arts of the boudoir," the dandy coquetry that both Jiménez Rueda and Campos accused him of indulging in himself. The participation of readers in these acts of dandyism determines for Novo their existence as "civilized" city dwellers. The frivolity and effeminacy of literature thus extend themselves to the act of consuming and exchanging texts, as well as to the consumers themselves. In this manner, Novo bonds with his readers through the experience of culture as a commodity. Many of Novo's chronicles comment on current events, as though he inspired himself by reading the same newspapers in which he published.[40] He is not only a producer of texts for sale; like his audience, he is also a reader. Just as Novo had made a point of extending his sexual ambiguity to include Campos in his polemic with the well-known writer, he also indicates that his readers, simply by virtue of being city dwellers, already participate in the frivolity of textual exchange.

Novo transforms the very critiques that dismiss him as banal into trademarks of his cultural production. It is tempting to say that Novo's cultural project is frivolity itself, but it might be more appropriate to argue that frivolity is Novo's *style*. In the context of mass culture, the concept of style draws away from the expected depth and intentions of a cultural project. As cultural critic Stuart Ewen has expressed, style "deals in surface impressions" (*Images*, 22), it "makes statements, yet has no convictions" (16). Susan Sontag refers to similar characteristics to define "camp" as a sensibility (rather than an idea) that "converts the serious into the frivolous" (*Against Interpretation*, 277) and that emphasizes "texture, sensuous surface, and style at the expense of content" (278). As Novo's fascination for flamboyant stars such as Barbara La Marr and Dolores del Río indicates, the camp sensibility of this chronicler works with underhanded humor to seduce readers and introduce performance and artifice as cultural ideals. The notion of style had already been singled out as a characteristic of the chronicle in the late nineteenth century. Rubén Darío argued that style was specifically what distinguished the chronicle's literary quality from simple journalism by keeping literature's aesthetic impulse alive (Rotker, *Martí*, 40). According to Darío, style rescues the chronicle from being fully contaminated by the pragmatics of the commercial sphere, but with Novo, style becomes precisely what marks the inclusion of the chronicle in the realm of mass culture. Novo's embrace of the rhetoric of mass culture does not detract from the pragmatic elitism that led him to define his audience within upper middle-class circles, for style also serves as a social marker, reinforcing class divisions by consolidating the unity of the social group that recognizes itself through its signs (Simmel, *Culture*, 547).

If superficiality indicates what is commonplace, cliché, overexposed, Novo becomes its embodiment, working from pejorative elements to stage his omnipresent public persona in his texts. His move toward a "light" culture was daring precisely because it was so forcefully out of tune with official intellectual concerns in the Mexico of the 1920s and early 1930s. Novo aimed to take culture outside of the institutional sphere of government, outside of a nationalist project, and into the sphere of commerce. He became a public figure, not because he was associated with spheres such as the government or education, but because he was continually made visible through his exposure in newspapers and magazines. The very ephemeral and banal nature of Novo's texts, therefore, worked to guarantee his continuous presence and visibility as a public figure. They enabled him to renovate his image and his style, day after day, chronicle after chronicle.

The blurbs that often accompanied Novo's articles in the *Ilustrado* enhanced his presence in the literary scene, as had, for instance, the editorial note that accompanied the article launching the polemic with Campos, "Anecdotal Generation":

> Our collaborator Don Salvador Novo sends us this tremendous article. In it, determined literary currents are attacked, and without a doubt, it will cause a true sensation in Mexico's artistic circles. Naturally Ilustrado does not express solidarity with the concepts expressed by its distinguished collaborator, but, at the same time, it considers the publication of these lines within its program of absolute eclecticism. (June 13, 1929)

The editor describes Novo's article as "tremendous" and emphasizes the sensationalist impact of his words. The importance of the chronicler's comments is measured in terms of its effect on the reading public, reinforcing the performative aspect inherent to a polemic, a public argument staged between two or more protagonists. In this aspect, the Mexican press of the 1920s became a theater on whose stage public prestige was debated, questioned, or confirmed, a process that clearly took place within the parameters of commercial writing. Novo was often presented as an avant-garde artist and as a young intellectual precisely because these terms were in vogue—they sold. The chronicler's public persona thus pragmatically responded to a shift in the very concept of the "intellectual." Habermas observes, "In the realm of mass media . . . publicity has changed its meaning. Originally a function of public opinion, it has become an attribute of whatever attracts public opinion" (*Structural Transformation*, 2). Likewise, Novo's writing persona continually adapts to changes in the political and social space allotted to public figures. He fashions himself as an intellectual in order to attract attention from a reading public, more than attracting readers by virtue of being an intellectual. In this aspect, Novo's theatricality does result in superficiality, as Campos had implied, but this superficiality makes a decisive cultural statement by responding to the increasing importance of reader interest at a time when many publications needed to display themselves as commodities in order to reach a public.

The Pleasure of Being Read

Novo's defense of literary production as consumable art was inseparable from his intervention in the heated discussion on the "feminization" of Mexican literature during the 1920s, for the supposed "effeminacy" of Novo's chronicles marked his incursion into the sphere of mass culture, a category consistently labeled as feminine since the nineteenth century.[41] Still today, the rhetoric of cultural consumerism is often sexualized. Either the passive consumer is feminized, or mass culture itself becomes a female figure, sometimes considered, more than simply as woman, as a "bimbo" embodying traditional female stereotypes: "distracted, absent-minded, insouciant, vague, flighty, skimming from image to image" (Morris, "Banality," 651). These adjectives easily apply to Novo's readers, the housewife who stays at home with the paper, the men and women who read the *Ilustrado* while at the *peluquería*. But they also apply to Novo himself, the flighty intellectual who focuses on the banality of daily life and who produces dispersed chronicles instead of a solid body of work. And as will be discussed in chapter 5, the description of the consumption of popular culture as a practice linked to gender and sexuality had far-reaching repercussions, not just for Novo, but also for the writing personas of women journalists and the reception of their work.

If popular literature is seen as a feminine figure aiming to seduce a potential reader, transforming him—and her—from wandering citizen to accomplice in the sexualized market of popular culture, what does that make the producer of popular texts? When reflecting on his extensive writings, the "prodigal sons" that roamed loose along the streets of Mexico City via various newspapers and magazines,[42] Novo in his typically biting humor compared his journalistic work to prostitution:

> One cannot demand [of a beautiful young girl] that she alternate the sacrament of maternity with the daily ritual of prostitution. If she lives from the latter, even if she did not voluntarily elect it, the most that can be demanded is that the ephemeral contact with all of those with whom that girl does her duty on the bed of the newspapers be, at least, pleasurable. (*Vida en México*, 19)[43]

Novo describes the writer as a figure divided between maternity (literature) and the daily ritual of prostitution (journalism). His predisposition toward journalism ties him to the sensual and the ephemeral, toward a type of writing that will touch many readers, only to be quickly forgotten. Yet at the same time, he claims to choose a sexuality defined by pleasure rather than a "sanctified" sexuality incorporated within a productive structure linked to heterosexuality, family, and nation. Far from moralizing the choice of writing for a massive audience, Novo plays with the prejudices involved, defending the pleasure of being read. By offering himself to his readers, the chronicler becomes not only the prostitute but also the pimp who caters to the sexual—and hence, textual—desires of a large population.

Novo considers his choice of prostitution over procreation as voluntary, although he once coyly admitted being dragged into the profession: "I simply confess, relatively regretfully, that I was dragged by prostitution, a circumstance of which I am consoled by the hope of having ennobled it a bit" (quoted in Monsiváis, "De la santa," 767). Novo here reinforces the parallel between the chronicler and the prostitute that *modernistas* such as Rubén Darío had flirted with, even if they had not articulated it with quite the same mischievousness (Ramos, *Divergent Modernities*, 139). Novo also references the promiscuity for which he was notorious and reinstates his sexual preferences as a cultural stance. But the chronicler's statement on prostitution, taken seriously by many, quickly gives way to a joking flaunt of his contribution to raise the profession to a more noble status. Once again, Novo inverts the paradigms at stake. Not only does he avoid being contaminated by the stigma of prostitution; he claims to have partly liberated it from its negative connotations by extending to the field of journalism some of the sacredness of literature. By claiming to choose prostitution over the socially acceptable option of procreation, Novo repeats his performative gesture of choosing popular over sanctified culture, just as, at the start of his writing career, he had opted for Barbara La Marr over Shakespeare for inspiration on his essay on bathing. Once again, this is not a democratizing gesture; rather, Novo strategically draws his journalistic practice into the "noble," and hence exclusive, realm of literature.

Novo's conceptualization of the role of literature, and more specifically of the chronicle, works from an intimate complicity between the intellectual and the public sphere. In the early twentieth century, most thought on Mexican culture had tended to reflect the rigid boundary between a didactic intellectual and a public eager to be incorporated into a new national modernity. The intellectual subject, such as José Vasconcelos and later Octavio Paz, defined himself as pure intellect (disembodied thought), while the masses described came into being through their corporality. Critics such as Juan Gelpí contend that with the chronicles of Carlos Monsiváis, Elena Poniatowska, and José Joaquín Blanco in the 1970s, the masses became the focal point of the texts produced by Mexican intellectuals who now spoke from within the city's public spaces ("Paseo por la crónica," 83). This shift is unquestionable, but I hope to have shown here that Novo's embrace of the flow of popular publications in the 1920s marked a crucial first step in redefining the role of the chronicle in Mexico's public sphere. Although he did not develop the political potential of his destabilizing cultural choices, and despite the great ideological gap that separated a conservative Novo from the chroniclers of the 1970s, he did pave the way for this next generation of cultural commentators.

Novo's public persona pushed his accessibility to an almost invasive level. He insinuated his chronicles into the very intimacy of his readers, transforming them from spectators to participants and even into accomplices. His status as an accessible yet flamboyant intellectual was not simply a side effect of the broad circulation enabled by journalism; it was the very element that defined him as a chronicler and reinstated his singularity as a public figure. The ephemeral pleasure of writing simply for the sake of being read was Novo's means of fusing with the constant ebb and flow of the modern city. Not only did he describe the mundane aspects of daily life in the Mexican capital, but he also managed, by transforming himself into a protagonist of his own texts, to become an essential actor in the urban consumer culture he described. Mexico City's streets, where Novo initiated his sexual adventures as a young gay man in the 1920s, were also where he seduced his public. This was where his articles were bought and sold, read and discussed. Novo's texts and his image thus wandered the streets as part of a sexualized commercial dynamic, flirtatiously seeking to be picked up by a curious reader.

Chapter 5

Overstepping Femininity
The Chronicle and Gender Norms

> "Feminine Chats," "Conversation Amongst Women," "Feminine," "Madam Mystery" . . . all these respectable sections are offered to the well-recommended female friend whom one does not know where to place.
>
> —Alfonsina Storni, "Femininities," *La Nota*, March 1919

> I think that because of the very fact that my section is called "Only for Women" men read it.
>
> —Cube Bonifant, "Vanity of Vanities!" *El Universal Ilustrado*, July 1921

Latin American cities in the 1920s were buzzing with conversations on modernity. New technologies and the effects of urban growth might have been the main topics of the day, but other, more intimate changes were also at stake. Some of the most pressing questions concerned the role women were playing in modern life and, in turn, the effect that modernity was having on women. The abundant representations of modern femininity that circulated were often contradictory. Newspapers, magazines, and films proposed images of young women dressed in flapper style, with short hair and bright red lips, holding cigarettes in exquisitely manicured hands. At the same time, activists organized feminist groups, distributing pamphlets and canvassing for equal rights; indigenous women in traditional dress were anointed nationalist symbols; and articles giving advice on hygiene and motherhood were broadly distributed.[1]

Such an abundance of descriptive—and prescriptive—representations of womanhood indicated that the very fabric of society seemed to be shifting. But they also reflected the increasing presence of middle-class urban women as independent cultural consumers. Women were entering the workforce in greater numbers, obtaining jobs as teachers, secretaries, typists, telephone operators, and sales clerks. Like working men, they were crossing the city at scheduled times, taking subways, streetcars, or buses, and picking up their reading for the day at corner kiosks. With their newfound income, women gained the possibility of being socially defined through means other than their belonging to a family or neighborhood network. The decisions they made as consumers were therefore conspicuous expressions of social belonging. Their choices in fashion and the places they frequented were scrutinized, as were the books and magazines they chose to read in public. How women exercised the choices available to them as consumers was becoming a matter of constant debate, and the question of taste—in literature as well as in fashion—was becoming all the more contentious.[2]

Many self-consciously modern women of the 1920s were avid for reading materials that reflected their newfound interests. As a result, savvy magazine editors began to revamp the pages they dedicated to "feminine" themes in their publications. Well in tune with the mores of their time, they were aware that instead of the expected notes on domesticity, full of cooking and beauty tips, young readers needed something new and different: regular columns that reflected how women were engaging with city life and with modern womanhood. That is how, in 1919, Alfonsina Storni was offered the feminine section in Buenos Aires' weekly magazine *La Nota* by its director, Emir Emin Arslan, and how, two years later, Cube Bonifant was invited by Carlos Noriega Hope to write a column for the *Ilustrado* in Mexico City. While the writing personas of these women chroniclers differed—Storni tended to be ironic while Bonifant was aggressively confrontational—their columns covered remarkably common themes and brought a willfully modern approach to women's journalism. They discussed expected topics such as fashion and relationships with a pinch of malice and also made a point of commenting on more mainstream topics such as current political and social events. More importantly, Storni and Bonifant shared an overt irreverence toward the very women's columns that they wrote, choosing to both exploit and mock the medium available to them.

Publishing regular columns in the "feminine" pages of newspapers and magazines gave these women chroniclers the opportunity to gain visibility as writers, in popular as well as intellectual circles. But while writing for the press enabled them to fashion original intellectual personas, the genre they practiced constantly reinstated their location on the outskirts of literary circles and imposed very clear-cut restrictions on *what* and *for whom* they could write. If their gender distanced these women writers from the homosocial networks of avant-garde circles in Argentina and Mexico, the heterogeneity of the genre they practiced was also too commercially oriented to be taken seriously, for it was linked to an industrial media that was in itself labeled as frivolous and, hence, feminine. Like the other male chroniclers in this book, Storni and Bonifant refashioned the perceived limitations of the chronicle to their advantage, but the dual markers of femininity—embodied by both their gender and the genre they practiced—made their struggle to gain prestige and recognition as writers even more difficult. For women chroniclers, mass culture was a treacherous ally. It enabled them to become accessible intellectuals who were admired and read, but it also reinforced their inevitable distance from implicitly masculine intellectual circles.

Storni and Bonifant are two unique examples of women chroniclers who interacted with the avant-gardes of their cities and absorbed some of their principal concerns with urban modernity. Both also wrote regular columns to earn a living and support their families, becoming the most visible professional women writers of their respective generations. Storni, the elder by twelve years, succeeded in gaining recognition for her poetry and her plays both in Argentina and abroad. While journalism was far from being her only outlet for writing, it helped foment her relationship with a local reading public and gave her the opportunity to comment on current events in a timely manner. Bonifant, who began publishing chronicles in 1921 at the age of seventeen, was a reader and admirer of Storni's poetry.[3] She relied much more on journalism than had her predecessor, not only as a means to build a readership but also as a source for aesthetic inspiration. Bonifant published chronicles regularly during most of her writing life, and even though she published thousands of articles in Mexico City's most important newspapers and became one of the country's most important film critics during the 1930s, she never acquired Storni's literary prestige. While Storni became a legendary figure in Latin America, mythified in part because of her dramatic life and tragic suicide at the age of thirty-eight, Bonifant would on the contrary disappear into virtual oblivion. Despite these contrasting trajectories, however, both women brought to their columns a will to fashion themselves as public figures, relating to their cities and to literary culture with an irreverence that chroniclers writing just a few years after them, such as Roberto Arlt and Salvador Novo, would also put into practice. This chapter therefore turns to the early 1920s to find in the women's pages a precocious manifestation of the rhetoric of accessibility.

Alfonsina Storni's Didactic Irony

Storni's rueful comment in the first epigraph to this chapter refers to the respectable magazine sections in which women journalists were expected to fit. She clearly considered them programmatic and safe or, perhaps more to the point, simply boring. That was where editors placed the "well-recommended" woman writer, not because of a belief in the quality and relevance of her writing, but rather to avoid offending whichever prestigious protector she might have.

In "Femininities," the first article in her column of the same name, Storni states two reasons for accepting Emir Emin Arslan's offer to head the women's section of his magazine. The first reason is without a doubt the most compelling: she needed the income. The second indicates, with underhanded irony, both a resignation to and a challenge in her role as chronicler for the women's pages. Storni first dismisses the offer by stating: "Cooking pleases me in my home, when I am waiting for my boyfriend and I want to prepare exquisite things" (*AS II*, 801). Thus she expresses that feminine domesticity, for her, does not infringe on her profession as a writer and that she has no intention to pen articles proffering culinary advice. But she then claims that the editor was flatteringly persuasive: "I have convinced myself that Emir, for his section 'Femininities,' wants a genius. I think that this genius is myself; I look in my hand mirror to verify if I am myself. I notice that in effect, I am without modification" (802). Storni then concludes that she will accept the offer, for "the feminine sex is resigned by habit" (802). The ironic contrast between the search for a supposed genius writer, her lukewarm self-recognition, and the subsequent resignation to writing a woman's column points to Storni's awareness of the low expectations for women's journalism. But it also signals one of the surprising opportunities that the newly anointed chronicler sees in her practice. If she is expected to write something new and different, she can use her regular column to cultivate an audience and engage with public life in her own way.

Storni's trajectory as a young writer reflects the ongoing tension between literary ambition and economic necessity that is revealed in her first article for *Femininities*. Storni was born in Switzerland, into an Italian-speaking family who immigrated to the provincial city of Rosario. The economic situation of her family was always precarious, and she worked multiple jobs from a very young age, ranging from factory to secretarial work. Two occupations, however, would have particular influence on her writing life. The first was theater; she briefly joined a traveling troupe as a teenager, and later in her life she wrote numerous plays as well as children's theater. The second was teaching; she was a normal-school student and formed herself as a *maestra rural* (a rural schoolteacher). This background in education would enable her to be included within the paradigmatic model for women intellectuals during the early twentieth century: that of the

Alfonsina Storni's first
Femininities chronicle.
La Nota, March 28, 1919.

maestra, the educator, perhaps the most famous example in Latin America being Chile's Gabriela Mistral. Storni moved to Buenos Aires from the provinces in 1911 and, shortly after, gave birth to a son out of wedlock. Once in the capital, she began to be recognized for her poetry, publishing in various well-known periodicals such as *Caras y Caretas* and *Nosotros*. She became a regular at literary gatherings and gained visibility as a *poetisa* with a particular talent for declamation.

Storni's poetry, like her declamation skills, enabled her to circulate in the capital's literary circles, but these activities also set her apart as "something less than a full-fledged poet" (Unruh, *Performing Women*, 43). Storni was well aware that the *poetisa* label was associated with a lack of technical rigor and aesthetic innovation. As Unruh has shown, Storni considered that the confessional intimacy that was expected of declamation restricted women's verses to their own experiences and hence limited the creative and intellectual potential of their work (43). But however hesitant Storni was about the label—and she made more than a few disparaging remarks about it—adopting it was also a means for the young writer to introduce herself into literary conversations.[4] The *poetisa* label also suggested a certain intimacy with mass culture, and Storni's consolidation as writer of sentimental poems that catered to readers of middlebrow magazines speaks to the impact that the culture industry had on all of her writing, regardless of genre. For this reason, Storni's public role as *poetisa* can be read as a pragmatic response to the requirements of the press and, in turn, to her own need to earn an income to support herself and her young son. Both Storni's poems and her chronicles thus reflect the pressures associated with writing for the press. They are shaped by the demands of editors, the desires of the public, and the need to respond to the mores of the times.[5]

Despite the similar pressures that framed both Storni's poems and her chronicles, she presents her choice to accept a regular column as a conscious decision to step away from her *poetisa* persona. Storni begins "Femininities" by describing her journey toward her meeting with Emir, the editor. It is a dreary day, and during the journey she has been reading about Verlaine's life. She then gives us a snapshot of the conversation that takes place with Emir:

> To the question: Are you poor? That I have been addressed, I feel the desire to respond: Emir, I write verses . . . But in that precise moment I look at the electric light and it suggests to

> me numerous things: modern times, the century in which we
> move, hygiene, the war against alcohol, vegetarian theories,
> et cetera. (*AS II*, 801)

Storni continues: "In an instant I understood that I must live in my century; I kill, therefore, the romanticism that the rainy day and Verlaine have contaminated me with, and choosing my most carefree smile (I have many), I respond: more or less, Emir, I'm living along" (801). Storni proposes a disjunction between the romantic verses, reminiscent of nineteenth-century sentimentalism, and the modernity of journalism, symbolized by the electric light and the will to engage with current trends covered in the press. It seems as if the persona of the poet cannot coexist with that of the chronicler, not only because of the atmosphere connoted by each genre (gloomy melancholy versus bright technological pragmatism), but also because Storni the journalist must engage with modernity and with her readers in a way that is different from how the *poetisa* had. Being a chronicler demands an involvement with the present and a focus on the communal experience of urban life rather than the nostalgic sentimentality that she associates with poetry.

Storni's insistence in differentiating her work as a poet from her role as a journalist reinstates one of the recurring disclaimers of chroniclers since *modernismo*.[6] Because Storni was recognized for her poetry before working as a chronicler, her prestige as a columnist was intrinsically linked to the persona that she had previously cultivated in her poems and declamations. Emphasizing a division between the poet and the journalist was hence a calculated move more than a true reflection of her writing life. It served to extend the literary prestige of her poetry into the sphere of the chronicle, even if this prestige was tenuous rather than full-fledged. By distancing her poetic work from the contextual referents of urban life and commercial culture, Storni minimizes the external parameters that had shaped her own poems, and evokes the idea of a protected, isolated realm where pure art can be created. In this way, she justifies her uniqueness as a chronicler by embracing the ideal of poetic purity. The irony of this double move—casting herself as a true poet in order to create an intriguing journalistic persona that would attract potential consumers—was hardly lost on Storni. On the contrary, it would provide the basis for her ongoing negotiations with both mass culture and the *letrado* sphere.

Fashioning a recognizable writing persona was very important for Storni, and she carefully cultivated her public image.[7] Storni's described initiation as a woman's columnist shows an obvious self-consciousness, revealed by her calculated smile and her glance in the mirror to check if she was the genius that Emir was supposedly searching for, as though she were verifying that her "journalist" costume was in place before walking onto the stage of her column. Framing a fresh start in *La Nota* did not, however, imply that Storni was truly new to journalism. On the contrary, not only had she published articles before, but it was through the press that she gained the opportunity to circulate her poetry and reach enough readers to publish her first book, *La inquietud del rosal*, in 1916. This makes Storni's choice to "live with her century" and leave behind the romanticism of Verlaine all the more striking. It indicates, not a turning point in her writing career, but rather a decision to privilege in her weekly column a certain aesthetic associated with modern life in the metropolis.

Storni's supposed choice of journalism over poetry was a means of honing an innovative voice that stepped away from the popular paradigms characterizing woman's journalism. In *El imperio de los sentimientos*, Beatriz Sarlo proposes that many of the popular texts that targeted the city's new readers in early twentieth-century Buenos Aires and were sold in newspaper kiosks followed aesthetic principles from the nineteenth century rather than avant-garde innovations (16). The stories published in the penny press were guided by melodrama and sentimentalism, and feminine columns in newspapers and magazines were expected to follow similar lines. This is apparent in *La Nota*, which featured a few other female pseudonyms during the years that Storni wrote, such as "La niña boba" (The silly girl) and "La dama duende" (The lady elf).[8] These columns shared similar themes and rhetorical approaches, ranging from humorous musings to melodramatic confessions, and often took the form of letters, staged private conversations, or diary excerpts. On occasion, Storni herself follows popular parameters in her chronicles, as in "Diario de una niña inútil" (Diary of a Useless Girl), an article that draws from the intimate tone that was expected of women's writing. Storni, however, turns to popular paradigms with a humorous irony that works to affirm her critical distance. This chronicle is narrated through the voice of a young girl who wants to write a diary, because it is in "good taste" to do so and "all great women have done it[;] even more, some became great after publishing their diary" (*AS II*, 827). The "useless girl," however, does not have much to tell other than her devotion to a list of guidelines that explain how to hunt for a boyfriend. While Storni's satire is directed to the notion of writing as a feminine bourgeois pastime, it also clearly mocks the parameters of a woman's column, where readers were expected to find advice on domestic topics such as marriage.

Storni's dismissal of Verlaine in her first article for *La Nota* had been a means to conspicuously step away from the already worn model of melodrama and, hence, of certain clichés reproduced in popular texts. Once again, Storni's self-definition as a chronicler hinges on a paradox. On one hand, she distances herself from the popular idea of what constituted the literary. But on the other hand, she recovers the cliché of the accursed poet to remind her readers that she is, in essence, a "literary" writer herself. In a gesture that caters to multiple readings and to both popular and literary audiences, the melodramatic story of the poet who must step away from her art to earn her living overlaps with the case of the young writer who turns to new, modern, avant-garde referents rather than to worn literary models.

Storni's chronicles claim a willfully novel way of conceptualizing mass culture and addressing a female readership. In her articles, she frequently infuses the sentimentality of the popular *folletín* with the irreverence of the avant-gardes. This strategy is already apparent in her first chronicle for "Femininities," in which she combines the image of herself as a young melancholic poet with her ironic self-portrait as the new "genius" of the woman's pages. Her irreverence toward an older—and in this case male—figure of authority, like the fragmented style of the chronicle and her abundant referents to urban modernity, are reminiscent of vanguardist literary techniques. Certain of Storni's chronicles from the same period can even be read as experimental prose poems or scenes from a play, as, for example, "Costurerita a domicilio" (The Little Home Seamstress). In this chronicle, Storni describes the plight of an archetypical young seamstress who, like many hardworking women of her generation, had to cross the city daily to deliver her work. Storni's chronicle is composed of fragmented scenes, where eerily disembodied images stand out as if through a sequence of cinematographic frames: the seamstress' dark silhouette, her hat, the package she carries, the streetcar fleeting through the city, the man's tie that symbolizes the middle-class professional she hopes to marry. By combining the codes of melodrama with daring literary techniques, Storni both coincided with the aesthetic norms expected from a popular text and went beyond them. In this manner, her chronicles bridged the parallel spheres of popular and avant-garde texts, forging a heterogeneous middle ground.

The mixed literary codes present in Storni's chronicles suggest that, despite the restricting frame of the women's pages, she imagined a diverse public for her column. This choice probably stemmed more from her desire to participate in the literary and intellectual conversations of the time than from the concrete reality of her public. Storni's column in *La Nota*, like the *Feminine Sketches* she would begin writing for the daily *La Nación* in 1920, was primarily directed toward middle- and working-class women. Like Roberto Arlt, with whom she would cross paths at the literary gatherings of the group Signo in the early 1930s, Storni belonged to the same population that she wrote for.[9] She was herself an immigrant who had recently arrived to the capital, one of the many who were working odd jobs to scrape together a living and who lived in one of Buenos Aires' inexpensive boardinghouses.

Like many of her readers, Storni belonged to the first generation of women who were leaving the home and entering the workforce. The chronicler insisted in numerous articles on her familiarity with the professional opportunities available for women. She further emphasized her own situation as a working woman when interviewed in 1927 for the newspaper *La Razón*. Asked how she spent a regular day, she responded: "I work, I go back to work, I work once more. What fun!" (quoted in Kirkpatrick, "Journalism," 111). With statements such as this one, Storni distanced herself from the notion of writing as an elite activity. As Kirkpatrick has shown, Storni instead stressed her identification with the working women who were her most likely readers (111). But the communal link that she draws with her public by no means contradicts her self-identification as a writer. Instead, it reinstates a classic gesture of the rhetoric of accessibility in that writing becomes both an inclusive and an exclusive practice. It is a type of salaried work like any other, yet it also indicates a privileged intimacy with a rarefied literary sphere.

Many of Storni's chronicles, especially those that are more essayistic in nature, confirm her interest in giving a trustworthy picture of women's rising professions, as well as the injustices that women experienced in the workforce, as, for instance, "Las mujeres que trabajan" (Women Who Work) and "La médica" (The Woman Doctor). Storni participated in women's groups such as the Asociación de Mujeres Universitarias (Association of University Women) and the Asociación pro Derechos de la Mujer (Association for Women's Rights). She also struggled to obtain legal rights for natural-born children (Diz, *Alfonsina periodista*, 8–9). Even though she supported feminist causes and on numerous occasions wrote pointed articles on women's rights and suffrage, she was ambivalent about the term "feminist" and oftentimes was distant from and critical of activist movements.[10] Nonetheless, it is when Storni writes about women's issues—such as motherhood, marriage, divorce, equality in the workforce, or poverty—that the didactic authority of the *maestra* most often surfaces in her journalistic work. For example, in "¿Por qué las maestras se casan poco?" (Why Do Few Female Schoolteachers Marry?), Storni speaks to an audience of professional women like herself. She explains why, according to her, it is so difficult for female teachers to marry, and she divides the reasons into four categories: economic, intellectual, social, and moral. Most poignantly, she denounces the effect that intellect and education have on gender relations: "It is curious to show how the intellectual factor, that is, the knowledge and intellect of a teacher, are an impediment to her marriage rather than favoring it or stimulating it" (*AS II*, 978). Storni takes her role as spokeswoman seriously and, much like Arlt, assumes the social responsibility that comes along with having a public voice. Even though she remains hesitant about writing "for women," she also seizes her role as an opportunity to advocate for women's rights.

Most of the chronicles that Storni published in the women's pages, however, were not about directly political or social matters; nor were they devoid of humor. She wrote frequently of the reading materials available to women and commented on the social implications of cultural consumption. In her chronicle "The Perfect Typist," from the series *Feminine Sketches* that she published in the daily *La Nación* and signed with the pseudonym "Tao Lao," Storni describes the types of working women one could find riding streetcars during morning rush hour. She categorizes them according to the reading material they carried:

> If a young reader has with her a detective-stories magazine, we can say she works in a factory or that she is a seamstress; a typist or a shop clerk if she presses to her bosom an obviously popular photo-magazine; a teacher or a student of high school education, if the magazine is of the intellectual bent; and if she carries nonchalantly an open newspaper, do not doubt it . . . she is an accomplished feminist, brave feminist, spirit of the times: punishable Eve. (Appendix 4)

This chronicle, like many of those included under the rubric *Feminine Sketches*, bears a striking resemblance to the *Aguafuertes porteñas* that Arlt would begin writing eight years later in the daily *El Mundo*. Storni's chronicles consist of *costumbrista* scenes of daily Buenos Aires life, balancing the distance of the ethnographic observer with the mutual identification of the practitioner. Yet, while Arlt views women readers with thinly veiled condescension, Storni grasps the complexities involved in the full-fledged participation of women in the cultural economy of the city. She shows us that, for women, reading in public—and consequently being judged according to taste—was a side effect of entering the workforce. It was also a defining act that included them within a specific social and intellectual hierarchy.

The process of earning a public identity through reading was on many levels promoted by the popular press itself. The daily *Crítica*, where Arlt began his journalistic career in the crime beat, gave itself the task of attracting female readers, even announcing that it gave out prizes to women seen carrying the newspaper in the streets. In December 1924, it advertised: "A gold ring, a pair of fine earrings, a necklace, a dress, a parasol, and a hundred more things are the gifts from *Crítica* to its women readers. Carry *Crítica* in your hands" (Saítta, *Regueros*, 113). Advertisements such as these confirm that reading in public was marketed as a way of being a modern woman. A few years later, in 1928, *Crítica* would also call for women to write, acknowledging that they were underrepresented in its pages. Even if women in Buenos Aires had established themselves in the workforce, the newspaper claimed, they were still lacking in something that modern women from Europe and the United States had acquired: "the fondness for public writing" (Saítta, *Regueros*, 113). Emir Emin Arslan's choice to offer Storni her own column in *La Nota* in 1919, a competitive marketing decision aimed at broadening the reach of the weekly, was a precocious move that put him almost a decade ahead of his competitors in Buenos Aires.

Despite the ethnographic distance apparent between Storni and the women she observes on the streetcar in "The Perfect Typist," the chronicler had done secretarial work herself and, by her own admittance, also read in public transportation. In a few of her articles, she mentions this practice in passing, making sure to clarify that she was reading a book as opposed to a popular magazine. In the already cited article "Femininities," for instance, she is reading about a literary topic: the life of Verlaine. In another chronicle, "The Lady in Black," she describes a trip on the subway and mentions that she travels with her "habitual book in her hands" (*AS II*, 805). Such a conscious choice to present herself as someone who did not read magazines in public, precisely written in the pages of one such publication, is another example of Storni's elusive self-fashioning with regard to popular culture. As a reader and a user of public transportation, she both resembles her public and differs from it, for she carries a book, an accessory that she refrains from including in her categorization of women readers.[11]

Storni's ironic praising of the "consummate feminist, valiant feminist" who chooses to keep up with the latest news by reading a paper shows keen awareness of how taste was intrinsically related to the expression of a specific type of womanhood. While consuming entertainment was associated with accepted feminine professions (typist, seamstress, or teacher), an interest in political and social information was instead associated with androgyny and even a form of masculinity. These masculine attributes are confirmed by the feminist's lack of interest in frivolous articles: she is the punishable Eve who tries to repress any form of self-expression associated with femininity. In contrast to the unflattering earnestness with which the feminist is portrayed, Storni defends the pleasure principle and adds a teasing aside to her readers: "But let the nonpunishable Eves rest assured. In the hands of the morning commuters there are plenty of popular magazines, those of love secrets. So, Eve is saved from seven to eight in the morning by the typists and shop clerks" (appendix 4).

Where then does Storni, a writing woman who chooses to read books on the subway, stand in this spectrum of modern urban femininities? Her critical, ethnographic eye, like her choice of reading material, distances her from other women riders. More importantly, unlike any of the examples she lists, Storni not only reads in public but also *publishes*. She does not need to display an intellectual pose, as does the "valiant feminist"; what circulates throughout Buenos Aires is her own writing in the press, which is read and discussed by other women on the way to work. Storni's stance regarding the hierarchy of reading is difficult to pin down. On one hand, she critiques the intellectual pretense and superficiality that can accompany the self-fashioning of a woman writer, as with the "useless girl" who struggles to write a diary because it is fashionable. On the other hand, she recognizes the vitality of consumer culture, even as she conspicuously distances herself from it. In this manner, Storni slips between the cracks of the categories of femininity that she reinstates in her chronicles, construct-ing a voice that is androgynous by default.

The elusive gender markings of Storni's chronicles can be partly attributed to the commercial requirements of journalism; they were a means to avoid staking a potentially divisive position that might alienate some of her readers. Yet her strategic ambivalence also reveals that she wrote at a time of great change in gender mores, a decade during which femininity was being dramatically redefined. There were many models for modern womanhood in the 1920s, but few solid routes for intellectual self-expression had yet been staked. Storni's aloof accessibility was a means of showing that there was more to her than a woman's column, even as she espoused wholeheartedly some of the opportunities it offered. While Storni took her role as a woman's columnist seriously, she also maintained an ironic distance from the popular parameters in which women's journalism was included. She thus juggled with two expressions of femininity, even if one seemed on occasion to undermine the other. On one hand, she adopted the programmatic, accepted version of the woman intellectual—that of the *maestra* who informed and educated her readers. On the other hand, she was the ironic, irreverent modern woman who toyed with androgyny and mocked some of the customs of her peers. This versatility as a chronicler is perhaps what enabled Storni to accrue such long-lasting prestige as a writer, something that Cube Bonifant, who wrote in similar circumstances from Mexico City, albeit with a bit less subtlety, would struggle to obtain.

Cube Bonifant, the Little Marquise de Sade of Mexican Journalism

In 1921, two years after Storni first began writing for the weekly *La Nota*, Cube Bonifant began her first column for the *Ilustrado*, the same magazine that would, a few years later, provide a stepping-stone for Salvador Novo's early writing career. She was seventeen years old and would continue to publish regularly for almost thirty years. From her start as a chronicler, Bonifant shared the irony that had characterized her Argentine predecessor, but she took it to a more aggressive level. Not only did she repeatedly address men from columns that were meant to be exclusively for women, but she was also so critical of her female readership that she was considered to be someone who wrote *against* women rather than *for* them. Being dismissed as a "light" journalistic writer became, nonetheless, an unexpected advantage that Bonifant consistently seized throughout her career as a chronicler, for it enabled her to get away with sharp social and political criticism that would undoubtedly have been censured in more serious sections of newspapers.

Cube Bonifant was born Antonia Bonifant López in the small mining town of El Rosario, Sinaloa, in 1904. She first moved with her family to Guadalajara to escape the violence of the revolution, arriving in Mexico City around 1920. Like Storni, she dabbled in theater, appearing in a few plays and writing poems before turning to journalism. Bonifant's forays into poetry, however, were short-lived. In her first article for the *Ilustrado*, which appeared in March 1921, she self-consciously introduces herself to her readers in a way that is remarkably reminiscent of Storni's "Femininities." She declares: "Verses? I don't write them since I read the last ones by Alfonsina Storni" (*Marquesa*, 52). This reference to Storni is framed as a supposed dismissal of literary ambitions, yet it works to associate the young chronicler in the making with a literary mentor who by then had been accepted as a public figure and a writer—even if grudgingly so by the literary elite in Buenos Aires. Notably, Bonifant's dismissal of her interest in poetry resembles Storni's own choice to distance her journalistic work from her *poetisa* persona. Bonifant conspicuously steps away from Storni's example, just as the latter had distanced herself from the model of Verlaine. Yet Bonifant's first article is playful and irreverent, and as Storni had done, she introduces herself to her readers through intimate confidences that highlight her idiosyncratic modernity. And like her predecessor, Bonifant recounts with nonchalant detachment the offer made to her by the editor to begin a column in the women's pages: "Mr. Noriega Hope has told me with pedagogical ingenuity: 'it is necessary that you take a section in *El universal ilustrado*.' And I, naturally, smiled, protested with some literature, and accepted" (54).

Bonifant's reference to "literature" in the first article for her column in the *Ilustrado* is worth noting. Although "literature" here refers to a certain facility of self-expression—or what is commonly known as good manners—it also has implications of superficiality that distance the term from any intellectual connotation. Bonifant's offhand statement reflects the open-ended use of the term in the Mexican press of the times—like the term *literato* (literary writer), it was used loosely and encompassed the efforts of anyone with literary ambition. But in the context of

Bonifant's first chronicle, this expression confirms that her offhand dismissal of literary ambition was anything but that. If the literary can be constituted as an inclusive and heterogeneous field, then Bonifant's entrance into the sphere of journalism would mark a first step toward obtaining recognition as a writer. In this respect, Bonifant's gesture upholds the tactical nature of the chronicle, or what de Certeau refers to as "the art of the weak," which seizes upon the opportunities available and makes the best of them (*Practice*, 37). Perhaps more significantly, Bonifant's apparent acceptance of her nonliterary ambitions echoes Josefina Ludmer's reading of another Mexican woman writer, Sor Juana Inés de la Cruz, who subverted ecclesiastical authority underhandedly by appearing to be compliant ("Las tretas"). Bonifant's apparent modesty, combined with her childish response to Noriega Hope's pedagogical intentions, helps her insinuate herself into literary conversations while claiming to shy away from intellectual ambitions.

As with Storni, Bonifant's commitment to the chronicle stemmed in part from economic reasons. She needed the income to help support her mother and sisters in Mexico City, for her father did not move to the capital with them, and it is unknown whether he contributed financially to the household. She gained visibility and recognition as a chronicler surprisingly quickly. True, there was little competition: no other writer at the time described what life in Mexico City meant for a young woman with a will to be modern. Bonifant's column quickly moved to the first pages of the magazine, with her signature and photograph featured prominently. She was also given important assignments, such as interviewing Mexico's first lady, Doña María Tapia de Obregón in 1921, and she was herself interviewed in the press with regularity. During the same year in which she began her column, she starred in Noriega Hope's first cinematographic project and the only film he would ever direct: *La gran noticia*, which was released in 1923 after many delays.[12] It was a film about journalism in which the main parts went to journalists who contributed regularly to the *Ilustrado*. Bonifant's participation in the film led to her being given the cover of the magazine in June 1921 and to several flattering reviews in the press after the film's release. Despite this success, she unabashedly declared her distaste for filmmaking and never acted for the screen again.

Although Bonifant took advantage of her public visibility during her first years as a chronicler, she gradually grew uncomfortable with the expectation that the image of women should appear regularly in the

Cube Bonifant's cover. *El Universal Ilustrado*, June 23, 1921.

press, as well as that women themselves should so arduously desire to be photographed and displayed.[13] By the 1930s Bonifant wrote film criticism almost exclusively, a medium through which her complex persona as a chronicler receded to a more analytical tone, even though her reticence to being tactful frequently resurfaced, especially when critiquing national film.[14] Bonifant eventually acquired considerable clout as a film critic and was described in a 1934 article for the *Ilustrado* as "the most popular film chronicler in Mexico."[15] It is ironic that Bonifant obtained such recognition in this realm, given the extent to which she criticized the influence that film had on young modern women in her early years in the press, yet her success can be attributed to the fact that cinema was still widely considered a minor form that was not quite art. Because of its relative novelty and its precarious cultural prestige, film was a territory where a woman chronicler's authority was less likely to be questioned.

From her first chronicles, Bonifant, like Storni, began to consciously mold her public persona. But instead of the didactic irony that characterized the Argentine chronicler, Bonifant would, from the start, privilege the role of the rebel. "I complicate everything that I find," she announced in her first article, presenting herself as a girl who was both "temperamental" and "versatile," had the appearance of a "messy schoolgirl," and liked bullfighting more than the cinema (*Marquesa*, 51). Her rebelliousness stemmed in great part from her unusual literary tastes. She claimed to prefer *El octavo pecado capital* (The Eighth Deadly Sin), by Álvaro Retana— a Spanish decadent writer who was well known for his erotic novels and his homosexuality—over the series *Claudina*, by the French writer Colette, a choice that was at the time much more in line with the expected taste of a young woman with a penchant for literature.

Even if Bonifant did not share the didactic persona that Storni frequently espoused in Buenos Aires, preferring to shock rather than edify, the figure of the *maestra* would nonetheless become one of the paradigmatic articulations of femininity in postrevolutionary Mexico. The importance of the *maestra* was only heightened by the highly publicized stay of the Chilean Gabriela Mistral, who was invited to Mexico by José Vasconcelos in the early 1920s, to contribute to his education campaign. But rather than molding her public image along the socially progressive norms of the *maestra*, as expected of any woman with intellectual ambitions, Bonifant chose instead to combine an untraditional sensuality with a calculated irreverence. In one of her first chronicles, Bonifant anointed herself with the memorable title of "una pequeña Marquesa de Sade" (a little Marquise de Sade), a label that she would consistently live up to through her references to decadentism and her indiscriminate critical gaze. Her attitude contradicted accepted forms of social decorum: "Do I like flowers and children?" she once asked. "Flowers . . . yes, but only to pluck them and eat their petals. Children cause me a profound unease, I feel a desire to pierce them with my sharpened nails" (*Marquesa*, 53). This statement is all the more provocative given the extent to which Mexico's government defined maternity in patriotic terms in the years following the revolution. In 1922, as a result of an initiative taken by the daily *Excélsior*, Mother's Day was institutionalized as a national holiday.

Like Storni's frequent espousal of romanticism and melodrama, Bonifant's references to decadentism remit to popular forms that gave continuity to literary paradigms from the late nineteenth century. Particularly in a country like Mexico, which was still feeling the aftershocks of the revolution, such dated literary references were the norm in the provinces, as well as for many middlebrow readers who resided in the capital. Having grown up in the states of Sinaloa and Jalisco, Bonifant was only too aware of this delay in literary mores. Describing her stay in the small Jalisco town of Ameca—a place that was always out of sync with the novelties of the capital, for the train that brought the news was derailed on a daily basis—she outlines the reading preferences of her contemporaries. While boys have "read from Bossuet to Beaumarchais," girls have barely outgrown the phase of "María and Carmen" (*Marquesa*, 56).[16] Bonifant's self-description in decadent terms can be read as a mockery of a sentimental provincial past from which she wanted to distance herself—at the mature age of seventeen. But it also shows to what extent she consciously catered to the types of literary references that middlebrow readers could easily recognize.

Although Bonifant assumed a decadent stance that was out of sync with the euphoric thirst for modernity of postrevolutionary Mexico, she did so by renovating it and using it as a means to carve a niche for her unique voice as a chronicler. Toward the end of the nineteenth century, the *Revista Moderna*, the bastion of Mexican *modernismo*, was already featuring the image of the decadent woman—the androgynous, cruel nymphomaniac that embodied all social evil—so as to critique the bourgeoisie of the Porfiriato that it simultaneously seduced with its glossy pages and its literary elitism.[17] Bonifant reroutes this imagery by defining herself, not as a decadent muse, but rather as a writing woman who chooses such a referent to question the mores of her times and undermine the expectations that come with her journalistic visibility. This gesture enables her to seize the reins of self-representation and design her various provocative poses through her articles.

Bonifant's multifaceted persona draws from two contradictory impulses. On one hand, she is the young curious writer who avidly discovers her voice in a modernizing lettered city: she has just arrived in the capital and relishes her freedom and status as a professional writer. On the other hand, she is the fatigued woman who remains bored and unimpressed by her surroundings: modernity has already ceased to interest her, and she is ready for the next fad to come and go. The duality of Bonifant's persona was emphasized through the images that decorated her column in the *Ilustrado*, which is ironic given her growing reluctance to be visually represented. We can find, on one page, a sketch of a young girl, smiling shyly under a gigantic bow that crowned her head; on another, a photograph of a serious Bonifant, framed on both sides with drawings of cats, suggesting that the chronicler had a feline and dangerous side. By embracing the double-edged pose of innocent childishness combined with seductive aggressivity, Bonifant could both give voice to the country's newfound modernity and nonetheless question a society that remained profoundly conservative.

Like Storni, Bonifant established herself as an unusual cultural commentator, frequently referring to decadentism as a means to justify her penchant for unexpected topics. Just as she nonchalantly announced her unusual literary tastes, Bonifant also expressed a preference for the heterogeneous cultural life of Mexico City. Her early chronicles describe events ranging from soccer matches and bullfights to plays, literary gatherings, and the opera. She also critiques fashion, frequents cabarets, listens to jazz, and avidly comments on the crime section of newspapers. By focusing on public events that were not limited to a protected bourgeois enclave, Bonifant expanded the horizon of the feminine column, challenging

Illustration of the childish Bonifant. *El Universal Ilustrado*, April 21, 1921.

The feline Bonifant. *El Universal Ilustrado*, August 4, 1921.

through her unorthodox choices the limitations of modern women's newfound freedom in the capital.

Bonifant's eclectic cultural preferences were not simply a means of undermining the expected domesticity of a woman's column. They enabled her to simultaneously embrace and question paradigms of modern femininity and also to contribute to ongoing conversations on the relationship between literary taste and gender. Like the New Woman that was frequently represented in the press of the day, Bonifant cut her hair in flapper style, smoked, wore fashionable shorter skirts, and was well acquainted with Mexico City's nightlife. But she was also wary of what she deemed the "flapperization" of her contemporaries, often reproducing in her criticism the stereotype of women as passive consumers of popular culture. Most modern women, according to Bonifant, were superficial readers and cinema aficionados who adopted intellectual poses without understanding them. Perhaps the best example of Bonifant's critique of the intellectual superficiality of women can be found in "Notes of a Married Woman," a series of sketches that she began to publish in 1927 in the *Ilustrado*. Following the model of Anita Loos' successful *Gentlemen Prefer Blondes* (1925), Bonifant tells the story of a scheming young woman, in this case from a rich Sonoran family, whose naivety and ignorance are equaled only by her will to fully experience the modern opportunities provided by Mexico City. Bonifant's protagonist decides to smoke, cut her hair, drink whisky, and dance the foxtrot, all to make her diary a more interesting read and to convince her bored husband of her worthy intellect. Bonifant's critique of feminine shallowness in this series is all the harsher given that it is directed toward the political elite from the northern state of Sonora, who wielded unchecked political power in the capital.[18]

Rather than modeling herself as an example of "good taste" and true intellectual insightfulness, Bonifant preferred to use her eclectic cultural choices to undermine cultural hierarchies. In her first chronicle for the *Ilustrado*, she declared: "I have read, as can be expected, good and bad books, although due to my great spirit of contradiction, the works that have been recommended to me as good have seemed to me excessively bad" (March 1921, 52). Bonifant was learning to become a reader. Like many other young women around her, she had no substantial knowledge of literary hierarchies and was confronted by a heterogeneous array of reading material. In an unusual move, however, she construes her uninformed criteria as an advantage that permits her to stand out from the crowd. In her own exceptional case, Bonifant informs us, she bypasses the norms that define good and bad taste *by choice*. It is not that she has indiscriminate taste but rather that she is not influenced by superficial intellectual fashions and has the autonomy to define good taste on her own terms. In this manner, Bonifant establishes herself as a woman of her time by discovering her modern identity through cultural consumption, without, nonetheless, relinquishing her claim to the unique persona of the rebel.

Bonifant's contrarian choices would surface most notably in her frequently misogynistic depiction of women writers and feminist activists. In her chronicle "Long Hair and Short Ideas," Bonifant describes her reluctant participation in a gathering of literary women. The title of the article references a phrase attributed to Schopenhauer that was frequently paraphrased in the press of the day, claiming that flappers cut their hair in rejection of the philosopher's belief that women were "long on hair and short on ideas." This phrase reinstates the notion that women's intellectual ventures were inexorably intertwined with their interest in fashion, and Bonifant appropriates this stereotype as a means to highlight both her heterogeneous cultural tastes and her provocatively androgynous appearance. Bonifant dwells on her difference from the other women present at the literary meeting. She finds them "rather thick, lacking in that virtue called good taste, and almost old" (appendix 5). The young chronicler decides to smoke, lighting her cigarette "with the same lack of elegance as men light them." She is reproached for her unladylike behavior and soon chooses to leave the meeting:

> Decidedly, I am taking leave, with the satisfaction of not being an authoress of short stories, of plays, of poetic prose

nor of impressions of the Motherland. I leave happy for not being a woman writer, and thinking that in fact, "woman is an animal of long hair and short ideas"; but also with the selfish and beaming smugness of my short hair and scarce femininity. (Appendix 5)

Bonifant's dismissal of this literary gathering is partly a result of a generational gap. But it also reveals that her relationship to literature and writing involved social parameters that starkly differed from those of the other women present. For the bourgeois women in attendance, writing was a private pastime that interrupted the monotony of domesticity; for the chronicler, it was a profession that enabled her to earn her living and enter public conversations. Bonifant's purposefully eclectic interests and her rebellious persona should be considered a response to her experience with journalism, which encouraged her to expand the boundaries of what was literary and to embrace a heterogeneous notion of culture. Bonifant needed to publish and be read by a majority and could not, for this reason, cater to the interests of an elite minority of readers.

Like Storni, Bonifant used her column as a stage from which she could perform a recognizable public identity, in her case one that relied heavily on provocation and satire. Building as broad a readership as possible did not, for Bonifant, mean being conciliatory. On the contrary, it meant extending her satirical gaze to such an extent that none of her potential readers could avoid feeling targeted by her sharp comments. To a much greater degree than Storni in Buenos Aires, Bonifant was wary of the "feminist" label and highly critical of feminist activism. In "Full-blown Feminism," a chronicle published shortly before "Long Hair and Short Ideas," she describes the women who attended the meeting with the same humorous disdain with which she would soon approach women writers. The president of the association makes a long-winded speech that leaves Bonifant unmoved: "I confess frankly that I stopped looking at my nails and glanced toward the door. It seemed to me as if the president would not be quiet until astronomers definitely stated whether or not we were being waved at from Mars" (*Marquesa*, 89). These feminist activists, the chronicler implied, liked above all the sound of their own voice and did not do much to put their beliefs into practice. Bonifant's description of these women recalls some aspects of Storni's dismissal of the "valiant feminist" who conspicuously read the newspaper on the subway: they are unimaginative, stodgy, and out of touch with modern reality. More importantly, and despite their ardent declarations, the feminists described by Bonifant are not immune from the seduction of social status.

Bonifant's portrayal of this meeting highlights what, according to her, fashionable flappers and earnest feminists had in common. Even though they represented diametrically opposed expressions of femininity in the 1920s, both were influenced by fashion, be it in intellectual mores or in dress. This reductive attitude regarding expressions of femininity seemed to leave no room for constructive choices, for even having intellectual ambitions was regarded as a desire to be in vogue. While Storni's journalistic voice was androgynous by omission—she purposefully excluded her persona from expected parameters of femininity—Bonifant would instead confront normative feminine behavior by exposing its inherent inconsistencies. Toward the end of "Full-blown Feminism," the chronicler recounts what happens when she is invited by the organizers of the meeting to voice her opinions on feminism. She first refuses to speak, then decides to shock: "I am not a feminist because I think that we women need to be feminine, kind and worthy of a home if we want to reign." She then concludes with an aside to her readers: "You yawn? I will stop my speech. But first know something: I am not a feminist nor an antifeminist. I do not like revolution, but neither do I like the insipid placidity of the home. You know what I am? A middle ground between bullfighting and the opera" (*Marquesa*, 91). Bonifant thus aligns her attitudes toward gender with her cultural tastes. Just as she enjoys elite culture (the opera) and popular spectacles (bullfighting), the chronicler expresses both masculine and feminine attributes. As Bonifant well understood in the Mexico of the 1920s, displaying a heterogeneous cultural taste was also a means of opening a space for an untraditional sexual identity.

As discussed in the previous chapter, questioning constructions of gender in Mexico during the 1920s was also a means of critiquing the narrow parameters that defined national culture. In this aspect, Bonifant shared Salvador Novo's irreverence and even preceded him in mocking the expected virility of intellectual production. Almost a year before Novo mockingly described Mexican literature as "a fresh and virile girl" in a survey that questioned leading intellectuals on the topic of national literature, Bonifant was also interviewed for a survey related to reading. This article, "What Type of Magazine Do You Prefer?"—which featured the opinions of a number of society women, local stage actresses, and the young journalist—was much less grandiose than the one that would shortly include Novo, "Does a Modern Mexican Literature Exist?" Nonetheless, Bonifant uttered a remarkably similar response: "I like two magazines, or rather, I read two . . . *Monsieur* and *El Hogar*. *El Hogar* because it is exclusively for women and *Monsieur* because it is only for men" (quoted in Ortega, "¿Cuál género?" 18). Although she never directly intervened in the debates on the "feminization" of literature that polarized Mexico's intellectuals in the mid-1920s—no woman, in fact, was invited to contribute to this heated conversation—Bonifant addressed from the sphere of journalism an issue that was clearly literary. Bonifant's chronicles thus exemplified the "fresh and virile girl" that Novo would soon describe, purposefully bringing referents from the middlebrow press into play within literary conversations.

That both Storni and Bonifant hesitated to align themselves with a particular feminist group or agenda in their chronicles can be explained in part by the requirements of a successful journalistic column. Even though they both used their articles as a means to open a space for women in public intellectual life, their own visibility depended on their ability to consistently cultivate individualism and establish their independence as writers. The chronicle, after all, existed in opposition to the anonymous work of reporters, and what gave continuity to a given column, despite the multiplicity of topics it usually covered, was the persona of the author. This does not mean that a chronicler's statements were necessarily consistent; in fact, most of the chroniclers studied in this book contradicted themselves on multiple occasions—they also tended to repeat themselves, one of the shortcuts necessary to survive the toil of a regular column. Bonifant's self-portrayal through exceptionalism, however, would eventually be unsuccessful. Not only did it limit the complexity of her ideas, but it also reinforced some of the very limitations that she struggled against in her career as a writer. It might also explain her gradual and mysterious disappearance from the world of writing. Despite her early recognition as a chronicler, when Bonifant died in 1993 at the age of eighty-nine, she had not written regularly for more than forty years.

A widely read column, even today, needs to sustain a difficult equilibrium between the familiar and the unexpected, the comforting and the provocative. Storni and Bonifant strove to obtain this balance by cultivating a form of androgyny, picking and choosing to their advantage from among the parameters defining masculinity and femininity in the 1920s. This gender ambivalence was immediately apparent in their choice of pseudonyms. Storni published her section in the daily *La Nación* under the pen name "Tao Lao," which had orientalist and masculine overtones, and Bonifant would be known throughout her life as "Cube," an androgynous nickname that suggested the sharp angles of industrial modernity. But if androgyny was posited as a form of liberation from the restrictions imposed on writing women, the same term, when applied to male writers, construed a dismissal of intellectual integrity—something that Salvador Novo and other members of the Contemporáneos group in Mexico City would come to know only too well. This duality reinstated the inevitable fact that, in the 1920s, intellectual respect was inextricably associated with masculinity. While this left women chroniclers with little room to maneuver, such limitations highlight the creative tactics through which they negotiated their public roles as chroniclers.

Writing in Public

Storni and Bonifant were only too aware of the restrictions implied by the place they occupied in the press. While feminine sections in popular newspapers or magazines of the period did not necessarily have a set location in the publications, their "difference" was signaled by drawings of mannequins, photographs of the latest screen stars, and childish decorative flourishes recalling the intimacy of the boudoir, such as brushes, combs, makeup, and handheld mirrors. The columns contained in such pages, with titles like Storni's *Femininities* or Bonifant's *Only for Women*—clearly suggested by the editors rather than by the columnists themselves— confirmed their expected orientation toward intimate matters that only women could share.

Such strongly demarcated territories in popular and middlebrow publications had distinct implications on expected patterns of readership. *La Nota*, like the *Ilustrado*, was a commercial magazine that targeted middle-class readers. As seen in the previous chapter, Mexico City's *Ilustrado* prided itself in being an eclectic publication that combined frivolous topics with in-depth articles on literature and culture. Buenos Aires' *La Nota* had a similar conceptualization. It brought together literary figures such as Leopoldo Lugones, Ricardo Rojas, and Paul Groussac, asking them to write in an accessible manner and encouraging the participation of readers through letters to the editor and the publication of polemics. It also combined a local focus with articles about European politics, specifically the consequences of World War I in Europe. In both magazines, feminine sections were designed to make women readers feel welcome in a mixed publication that also covered matters codified as "manly," such as local politics or international news. The overinscribed demarcations of femininity also served as a warning to the male reader to steer away from the frivolously feminine pages included in such hybrid publications, while at the same time, as Bonifant pointedly reminds us in the epigraph to this chapter, flirtatiously provoking his curiosity.

The journalistic trajectories of women writers such as Storni and Bonifant bring an added level of complexity to the notion of the "accessible intellectual" that has guided the previous chapters of this book. Writing chronicles enabled Arlt, Mário, and Novo to imagine a large and diverse audience, to reach readers that they might not have found through other genres, and to propose themselves as an indispensable part of modern life in their respective cities. Their public personas were intrinsically linked to their familiarity with urban public life and to the ample circulation of their articles. Even if their rhetoric of accessibility had its implicit limitations, expressed most notably through the underhanded exclusivity of their status as well-known intellectual and journalistic figures, it was based on the experiences of communal life and on the unifying rhetoric of a shared urban routine.

Although women were entering the workforce in greater numbers by the 1920s, the role these new players had in the imagined comradeship of the modern Latin American city remained unclear. Women were beginning to be recognized as significant readers and consumers, but they seemed to have no stake in lettered culture, lest, of course, the definition of "lettered culture" was broad enough to include popular forms such as the cinema and the press. While male chroniclers were conscious of the increasing diversity of their public in terms of gender, women chroniclers were expected to write for an audience that was exclusively composed of women. It seemed as if women chroniclers were called to cater to the needs of the "overflow" of female readers who were now reaching out for more diverse material, thus complementing journalistic production through some of its less respected sections rather than breaking new ground.

Conceptualizing accessibility in the writings of Storni and Bonifant is a laden process, for one must first consider what was accessible *to them* as women chroniclers. Even if women were working outside the home and circulating through their cities alone in greater numbers, the physical mobility of women in the 1920s was restricted and a woman's familiarity with city streets had dubious moral repercussions.[19] For a professional woman, the notion of accessibility points firsthand to the profession of prostitution—which Salvador Novo could afford to joke about—instead of that of journalism. Any chronicler was expected to be involved in public life, yet such public endeavors had charged implications in the case of women. What had made Novo's numerous references to prostitution so humorous was not only that they pointed to what remained unsaid—namely, his own homosexual promiscuity—but also that the idea of a respected writer having to sell himself in the streets was absurd. In the case of women, the parallel between journalism and prostitution was no laughing matter, for any working woman of the 1920s was already risking the label regardless of her occupation or her schedule. Storni subtly acknowledges this prejudice in her chronicle "Historia sintética de un traje tailleur" (The Concise Story of a Tailored Dress), in which a thirty-year-old widow who works to support her children provokes comments behind her back because she returns home late at night (*AS II*, 751).

Despite their interest in street life, there is no doubt that the freedom of women chroniclers to walk through the city was limited in comparison with that of their male counterparts, who could take for granted unrestricted hours, the anonymity provided by city crowds, and the opportunity to explore. Similarly, the mobility of female chroniclers was also restricted in the layout of the publications in which their articles circulated. Rarely could a female chronicler walk out of the feminine page to other sections of a publication without an anxious editor pointing out the unique status of her gender. Bonifant managed to do so on occasion, but such excursions tended to be short-lived. In 1922, for instance, Bonifant began to write daily for *El Mundo*, the evening paper directed by Martín Luis Guzmán. Her column was initially called "Sólo para ustedes," but it was quickly changed to "Sólo para vosotras," a subtle alteration guaranteeing that the feminine gender of the addressee did not go unnoticed. Bonifant managed a few other times to sidestep the constraints of the women's pages in her early years as a writer, with columns such as *Confetti* (1924) and *Estación radiodifusora del Ilustrado* (*Ilustrado*'s Radio Station, 1931–1933), the latter of which she signed with QB, an even more androgynous version of her nickname and usual pseudonym Cube. Both were dubbed humorous columns, which might explain why she was able to address an audience that was not necessarily feminine.[20] Yet it would only be by writing on film that Bonifant would manage to consistently avoid having explicit gender markers frame her writing. There was no doubt that in the Latin America of the 1920s, writing for a public—like walking in public—was subject to social, familial, and editorial control.

That Storni and Bonifant's columns prominently featured their signatures enabled them to consolidate their presence in the public eye. The privilege of a regular column and the journalistic visibility it entailed led to regular interviews, frequent photographs, and invitations to social events. Both women chroniclers became public figures like Horacio Quiroga or Salvador Novo, writers who were also frequent fixtures in middlebrow publications. In particular, the early portrayals of Bonifant in the *Ilustrado* were closer to that of a stage or film performer than that of a writer. Undoubtedly, such representational paradigms were a way of once more putting women writers in a certain place. They might well be read, discussed, and recognized, but they clearly belonged to a sphere of mass culture rather than to intellectual circles. The reinstated parallel between the performer and the chronicler was also a means to cast a dubious morality on any woman who aspired to be a public figure. Evidently, the connotations implied by the term "public" woman, as opposed to that of a public—and inherently male—intellectual were radically different.

In the previously cited article "What Type of Magazine Do You Prefer?" for which Bonifant had been interviewed in 1924, popular publications such as illustrated magazines are described as part of a sexualized urban economy that seduces an implicitly heterosexual male reader as would a flirtatious woman: "From the multicolored stands, the illustrated magazine offers herself with the studied coquetry of a pretty woman," remarks the author, who signed his piece "Aldebarán." Referring to the Parisian magazine *Les Pages Folles*, he adds: "There is always a woman who smiles at us from the portico. She is half naked and with that unique coquetry of the women of Lutetia, she warns us: 'skip the page quickly, for I am not dressed yet'" (Ortega, "¿Cuál género?" 18–19). The commercial exchanges through which popular magazines were bought and sold, read, and passed along are compared to female prostitution in no uncertain terms. The reader is described as a man easily tempted by the art of feminine seduction. The fact that this description appeared in an article that focused on women *as readers* is ironic if not coincidental. It served to reassure anxious male consumers that their interest in illustrated magazines was not a sign of a lack of masculinity. On the contrary, men's participation in the frivolity of the middlebrow press is here presented as a confirmation of manliness and leaves no doubt as to the implied roles of any woman who figures in these pages—regardless of whether they write or are photographed. Women who publish in illustrated magazines are here directly assigned the role of provider in a sexualized urban cultural economy.

The recurring association of women chroniclers with seductive stage stars was, however, part of a much more widespread process that was not restricted only to women writers. In fact, their representations condensed the workings of literary celebrity that were becoming common during the 1920s as an extension of Hollywood influence into the Latin American press, affecting the public personas of all the chroniclers discussed in this book.[21] The chroniclers studied in the previous chapters were well aware of their female audience, yet an undercurrent of discomfort with their presence is often obvious, most notably in Roberto Arlt's *Aguafuertes porteñas*.[22] These chroniclers might have playfully embraced the effects of technological modernity and their incursion into the sphere of mass media, yet the reality of their growing female public—like their own participation in the consecration of chroniclers as literary and journalistic celebrities—led to more than a few snide comments.

At the time, most women who were employed by newspapers were secretaries, copy editors, or translators. The female columnists who worked with men in the newspaper room were scarce.[23] If the presence of the few professional writing women who, like Storni and Bonifant, earned an income by writing for the press made their male colleagues uncomfortable, this discomfort arose from the unsettling reality that these women chroniclers were gaining significant presence in the press, becoming colleagues and rivals more than muses.[24] In fact, the columns of Storni and Bonifant marked a turning point in women's journalism. Such columns were no longer the territory of bourgeois women who considered writing a pastime, as had frequently been the case in the late nineteenth century; rather, they were expressions of professional journalists who wrote for an audience composed of women who, like the authors, worked for a living. This condition explains why both Bonifant and Storni tended to identify with other professionals, even if they were male, over bourgeois women who wrote for pleasure.

Storni and Bonifant fit in well with many of the characteristics of intellectual accessibility that defined urban chroniclers of the 1920s. They were approachable, familiar figures who frequently received letters from readers seeking advice and who addressed those readers in their columns. They formed part of a struggling middle class who wrote in order to earn a stable, if meager, income. Since they had little access to the luxury of travel, they relied on newspapers, magazines, and the occasional local gathering to discover literary novelties, in much the same way the other chroniclers in this book did. The relationship of these women chroniclers with their audience, however, had an added level of complexity, for making their columns "accessible" to a heterogeneous—and hence potentially male—public was a rebelliously inclusive gesture that questioned the hierarchies implicit in a woman's journalistic practice.

Bonifant and Storni were repeatedly put in their place by their fellow writers, even when they were ostensibly being complimented for their work. In 1925 the Estridentista Arqueles Vela wrote a regular column for the *Ilustrado* entitled *Frivolous Commentaries*, which was situated next to Bonifant's own. He dedicated one of his columns to his neighbor with the following epigraph: "To Cube Bonifant, so that she reads one of my chronicles, this one so full of femininity." Vela's chronicle was about women who used eyeglasses, which according to him worked as "a windshield for flirting." But instead of flirting with his neighbor, Vela's dedication offers an aggressive lesson in femininity that reveals his own discomfort with having to write articles on fashion. Vela would not be Bonifant's only critic. On the contrary, the young chronicler seemed to enjoy encouraging polemics and would provoke the anger of writers such as Francisco Monterde García Icazbalceta and the cartoonist Ernesto "El Chango" García Cabral, who in 1923 lampooned her with a series of caricatures in the daily *Excélsior*. Like Bonifant, Storni would also be the target of remarkably harsh comments, although they were mostly directed toward her poetry rather than her journalism. Borges, to offer one example, disparaged her as "la Storni" and grouped her into the category of "shameful *rubenistas*" who repeated worn poetic paradigms (quoted in Kirkpatrick, "Journalism," 107).

Despite their critics, both Storni and Bonifant earned the right to be considered colleagues by their fellow writers. At Storni's death in 1938, Roberto Giusti, the founder of the magazine *Nosotros*, commented on the impressions Storni provoked when she first began to frequent literary gatherings in Buenos Aires. He described her as a "cordial little teacher" who offered a "vague promise" but soon would become "an honest comrade at *tertulias* [literary salons]" and "an authentic poet." Not surprisingly, Giusti complimented Storni by calling her "un auténtico poeta," the masculine term that granted a prestige unattainable by the feminine *poetisa*.[25] Gaining literary status implied, in this case, literally shedding a feminine gender marker for a male universality. The warmhearted inclusivity of such comments, however well intended, nevertheless reinstated the difference of women chroniclers from a masculine norm. In a similar manner, the journalist Oscar Leblanc, when complimenting Bonifant for her work in the *Ilustrado*, couldn't help but highlight the particularity of her gender and the fact that she did not quite belong: "Cube is a good and firm comrade who understands *our* problems, discusses heatedly *our* destinies and completes every week her mission with talent and renewed joyfulness. She puts the feminine seasoning in our weekly, but sometimes, with concentrated malice, she exchanges the salt for the pepper" (emphasis mine).[26] It is ambivalent whether Bonifant is included within the "we" that Leblanc alludes to.

In contrast to the experience that Storni and Bonifant had in the press —that is, the insistent restriction to a defined place from which women were expected to write publicly—there remains a keen sense of literary homelessness in their writing, as if their forced "home" in the women's pages made it impossible for these chroniclers to build a sense of literary belonging within avant-garde groups. In fact, neither chronicler fit in well with the vanguard circles of their respective cities. Storni was a few years older than most avant-garde writers and hardly fit into the paradigm of the muse, while Bonifant frequented the company of journalists and had little patience for bohemian poses. The condition of literary nomadism for women writers in 1920s Latin America has been thoughtfully argued.[27] Yet this perpetual sense of displacement and wandering also defines the public personas of all urban chroniclers studied in this book. Homelessness, in fact, can be construed as an inherent characteristic of the chronicle. It reinstates the rhetorical flexibility of the genre, its propensity to improvisation, and its formal multiplicity. For these reasons, reading the chronicles of Storni and Bonifant within the greater framework of the genre's rhetoric of accessibility during the 1920s gives an invaluable insight as to how women chroniclers negotiated a space for themselves within an increasingly heterogeneous literary modernity.

The Chronicle and Gender Norms

The question of gender has frequently hovered around conversations on the nature of the chronicle, especially those referring to the genre's intimacy with both literature and journalism and the discursive implications of this proximity. But instead of providing a consistent definition for the chronicle, such references to gender have brought about a flurry of contradictory associations. As we saw in chapter 1, the *modernista* Manuel Gutiérrez Nájera defended the literary quality of the chronicle by comparing it to the epistolary form and to the kindly femininity of his white-haired aunt, thus defining the genre in opposition to the brutal—and masculine—telegraph that was associated with technology, modernity, and commerce. In this case, femininity ensured the literary and aesthetic quality of the chronicle. But a significant shift took place during the 1920s, when literature was instead linked to masculinity, particularly in respect to literary projects that contributed to nation building. As Francine Masiello has shown in the case of Argentina, "manliness" was considered a patriotic virtue in the early twentieth century (*Civilization*, 142). During the same period in Mexico, truly "masculine" national literature referred to works that fit within the paradigm of the novel of the revolution. By that time, femininity, especially as espoused by the daring New Woman, was coming to signify the dangerous heterogeneity that accompanied the destabilizing process of modernization and the "inability to maintain a boundary between popular and elite traditions" (139). Not only did the feminine signal the growing visibility of the cosmopolitan aesthetics that circulated in illustrated magazines and frequently undermined national paradigms, but it also marked the rise of a middle-class reading public that was increasingly difficult to imagine and define.

The consideration of the chronicle as a genre that embodies both masculine and feminine attributes hinges around its role as a mediator in an expanding middle-class culture. During the 1920s the question of cultural taste—and how it could be conspicuously cultivated—was moving beyond bourgeois circles and into broader social spheres. Masiello points out that in Argentina, women became "an emblem of middle-class culture" (*Civilization*, 168), an observation that could easily be extended throughout Latin America. The chronicle's association with femininity and mass culture was hence a reflection both of the growing presence of women as cultural consumers and of the emergence of women chroniclers such as Storni and Bonifant, who became active discussants on issues of cultural taste through their regular columns. Yet, if the chronicle enabled these women writers to enter cultural conversations, it also kept them within the parameters of a middlebrow culture that was defined by the marketing of authors through images in the press and the cultivation of a broad public—a role that they only reluctantly embraced. According to Faye Hammill, the middlebrow was an "intermediary field of literary production" that dialogued with both the avant-garde and mass culture (*Literary Culture*, 11). For Hammill, the heterogeneous sphere of middlebrow writing not only diminished the distance between the fields of high and mass culture but also suggested ways to move beyond rigid definitions of art and literature and subvert cultural hierarchies.[28] In the double bind of the chronicle, therefore, women writers such as Storni and Bonifant were faced with their discursive limitations and, at the same time, were offered the tools for overcoming them.

The chronicle of the 1920s thus condensed the characteristics of a thriving middlebrow culture and worked to question the hierarchies that divided different modes of cultural production. The accessible intellectuals studied in this book fomented the overlapping aesthetics and the reciprocal influences that surfaced in the chronicle, as a simultaneous expression of the commercialization of literature and the incursion of avant-garde experimentation into consumer-oriented media. The chronicle of the 1920s, like the self-fashioning of chroniclers as accessible intellectuals who both guided and identified with their publics, was inseparable from the articulation of an urban middle-class culture. Such a social group was not homogenous throughout Latin American cities—Buenos Aires' middle class was robust when compared with Mexico City's or São Paulo's—and the existence of an urban middle class in Latin America is debated today more than ever. Yet in the 1920s the works of women chroniclers such as Storni and Bonifant, like their relationship to a growing and heterogeneous readership, came to embody—in all of its threatening and unsettling aspects—a modern reality where categorizations of gender and social class were becoming productively blurred.

Afterword

On June 19, 2010, Carlos Monsiváis passed away in Mexico City after a long fight with pulmonary fibrosis. Although he had been ill for many months, his death caused a collective shock in Mexico. A multitude of heartfelt testimonies from fellow writers, artists, and activists, as well as from regular readers, were published in national dailies such as *La Jornada, El Universal, Excélsior,* and *Milenio.* The chronicler's neighbors left flowers and posted messages on the walls of his home in the Portales neighborhood. Readers and admirers traveled for hours by bus to pay their respects in person.

Monsiváis' wake was held at the Museo de la Ciudad de México, a museum devoted to the history of Mexico City and located in the historic district. On the morning of June 20, his casket was taken to the Palacio de Bellas Artes, the nation's most important cultural center, for a public homage. As a crowd overflowed outside, his family and friends— composed of many of Mexico's most respected writers and intellectuals— stood guard, surrounded by news cameras. Monsiváis' longtime friend and fellow chronicler Elena Poniatowska spoke, eloquently summarizing the sense of loss and bewilderment that was being felt by so many. "What will we do without you, Monsi?" she asked. "How will we understand ourselves?" Meanwhile, the crowd that was unable to enter Bellas Artes grew restless. Frustrated cries rang out: "Let the people in!" "Monsi is of the people!" "Monsi is of the underdogs!" "This is not a show!"

The collective grief that was manifested after Monsiváis' death attests to the chronicler's omnipresence in Mexican public life. But the tension that surfaced between the official homage given to one of the nation's most admired and respected intellectual, and the many who felt excluded from this ceremony, also showed that he was a familiar figure whom diverse sectors of society claimed as one of their own. Monsiváis was mourned as a daily interlocutor, as an admired mentor, even as an intimate friend, by the many people who read him regularly, listened to him on the radio, or saw him on television. He was the one people turned to when they needed to understand major public events, and at the same time, he remained an idiosyncratic guide to the everyday street culture of the Mexican capital. With his death came not only a collective sense of loss but also a sudden, disorienting silence.

Monsiváis condensed, perhaps more so than any other contemporary chronicler, the characteristics of the rhetoric of accessibility that I have traced throughout this book. His interests indiscriminately spanned all areas of urban culture; his tone was witty and self-deprecating yet astonishingly confident, and he participated in a variety of facets of Mexican culture, making appearances at the most unlikely moments. Here was Monsi giving a talk in the bustling metro station La Raza, interviewing Subcomandante Marcos in Chiapas, and opening El Estanquillo, a museum in Mexico City that houses his private collection of eclectic artifacts. There he was, making a cameo appearance in the final episode of *Nada personal*, the political soap opera that parodied the absurdities of the Salinas presidency in the 1990s; reading jokes on *El circo*, an album by the Mexico City rock group Maldita Vecindad; or showing his support for left-wing candidate Andrés Manuel López Obrador in 2006, after a dubious election gave the presidency to the right-wing party of Felipe Calderón. Monsiváis was ever present in Mexican cultural life, but in many ways he was also impossible to reach and difficult to decipher.

Monsiváis gave the rhetoric of accessibility that characterized the chroniclers from the 1920s a postmodern twist. He was much more than an everyman who doubled as writer. He was a cultural and political actor who remained remarkably self-conscious about the ironies implied by his visibility in the media. This was made obvious in the illustration that appeared on the cover of his 1995 collection of chronicles, *Los rituales del caos* (The Rituals of Chaos), a book that focused on collective rituals through which mass culture is lived and practiced. The cover illustration depicts what first appears to be a fairly typical image of Mexico City:

a crowded subway car during rush hour. But a closer look reveals that the passengers of this car are far from ordinary citizens: the pop singer Gloria Trevi poses daringly in a bikini, the romantic crooner Luis Miguel smiles seductively, and the iconic wrestler El Santo sits to the right in a flowing cape that likens him to a Mexican Superman. Toward the back, the global rock star Bono stands next to a very local icon, the Virgin of Guadalupe. The image is framed by two Mexican archetypes—a middle-aged campesino stands to the left, his face partly shielded by the brim of his hat, and to the right a young man with spiky hair and sunglasses represents urban youth culture. In the midst of all of these characters Monsiváis stands, unobtrusively taking notes, his presence revealed by his unmistakable mop of gray hair and his thick glasses. This incongruous image—the chronicler nonchalantly riding the subway while surrounded by celebrities—highlights the inherent contradictions of his status as chronicler. At once spectator and protagonist, Monsiváis continually managed to stand out while fitting in, becoming an icon precisely because he possessed the elusive ability to put into words the experiences that city dwellers shared on a daily basis.

Monsiváis, a chronicler hiding in plain sight. Cover of *Los rituales del caos*, 1995 edition.

What has changed between the chronicles written during the euphoric modernity of the 1920s and those penned at the turn of the twenty-first century? How has the rhetoric of accessibility shifted in the transition between an incipient modernization and the era of globalization? The image of Monsiváis described above implies that the contemporary chronicler functions more than ever as a mediator who stakes a place for local cultures in an overwhelmingly globalized world. This disjunction between a local community and a global imaginary was just beginning to surface in the 1920s, notably in the tension between cosmopolitanism and nationalism that has been highlighted in the previous chapters. Roberto Arlt defended a Buenos Aires of immigrants that existed in tension with the national emblems of the gaucho and the pampas. Mário de Andrade struggled to place São Paulo on the cultural map of Brazil before turning his gaze toward the vastness and diversity of his country. Salvador Novo focused on a frivolous capital to question the assumption that national culture had to deal with the rural and manly struggles of the revolution. Alfonsina Storni and Cube Bonifant both found in growing cities new possibilities for forging intellectual personas and questioning a woman's place in the national patriarchy. Defending a cosmopolitan lifestyle in the 1920s was thus a means to turn the gaze toward the multiple symbols provided by modern urban life at a time when national discourses still privileged a rural identity, even if traditional rural lifestyles were quickly becoming obsolete. Focusing on the city did not imply a lack of concern for the nation; rather, it was a means of reminding readers to look to the present rather than the past for clues to their cultural identities.

Perhaps the greatest difference between the chroniclers discussed in this book and those who inhabit today's cultural landscape lies in their status. The chroniclers of the 1920s were still struggling to reconcile their work as journalists with their ambitions as writers. Even though they used their chronicles as a means to broaden the limits of the lettered city and circumvent the literary establishment, they were still on the defensive. They could not take for granted that the chronicle offered the literary recognition they so desired, and in many cases they did not obtain this appreciation in their lifetime. By the end of the twentieth century, a successful chronicler no longer needed to defend the relevance of the genre. On the contrary, chroniclers were fully confident not only that the chronicle had literary value but also that it occupied a privileged position within a literary sphere that was increasingly focused on the aesthetics of the "real," as is apparent with the success of the *testimonio* genre and the proliferation of novels and films since the 1990s that focus on gritty urban themes.[1]

The conditions of production and reception of the chronicle have now clearly changed. The chronicles penned in recent decades can no longer be portrayed as "literature under pressure," as Rotker defined the genre in nineteenth-century Spanish America. Chroniclers such as Edgardo Rodriguez Juliá (Puerto Rico) and Pedro Lemebel (Chile) craft their texts with a great attention to detail and a complexity that, paradoxically, recalls the stylistic ambitions of the *modernistas*. The highly crafted style of contemporary chronicles, however, does not reflect an anxiety over the mechanization of writing, as was felt by nineteenth-century chroniclers but rather indicates an engagement with the genre's heterogeneous complexity. As other indications of this shift in the genre's cultural status, chronicles are now regularly published and marketed successfully in book form, and prominent chroniclers are now more likely to be identified by their books than by their columns. The chronicle thus seems to have lost some of the vulnerability that characterized the accessible intellectuals of the 1920s. But if the chronicle is no longer an ephemeral genre located on the margins of literary culture, it still draws from the discursive strategies that characterized the rhetoric of accessibility and even exacerbates some of its main characteristics, such as hybridity, fragmentation, humor, a focus on happenings that have generally been dismissed as minor, an irreverence for cultural hierarchies, and a complicity with a readership that is imagined as broad, diverse, and yet familiar. Unbeknownst to themselves, the chroniclers of the 1920s were postmodernists avant la lettre. While they described the overarching processes of modernization that were transforming daily urban life in their respective cities, they also pointed to the inconsistencies in these changes, coining a form of intervention through supposedly "minor" means that would become all the more relevant as modernity went from being a promise within reach to a fatiguing disenchantment.[2]

The previous chapters argued that the 1920s brought about the consolidation of the urban chronicler as a new type of intellectual, one who informed and shaped public opinion by identifying with a diverse audience rather than by wielding the distant authority of nineteenth-century *letrados*.[3] This intimacy between a chronicler and his or her public was enabled by an incipient mass media, which promised ingenious ways of bridging the gap between writing and reading, between literature and modernity. A few decades later, with the repressive political atmosphere of the 1970s and the establishment of media conglomerates that were fully entrenched with government power, this creative complicity between the chronicler and the culture industry receded. The chronicler's public role took on the urgency of political responsibility and revealed a deep concern with the ethics of representation.[4] One way the distance between the chronicler and mass media manifested itself was through the heightened orality of the genre, which turned to fragmented voices as a means to contest the censorship of images by government-controlled media empires.[5] The most emblematic example of this shift would be Elena Poniatowska's chronicle of the 1968 student massacre in Tlatelolco, *Massacre in Mexico*, which was published with the subtitle *Testimonies of Oral History*. This chronicle bypassed the censorship of the press by appearing directly in book form, a move that highlights the growing independence of the genre from the newspaper page and its alliance to other Latin American genres such as the *testimonio*. In *Massacre in Mexico*, the vulnerable accessibility of the chronicler hinges on her willingness to listen and to become politically engaged. Poniatowska assumes the task of a transcriber and cedes the role of protagonist to the masses. The chronicler thus blends in with the voices of the crowds in a radical manifestation of the rhetoric of accessibility that had been expressed by chroniclers such as Arlt, who consistently highlighted his public anonymity in the streets of Buenos Aires. In many ways, the chroniclers from the 1920s set the foundations for the engaged chronicles of the late 1960s and 1970s, even if they did not themselves necessarily exercise the genre's potential as a form of intervention.

If the highly politicized chronicles of the 1970s tended to distance themselves from mass media during a crucial historical juncture, this did not mean that media ceased to be an object of fascination for the genre. By the 1980s and 1990s, as Monsiváis' collection of chronicles *Los rituales del caos* well shows, mass media had returned as an emblem of collective experience, if not as the accomplice it had momentarily been in the 1920s. Quite a few other chroniclers, such as Jaime Bedoya (Peru), María Moreno (Argentina), and Mario Prata (Brazil), gave space to the experience of global culture in their chronicles, dwelling on the local influence of Michael Jackson, Lady Diana, or *Playboy Magazine*. The chronicle is now defined more than ever by its constant migration between local and global referents, between literary and popular discourses. This rhetorical mobility surfaces in the chronicle's aesthetic take on banal and unexpected topics and in its recurrent questioning of the arbitrary norms that draw the line between good taste and kitsch.

The question of gender and its relationship to the chronicle surfaced many times throughout this book, particularly in the frequent association of the genre's hybridity with the questionable masculinity or the rebellious androgyny of its practitioners. If the genre's journalistic nature caused it not to be taken seriously by the literary establishment, this secondary position also propelled the careers of unexpected figures such as the flamboyant Novo, the outspoken Storni, and the contrarian Bonifant. Years later, the chronicle's condition as a "lesser" genre undoubtedly helped Elena Poniatowska slowly and unobtrusively ascend the literary ranks in Mexico. Clarice Lispector, perhaps the best-known Brazilian woman writer of the twentieth century, was also a prolific chronicler, a factor that only enhanced her public visibility and fomented the literary admiration of her peers. That both Poniatowska and Lispector, like Storni before them, were born in Europe and emigrated to Latin America as children might also have played a role in their dedication to the chronicle. They needed to establish themselves as cultural insiders, and the chronicle provided them with the ideal means to do so.

Perhaps because of the chronicle's formal flexibility and the difficulties inherent to defining it, the genre has shown a remarkable affinity for opening new discursive spaces for gay subcultures since the 1980s, in an apt continuation of Salvador Novo's work throughout his life as a chronicler. Both José Joaquín Blanco (Mexico) and Pedro Lemebel (Chile) propose the chronicle as a playful and contestatory locus for the articulation of sexual differences. In editions of collected chronicles such as Blanco's *Función de medianoche* (1981) and *Un chavo bien helado* (1990), or later Lemebel's *Loco afán* (1997) and *La esquina es mi corazón* (2001), these chroniclers strive to create an alternative cartography of their cities, in which informal gay landmarks can be incorporated into a broader urban history. Works such as these confirm that the chronicle, as both a literary genre and a cultural practice, can have potentially transformative effects on civil society.

This book has tried to shed light on one crucial moment in the trajectory of the Latin American urban chronicle. Without a doubt, one of the principal reasons for the genre's contemporary relevance is the long tradition of Latin American intellectuals working for the press and deriving their visibility and impact from their salaried journalistic work.

The urban chroniclers studied in this book formed part of a durable—if often tense—affinity between intellectuals and the press in Latin America. As professional writers, they seized the opportunity offered by the chronicle, using the hybrid genre to propose novel collaborations between the intertwined discourses of literature and journalism and to offer themselves as spokespeople of the collective experience that is city life. Almost a century after their columns ceased to circulate, the chroniclers from the 1920s continue to inform the most pressing questions broached by Latin American thinkers and writers. As the chronicle moves from the newspaper page to the Internet and urban communities turn increasingly virtual, this multifaceted genre continues to suggest new ways in which literature can mingle with everyday life.

APPENDICES

FIVE CHRONICLES IN TRANSLATION

Translated by Jacinto R. Fombona

Corrientes, at Night
Roberto Arlt

Fallen among the grand cubical buildings, featuring panoramas of chicken "on the spit" and golden halls and cocaine stands and theater lobbies, how delightfully brazen is by night Corrientes street! How lovely and how idle! More than a street it seems a living thing, a creation that oozes warmth through all of its pores; our street, the only street with a soul in this city; the only one that is welcoming, truly welcoming, like a trivial woman and prettier for that.

Corrientes, at night! While the other honest streets sleep to awake at six in the morning, Corrientes, the vagabond street, lights up all its signs at seven in the evening and, garlanded in green, red and blue rectangles, throws into white walls its methylene blue reflections, its picric acid yellows, like the glorious provocation of a pyrotechnist.

Under those phantasmagoric lights, stylized women like those drawn by Sirio, pass by lighting a volcano of desire among the stiff-neck bums rusting at the tables of "jazz band" saturated cafés.

Confraternity

Guards, paperboys, pimps, actresses, theater porters, messengers, resellers, company officers, comedians, poets, thieves, men of unnamable occupations, authors, tramps, theater critics, ladies of the lowlife; a unique humankind, cosmopolitan and bizarre, shakes hands in this sole waterway that the city has for its beauty and joy.

Yes; for its beauty and joy.

Because it is enough to enter this street to feel that life is otherwise and stronger and more lively. Everything offers pleasure. Everything.

From the "trattoria", with its windows filled with seafood arranged among iron pebbles, to the confectioneries that, instead of exhibiting sweets, showcase satin and silk-cloth dolls and dogs that smile with children's eyes. And books, women, bonbons and cocaine, and greenish cigarettes and unknown assassins; all socialize in the stylization modulated by the super-electric light and a voiceless shudder of sorts, that no one knows if it pours from the earth's innards or falls from the purest sky, high, with a glacial white moon chopped up by the cornices of skyscrapers.

Babel

The sidewalks are so narrow, and there is so much rubble in the wider areas, that people go by doing balancing acts with their feet between the cars' fenders. As in theater stages once the lights are off and the backdrops are left standing, one can see the houses chopped in half, rooms where municipal public works have left, by sheer miracle, a golden rectangular piece of paper or a clipping from "La Vie Parissien" [sic].

Casings made of reinforced concrete prettier than a woman. Black drainpipes suspended among frames of wood and beams. Voltaic arcs rumbling cellars of yellow soil, while the chain of the electric crane creaks. One-hundred-ton trucks. Trams in trinity, hallways with doors wrapped in green paper and inscriptions in gold letters: "Reserved sitting rooms." Women's hair salons where men come in and out. Apartment houses where every apartment provides a huge profit for the owner . . . and the police agent. Taverns where you eat "macaroni" adorned with little buns and haggard lampreys. Bookshops for old and new books with volumes fattened by pornography next to the one-millionth printing of *Martín Fierro*. Strings of photographs that would excite Methuselah. Photography studios that, aside from photographs, sell other items. Newspaper salesmen who address admirably dressed ladies in very familiar terms. Gentlemen with diamonds on their dickeys who shake hands with a black man from a dancing club. Top theater stars with the look of a pension lady out shopping. Honest ladies that look like artists. Poor folk who could pass for eminent delinquents. Bandits with cold-cream faces and tortoiseshell glasses. Sharp guys who look dumb and idiots [*lonyis*] who look like assailants.

Everything here loses its value. Everything is transformed. A gentleman passes by and says:

—Good evening, my corporal.

And the corporal salutes. That man he saluted has eight police round-ups [*manyamientos*] and two women who dress him so he can promenade his dashing figure along the way of the madmen and bagatelles.

Everything here loses its value: it is transformed. A princess gets out of a car and tells the ruffian at the newsstand:

—Che, Serafín, don't you have drugs [*menezunda*]?

The moon, white like zinc salt, round and pure, passes obliquely cutting the cornices of the skyscrapers. From time to time, a criminal raises his head, looks at her and then says to his partner:

—Che, are we going to the casino?

Unique Street

Unique street, absurd street, pretty street. Street to dream, to get lost in, to get from there to every success and to every failure; street of joy; street that makes women more daring and rowdy; street where tailors give counsel to authors and where policemen fraternize with the petty crooks; street of oblivion, of madness, of *milonga*, of love. Street of Russian and French women, of criollas who left their home too soon to join a young brawler on a bender; street that the jailed remember in the fifth cell; street that at dawn turns bluish and darkens because life is possible only under the artificial glow of methylene blues, of the greens of copper sulfate, of the yellows of picric acid that inject it with pyrotechnic madness and jealousy.

—*Aguafuertes porteñas*, *El Mundo*, March 26, 1929

The Cult of Statues
Mário de Andrade

A most curious expression of social psychology is the distortion that in cities often shapes the cult of the more or less illustrious dead. The real cult of men toward the dead, however secondary, very rarely exists. People easily adore God, the gods, the saints and spirits because toward those manifested forces from Beyond the cult is more a bargaining for favors, a constant "give me this and you take this" in which we always have the hope of gaining more than we give. Another helpful cult is the one practiced toward the powerful or well-known living. The powerful are capable of giving us a bit of their strength. And to live at the foot of the powerful is the most certain way to appear in photographs.

Nowadays the cult of the dead is insufficient and of little benefit. Except for those writing stories about the Marquise of dos Santos. For that reason, men have been gradually replacing it by the cult of statues.

Deep down, this cult is not without its beauty. The statue stays fixed in its square and we replace the memory of the dead, uneasy and hard to keep alive, for a lively minute of beauty. In fact, the most basic and permanent role of statues is not to preserve anyone's memory but to be pleasing to view. However, the fact is that very few statues do please. Not only because the beautiful is more attractive than the ugly and in the entire world a pretty statue is extremely rare, but also because knowing how to please with ugly things already implies a degree of knowledge too elevated to be shared by many.

Up to here it was not painful for me to speak, but it starts to be so. That is because I am being forced to engage in some rude musings: not only is the memory of the dead exceedingly relative in a statue, [but] is it true that so many of the illustrious dead deserve to be eternally remembered through sculpture? It is clear that I am not talking of any mediocre character one finds around town set to bronze. I am talking of those that are really illustrious, so rare that I dare not name any at this point.

Every public statue has to represent a public cult. The street is for all, and everything that is on the street is for all. I know well that unanimous applause is an impossible thing, although some men, occasionally for themselves and more often for the idea they represent, may deserve a universal, national or city-folk cult. It is possible, for example, that for a historian, Tiradentes means nothing within the historical phenomenon of Brazilian independence, but such a historian, facing the figure of Tiradentes, will never ignore the notion of our independence. The argument that possibly thousands of Brazilians ignore even the name of Tiradentes (not that many, but I agree I exaggerate it to argue this point) forgets to acknowledge that the statue may have an educational function.

It is at this point where the shoe pinches. I can see only one way for the monument to be educational: through its obstructing and discomforting grandiosity. The monument, to really stand out, the monument that forces people to stop, cannot be part of the street. The monument has to bewilder. A woman in her dancing dress is much more monumental on Quinze Street, even if a she is a little midget, than the monument to Olavo Bilac or Carlos Gomes' stairwell. People stop and think, "Who is she?" The merchants understood that very well, particularly after the arrival of the United States and electricity. It is unquestionable that the ads placed to the memory of the Castelões cigarettes or the Marmon automobile in Anhangabaú are monuments that Carlos Gomes or Olavo Bilac never had.

Its own beauty is not enough to turn a monument monumental. People get used to passing by without noticing it.

All of these remarks are obvious by themselves without my having to mention them. In São Paulo, with the exception of the Ipiranga monument and the Count Matarazzo one, the only ones monumental and . . . educational, every other statue is nothing more than a petty mockery. Of why they are there I will talk in a forthcoming táxi.

—*Táxi, Diário Nacional*, September 29, 1929

On the Advantages of Not Being Fashionable
Salvador Novo

The charm of ignoring the bustling everyday news never feels stronger than when one is sick or away from the city. Both situations take the subject away from cinemas, newspapers and busy streets where shop windows with books or suits are never missing, their offer so different from what one is wearing or carrying, that one feels the urge to acquire them. Nurses and peasants do not change their looks. They are a return to chemistry and botany, the return to nature that the wise recommend in times of hardship. One becomes then a character from an exemplary novel. People that assist one have names we thought had died out, and they carry them proudly: Anarda, Clorila, Partenio, Filis. One can hear the sweet lament of two Castilian shepherds, read Valle-Inclán and the street band plays Arditi's works. Suddenly, every romantic's moon appears glued to the paper backdrop and the stage is complete. The faraway stars proclaim no subversive manifesto whatsoever and, at most, they dust into the paysage a bluish chalk that makes the canvas a Ramos Martínez without reaching the exuberances of Diego Rivera. So that nothing is missing, the cowbell rings . . .

But in the city, who dares to do this? A sanction not listed in the code is the half sideways smile of those listening to you talking of things passé, or wearing a bad suit, or confessing you do not understand the latest "-ism." For, regardless of the branch of the social tree that you are attached to, if you live in the city, enjoying its well-known advantages—the roads, electric power, the telephone, French novels, public sector employment, Turkish baths—you must pay civilization a tribute by being up-to-date on its last cries and being able to discuss them uprightly. If you are a woman, you should wear organdy, shave your neck and chew gum, as well as other obligations shared by all citizens, such as going to the weekly movie openings, going every once in a while to a classical music concert, and being up-to-date on the daily news. If you are a man of society, I do suspect your day-to-day obligations are always new and complicated. They will mainly consist of spotlessly wearing the tips of your suit and your hair, of not having a shiny nose at parties, and of drinking tea without sugar, with lemon, with cream, without sandwiches, or whatever the fashion is. You should be fastidiously up-to-date on the society news published in newspapers, where sensible deaths are recorded, happy births, elegant weddings and distinguished travelers; so as to know everything necessary to polish your wit, brush your suit and choose your compliments.

Let us assume you are one of those things they call a dilettante; that you go after everything; that your merit is to know a bit of what music is, another bit of what literature is, a little bit of what painting is and another bit of what sculpture is. Then, to come out unscathed when facing specialists, you have to deftly distinguish Classical music from Romantic and Modern, and confess that you prefer the Russians above the Germans, who tend to be deaf or leave us, and that Mussorgsky is above Stravinsky, and naturally below Amani, whose *Bird of Paradise on a Waterfall* you like as much as the *Dialogue between Two Typewriters and a Cat*, by Erik Satie; but not as much as *Fireworks in a Green Cup* and *Pear-Shaped Fragments*, by Nieman the German one, although you are not quite certain. Of course, Debussy is not to be mentioned ever again.

If conversation veers toward a literary route, Cocteau, Morand and Max Jacob "fit" well. A bit Blaise Cendrars, but not even by mistake that mastodon of Victor Hugo, since there is quite a difference between Notre Dame and the Eiffel Tower. Later, of course, one has to perorate about Apollinaire, about the PEN Club and about the Museum of Letters. But it is already bad form to talk of Manuel José Othón, of Rubén Darío and of José Asunción Silva, and even worse of the ones before them. It would show that you are behind in important news.

If painting is the subject, it is necessary to say that you find in the new canvasses, in front of which you stand in ecstasy, the stroke "well resolved," "admirable" the coloring and "superb" the volume . . .

It is, furthermore, essential for every man to find out and discuss every recent social scandal. This is easier since you can find them in newspapers.

In the countryside nothing like this happens. Neither in the sanatoria. You wear the suit you most please, talk to who accommodates you better, and you do not broach rough subjects. You do not get exposed, moreover, to the possibility that your partner in conversation has the advantage in matters of art news.

Clearly, once you return to civilization you are bound to find things quite changed. Twenty volumes you have to read will have arrived. Painters will have painted more canvasses, and their meaning you will need explained. A new pianist will have made his debut with ultraviolet music. Your first duty is to check society pages. Under the heading "Recovered" is your name in a rather compromising paragraph. Fashion has caught you again. You have to arm yourself with clothes and knowledge; the dilettante's martyrdom starts . . .

If Manuel Acuña has rebutted Fray Luis (two gentlemen no longer quoted) on life in the countryside, I assure you that you have no escape: the hospital or the country house. Perhaps suicide remains; but of this society pages will also have their say.

—*El Universal Ilustrado*, July 24, 1924

The Perfect Typist
Alfonsina Storni

If you take a streetcar between seven and eight in the morning, you will notice the tram partly filled with women commuting to work and spending their time reading.

If a young reader has with her a detective-stories magazine, we can say she works in a factory or that she is a seamstress; a typist or a shop clerk if she presses to her bosom an obviously popular photo-magazine; a teacher or a student of high school education, if the magazine is of the intellectual bent; and if she carries nonchalantly an open newspaper, do not doubt it . . . she is an accomplished feminist, brave feminist, spirit of the times: punishable Eve.

But let the nonpunishable Eves rest assured. In the hands of the morning commuters there are plenty of popular magazines, those of love secrets.

So, Eve is saved from seven to eight in the morning by the typists and shop clerks.

The Typists

They are at the forefront of the female foothold in commerce, they add up to thousands of employees.

They invade the private firms, trading companies, public offices and studies.

Rocking in their machines' monotone tic, tic, tic-tic, tic, tic, they attack from the poor girl who writes addresses on envelopes and is paid by the hundred, to the high-level employee who knows typing and is in charge of foreign mail.

But what impresses us is not "a class" of typist, but the perfect typist, the typist born to type, the one we could call the typist-symbol, with her fixed and unmistakable characteristics.

Let's see some of them:

Guild Aristocracy

The perfect typist suffers from some aristocratic afflictions, among others, that of being under the astounding influence of a king.

This modest king of typists carries no crown whatsoever.

In its stead he carries something else: a bag with minute tools he uses to put typewriters together and take them apart.

Of course, like all kings, and Americans on top of it, he is hard to reach for the typists and, in his job of diagnosing the ills of the machines, despicable viceroys frequently replace him.

And I'll bet you all don't know what attribute bestows on the man with the bag his mysterious, regal character?

The man with the bag, if he is a real king, uses all ten fingers of his hands to type and, oh wonder! He does not watch the keyboard at all.

As if he had it grafted into his retina, he lets his fingers slide on it while contemplating the beautiful eyes of the perfect typist and, facing such an exquisite landscape, he calmly types over one hundred and twenty words per minute.

Each of his fingers is a soldier that does not miss his orders, and even the little pinky stores the perfect memory of the precise and fixed task assigned to it.

And this is way too much for a girl, a perfect typist.

She, who has spent three months of training unable to make her middle finger nor her pinky do their function, finally opting out for a two-fingered pecking (the index and middle fingers), all of this while checking the keyboard with her eyes, she succumbs, defeated by admiration, to the occult magic (undoubtedly of divine origin) wielded by that active and obedient pinky. Her minute and pink mouth, in such a solemn trance, takes the rounded shape of a large O.

And for a good reason . . .

Of Spelling and Other Things

We do not know if all of the comments floating around have a grain of truth; but according to them, the perfect typist's spelling would be in permanent default.

Crystal "*vasos*" [glasses] become, by calling forward a "z," an organ of the digestive system [*bazo*, the spleen]; "*vastos*" [vast] businesses lose their magnitude and elegance with the simple absence of a vertical dash [*bastos*, rough or crude]; the Spanish imperfect ending in "*-abas*" pitilessly slaughtered; zeds and esses that keep no hierarchy between themselves, aitches dropped or multiplied, and the punished and terrible word "*ocasión*" [opportunity], a word key for commercial spelling and ten thousand times spelled "*ocación*" would finally overcome a manager's patience to make him cry:

—Miss, once and for all, "*ocasión*" is spelled with an s, like "*casamiento*" [marriage]!

But, aside from the spelling, the perfect typist is accused of overusing the mirror, of being graceful, and playful, of living like little birds out of barely nothing, of wearing blouses with powder stains on them, and carrying red lipstick in their purses, of unrestrained laughter in the streets, of contributing, in one word, to the happiness of the streets of Buenos Aires with their twinkling glances and clicking high heels. And since from all these charges, trivial all of them, one can surmise that Buenos Aires without typists would be like Paris without "*midinettes*," we offer here a recipe for whoever would like to mass-produce them, and thus bring an end to the traditional boredom of the *porteño*.

Recipe for a Perfect Typist

To obtain a perfect typist follow these steps: choose a young woman eighteen to twenty years old living in an apartment building of any faraway barrio.

Lightly make up her eyes.
Use peroxide to get blond hair.
Polish her nails.
Tailor for her a fashionable and very short dress.
Tuck in her belly.
Harden a callus on the tip of her ring and pinky fingers.
Sprinkle copiously with bad spelling.
Put a bird inside her head (better if it is a blue one).

Send her to a business academy for two or three months. (Up to five pesos per month,)

Now make her follow the employment ads for one, two or three years.

Employ her for little money.

Note: Sometimes the typist does not wear makeup or polish her nails: such humbleness might come with staggering good spelling and a lack of paralysis in the ring and pinky fingers, but this is not the case, even remotely, of the perfect typist.

—"Tao Lao," *La Nación*, May 9, 1920

Long Hair and Short Ideas
Cube Bonifant

I do not know if you are aware that Mexico has women writers and who they are. Nor do I know if you happen to be acquainted with a few and even admire others. Since until now I have had the good taste to not read any woman writer (with the exception of a few French women writers that are worth something precisely because they do not write like women) I know nothing of literary ladies; but right now I intend to find out something about them, to tell you all, to the dot, the results of my research.

Of course, you should all know I am at a meeting that some of them attend. I am not sure how many they are, and seeing them like this, superficially, they all seem to me rather thick, lacking in that virtue called good taste, and almost old.

So, it is a meeting for lonely ladies. I am here, because I suppose they are not going to turn into suffragists, or issue an edict condemning bullfighting. I trust as well that I am not to be expelled for being "daring," as one of them proposed, I do not remember on what occasion.

Given this precedent, you will all understand that I cannot be better.

I ruffle my hair a bit, to let time pass, and take out my cigarettes. I light one with the same lack of elegance as men light them. (I have always liked masculine gestures immensely; I think I was born a woman by error.) I take a drag.

The first one who sees me—an ugly lady, she is an author and an actress—says nothing, but she frowns. She quickly passes on the news to the rest, because all of them turn to watch me.

I take another long, long drag . . .

The matriarch comes to the corner where I am:

—What are you doing? —she asks.

—Oh! My lady, I smoke and think. Moreover, I remember the great Fradique Méndez when he used to say: to smoke and to think are the same action: to send some little clouds to the wind.

—But, don't you know that smoking bothers the ladies, and besides, that this is not a smoking room?

I bow silently and she takes leave.

I am alone again, and unable to smoke! All because I have to be a gentleman with these ladies.

After long meditating on it, the actress and authoress approaches me exuberant in gaudiness, but kindly.

—Come, come here, we are all friends.

I stand up and approach the group. They have so little wit that I have no idea what to do.

A pretty zarzuela artist, who not long ago published a book, not sure if called handful of thornbushes, or woman's feeling, decides to play the piano and sing.

I, who have listened to her sing on the stage, prepare myself to not listen, because discordant sounds are not always of my taste. If you please, while she sings we shall talk about her.

She is in fact beautiful; she looks like an elegant Cybele, the goddess, although she has the fixation of believing she lives in 1830. Yes, this lady writer quite often turns Romantic; sings to "her poor wrecked soul"; tells her heart: "be quiet, these dark times will come to pass," and engages in so many gaudy things worthy of maudlin girls from the provinces. She is an operetta singer who has been ten years, at least, on the stage, filled with dirt and bawdry, it is clear she has yet to adapt to her environment, and if she shows no special temperament, she abandons it.

Yes, it makes sense. This pretty artist is like all women in theater: her talk is only to the flesh. Doesn't it strike you as curious, then, that she writes prose (never have I read her work, but I can imagine it) for the pleasure of hysterical and dumb girls?

But she stops singing and I keep quiet. Everyone here praises her voice.

They ask another to recite and she accepts. She is tall and slender. She seems to me the least gaudy of them all, although she is a bit of a broken record, because of every actress she interviews she asks the same question: "What is the happiest moment of your life?" "What is worth more for you: an hour of triumph or an hour of love?"

Well, she is saying something completely devoid of interest to me or to you all. People assure me she writes acceptable short stories. I understand she is cultivated; I am not certain about it; I have not read her either. And they add that she writes letters of a very subdued affected style. Perhaps: There is so much difference between short stories and letters, and letters and short stories . . . !

I look somewhere else. There she is, the authoress and actress, chatting with the other lady—the biggest of them all—who, I know, has written a sociological-sentimental novel, bursting with laments and dedicated, wholeheartedly, to her husband, a military man. A truly curious pair. More than intellectuals they look like a couple of bourgeois ladies who have sent their children out for a walk, and now rest, bemoaning their fleeting youth. (I assure you, it is way gone.)

The reciting woman finishes and discreetly takes a seat.

There is a sense of anticipation in the group now: readying herself to talk is a blond young lady, she looks like a maelstrom of curly hairs, and she knows Spain—but, what is she going to say of the Motherland? She starts, "for the first time a woman's heart served as a messenger" . . . to carry what, I have no idea.

I then start a silent and feline getaway.

Decidedly, I am taking leave, with the satisfaction of not being an authoress of short stories, of plays, of poetic prose nor of impressions of the Motherland. I leave happy for not being a woman writer, and thinking that in fact, "woman is an animal of long hair and short ideas"; but also with the selfish and beaming smugness of my short hair and scarce femininity.

—*Sólo para Mujeres*, *El Universal Ilustrado*, December 8, 1921

Notes

Introduction

1. This anthology was reissued in 2006 with the addition of more recent chronicles by Mexican writers such as Héctor de Mauleón and Fabrizio Mejía Madrid.

2. I am thinking particularly of Sylvia Saítta's ongoing work on Roberto Arlt, as well as Aparecida Maria Nunes' book on Clarice Lispector's journalistic career (2006). In the specific case of the Brazilian *crônica*, scholarship tends to be grouped in terms of author rather than period, with chroniclers such as Machado de Assis, Rubem Braga, Carlos Drummond de Andrade, Mário de Andrade, and Lispector garnering the most substantial critical attention. For scholarship on the *crônica* as specifically written in Rio de Janeiro, see Beatriz Resende, *Cronistas do Rio*, and for a broader overview of the genre in Brazil, see Antonio Cândido, *A Crônica*.

3. To give just a few examples, *As cem melhores crônicas brasileiras* (Objetiva, 2005, 2007); Rubén Gallo's *México, DF: Lecturas para paseantes* (Turner, 2005), published in English as *The Mexico City Reader* by the University of Wisconsin Press (2004); and Mexican press Cal y Arena's series Imprescindibles, which has reissued the chronicles of Manuel Gutiérrez Nájera (2006) and Ángel de Campo (2009).

4. I here loosely use the term "self-fashioning" as described by Stephen Greenblatt in *Renaissance Self-Fashioning: From More to Shakespeare*. I use the term "self-fashioning" to refer to the creation of a public writing persona both through writing (the chronicle as a form of self-portraiture) and through the chroniclers' awareness of the photographs and caricatures of them that circulated in the press along with the articles.

5. Even if Buenos Aires and Mexico City both saw the growth of a middle class during the 1920s, there was a great difference of scale between both cities, with the

former seeing a much more significant increase in numbers. These differences and their effect on the public personas of chroniclers is detailed in chapters 2 and 4.

6. For more on the effects of modernizing media on daily life in the early twentieth century, see Friedrich Kittler's *Gramophone, Film, Typewriter* and Stephen Kern's *The Culture of Time and Space, 1880–1918.*

7. To give just a few examples, it is no coincidence that the chronicles from nineteenth century that have received critical attention are the ones penned by *modernistas* such as Rubén Darío, José Martí, and Manuel Gutiérrez Nájera.

8. The choice of highlighting literary value over journalistic origins can be traced back to the inferior place in the cultural hierarchy that Spanish American *modernistas* assigned to the chronicle and that continued well into the twentieth century. If one glances through early publications in book form of some of the articles studied in this volume, one finds that most of these editions specify neither the newspaper that first published the chronicle nor the date in which it first appeared. For example, see the first edition of Novo's *Ensayos* (Taller Gráfico de la Nación, 1925), Mário de Andrade's *Os filhos da Candinha* (Livraría Martins, 1943), and Arlt's *Aguafuertes* (Editorial Victoria, 1933). This is not the case for Alfonsina Storni, however, as a selection of her chronicles was not published until much later (Alfaguara, 1998).

9. Few of the chroniclers studied in this book had any of their journalistic pieces published outside their respective countries, even if some of Novo's and Storni's poems were published abroad. Roberto Arlt would be an exception. Rose Corral explains that after 1928 his "Aguafuertes porteñas" were reproduced in newspapers from Uruguay and Chile, as well as Argentine newspapers from the provinces. From 1937 to 1941, the Mexican paper *El Nacional* published seventy-three of Arlt's chronicles, which have been reissued in Rose Corral's edition, *Al margen del cable: Crónicas publicadas en El Nacional, México, 1937–1941.*

10. In this context, I approach the chronicle through Pierre Bourdieu's notion of the cultural field (*The Field of Cultural Production*, 29–73). I take into account the radical contextualization necessary to understand the mechanisms of consecration and legitimation that define cultural products such as the chronicle.

11. Leduc was closely affiliated neither with the Estridentistas nor with the Contemporáneos. He spent most of the 1920s away from the capital and worked as a telegraphist for the Mexican army from 1912 to 1929 (*Cuando éramos menos*, 102).

12. Tarsila do Amaral, Oswald de Andrade's partner during the 1920s, was one of the founding members of the modernist movement in São Paulo. She is known primarily for her innovative work as a painter, though she also wrote chronicles irregularly throughout the 1930s for the *Diário de S. Paulo* and *O Jornal* (Rio de Janeiro). Her practice of the chronicle, which mostly took the form of art criticism, can be explained by the economic hardships of the 1930s, for she lost much of her inheritance as a result of the 1929 world financial crisis. Patricia Galvão, who succeeded Tarsila do Amaral as Oswald's partner, wrote chronicles regularly beginning in the 1940s. In 1931 she

published the column *A mulher do povo*, as well as caricatures and film criticism in the newspaper *O Homem do Povo*, which she cofounded with Oswald (the publication lasted eight issues). The primary reason I have not devoted a section to Galvão in this book, apart from her having written few chronicles in the 1920s, is that her interaction with the Brazilian vanguards was mediated by her relationship with Oswald. In this sense, she does not fit into the paradigm of the chronicler who depends on his or her writing to generate a sustainable income and to initiate conversations with avant-garde circles.

13. Other women chroniclers who might have fit into the parameters of this book are Mariblanca Sabas Alomá and Ofelia Rodríguez Acosta, Cuban authors who wrote regularly for the press throughout the early twentieth century. Though their journalistic work warrants further study, I have chosen not to include them, in order to restrict the frame of this study to Buenos Aires, São Paulo, and Mexico City.

Chapter 1

1. Salvador Novo's "El joven" was first published in 1928, but it is estimated that it was written around 1923 (*VE II*, 647).

2. For more on the sensory transformation of urban life through modern technologies in the specific case of Mexico City, see Rubén Gallo's *Mexican Modernity: The Avant-Garde and the Technological Revolution*.

3. See José Luis Romero's chapter "Las ciudades burguesas" in *Las ciudades y las ideas* for an overview of urban change from the 1880s to the 1930s. Capital cities and ports were particularly open to growth and to foreign cultural influences, and concentrated commercial enterprises linked to an expanding international economy.

4. I here single out the worries of Gutiérrez Nájera, but many of his contemporaries voiced similar preoccupations regarding the status of the chronicle in the face of technological progress and the industrialization of the press. For more, see Aníbal González' *La crónica modernista hispanoamericana*.

5. Throughout this book, I will refer to both nineteenth-century Spanish American *modernismo* and the Brazilian modernist movement of the 1920s. To avoid any possible confusion, I will refer to the first through its title in Spanish, *modernismo*, and the second through its English translation, "modernism."

6. For more in-depth reflections on modernity in Latin America, see Carlos Alonso, Cathy Jrade, Julio Ramos, and Aníbal González.

7. Many scholars have contributed useful definitions of modernity. See, for instance, Marshall Berman's *All That Is Solid Melts into the Air* and volumes such as Leo Charney and Vanessa Schwartz' *Cinema and the Invention of Modern Life* and Hal Foster's *The Anti-Aesthetic: Essays on Postmodern Culture* (especially Jürgen Habermas' essay "Modernity: An Incomplete Project"). Also see Nestor García Canclini on Latin America in *Hybrid Cultures: Strategies for Entering and Leaving Modernity*, in particular the chapter "Latin American Contradictions: Modernism without Modernization?"

Here, García Canclini aptly argues that "we have had an exuberant modernism with a deficient modernization" (41), and develops his notion of a "hybrid" modernity that draws from the contrast between a modernism as a global project led by the elites and a socioeconomic modernity that lags behind.

8. See the chapter "Arqueologías: Orígenes de la crónica modernista" in *La crónica modernista hispanoamericana*, by Aníbal González. For a more detailed discussion on the relationship between journalism and modernity, see González' introduction to *Journalism and the Development of Spanish American Narrative*.

9. In *The Structural Transformation of the Public Sphere*, Jürgen Habermas associates this transition of the press—from an organ of the state to an independent commercial vehicle—with the consolidation of the bourgeois public sphere.

10. See Rotker's commentary on Habermas in the context of Latin America (*Martí*, 32).

11. For more on the influence of *costumbrismo* on the chronicle, see chapter 2.

12. Machado de Assis (1839–1908) was born in Rio de Janeiro into an impoverished family. From a young age, he worked in publishing, first as a proofreader and later as a chronicler. He became a highly respected man of letters through numerous novels (such as *Memórias póstumas de Brás Cubas*, 1881), poetry, plays, and short stories. The majority of his publications, however, were chronicles, and he practiced the genre for four decades: first in *Diário do Rio de Janeiro*, then in *Semana Ilustrada*, *O Futuro*, *Ilustração Brasileira*, *O Cruzeiro*, and finally in *Gazeta de Notícias*. He also used numerous pseudonyms, such as Foi Lara, Lélio, Malvólio, Job, Eleazar, and Sileno, among many others. For more on his work as a chronicler, see Antonio Cândido's *A crônica*, which devotes an entire section to various essays on Machado de Assis and Lucía Granja's *Machado de Assis, escritor em formação (à roda dos jornais)*. For more on Machado de Assis in relation to the works of Mário de Andrade, see chapter 3.

13. The virtual absence of comparative criticism tends to increase the apparent conceptual differences between the Brazilian *crônica* and the Spanish American *crónica*, although many of the observations made about one can be extended to the other.

14. In Brazil, for instance, one can trace earlier and more numerous book editions of chronicles originally published in the daily press. There is also earlier critical work on the genre, most notably in the case of Machado de Assis.

15. Antonio Cândido defines the chronicle as a "minor" genre in his introduction to *A crônica* and uses this conceptualization as a starting point for his analysis of the genre.

16. Ramos, Rotker, and González have made this point.

17. See Ramos' *Divergent Modernities*.

18. Both Aníbal González and Susana Rotker coincide in this argument.

19. This tension between journalism and literature, while a point in common between *modernistas*, expressed itself on different levels. Martí, for instance, saw advantages to journalism. However, he considered that earning a wage gave him freedom to dedicate time to literary production, which took place *elsewhere*: journalism was

the flip side of literature; it was not a part of literature. Martí also insisted that even his journalistic writing never relinquished a degree of autonomy. Furthermore, he defended the didactic angle of literature; he aimed to elevate the public to literature rather than adapting literature to the interests of the public.

20. Renato Leduc's chronicles and poetry are marked by an antiacademic bent that mocked Mexico's prominent intellectuals. For example, his play *Prometeo sifilítico* (1934), in reference to José Vasconcelos's *Prometeo vencedor* (1916), parodied the Hellenic orientation of the group Ateneo de México.

21. See Flora Süssekind's *Cinematograph of Words: Literature, Technique, and Modernization in Brazil* for an excellent analysis of the Brazilian chronicle in the first years of the twentieth century. For the relationship between technology, literature, and practice, see in particular the chapter "Traces of Technology."

22. Throughout this book, I will often refer to Mário de Andrade by his first name, Mário, as many scholars have done previously. This is to avoid confusion with the other Brazilian writers who shared the same last name, such as Carlos Drummond de Andrade and Oswald de Andrade.

23. Cathy Jrade compellingly makes this point in *Modernismo, Modernity, and the Development of Spanish American Literature*.

24. See Huyssen's *After the Great Divide: Modernism, Mass Culture, Postmodernism*.

25. Renato Leduc, for instance, introduces his collection of chronicles *Historia de lo inmediato* in this way: "Among the dozens or hundreds of kilos of typewritten pages that are the product of more than thirty years of journalistic work, it is very difficult to make the rigorous selection of the best two hundred pages" (11). Roberto Arlt also made numerous similar allusions (see Saítta, *El escritor en el bosque de ladrillos*).

26. Esther Gabara sees a similar alliance between photography and the avant-gardes in her book *Errant Modernism: The Ethos of Photography in Mexico and Brazil*.

27. With the rise of advertising, argues Habermas in *The Structural Transformation of the Public Sphere*, "the public sphere becomes the court *before* whose public prestige can be displayed, rather than *in* which public critical debate is carried on" (201, emphasis in original).

28. By "men of letters," I refer to the concept of the *letrado*, as used by Angel Rama in *The Lettered City*. Roberto Arlt, Mário de Andrade, and Salvador Novo are "men of letters" in that they are professional writers who earned a living through the pen. However, these chroniclers (to varying degrees) shied from committing to political or critical projects as had the *letrados* before them (Bello, Sarmiento, Martí), and engaged with media in novel ways. Of the three, Mário de Andrade comes the closest to fitting the mold of the *letrado*, in that he engaged with his readers and with national culture in a more didactic manner and had the benefit of speaking from a more established literary authority.

29. In the first decades of the twentieth century, the Latin American book market was far from strong. In postrevolutionary Mexico, books did not circulate with ease, despite the efforts of José Vasconcelos and publications such as *El Libro y el Pueblo*, a

monthly magazine devoted to orienting the general public on the selection of reading material. Sergio González Rodriguez mentions that in the 1930s there were only around 150 bookstores in Mexico City and that the city's reading public ranged perhaps between 6,000 to 7,000 people. In Brazil, as in Mexico, illiteracy was rampant, and until 1930 the average printing of a novel was of 1,000 books (Ortiz, "Popular Culture"). The only exception would be Buenos Aires, where Editorial Claridad, for example, published inexpensive editions of 10,000 to 25,000 books in the 1920s and 1930s (Luis Alberto Romero, *Libros baratos*).

30. The underlying argument in Susana Rotker's *The American Chronicles of José Martí: Journalism and Modernity in Latin America* is to defend the chronicle as a literary genre in its own right. While I clearly agree with her proposal, I contend here that the chronicle should also be read through an approach that goes beyond a purely literary focus.

31. Throughout the rest of this book, I will refer to the chronicle both as a genre and as a practice, sometimes to avoid repetition and sometimes so as to highlight the dual ramifications of my reading. In *The Contemporary Mexican Chronicle: Theoretical Perspectives on the Liminal Genre*, Corona and Jörgensen also consider the chronicle as a social practice.

32. Elena Poniatowska and Carlos Monsiváis, to name just two examples, clearly fit into this paradigm.

33. De Certeau defines a tactic as follows: "A tactic is a calculated action determined by the absence of a proper locus. No delimitation of exteriority, then, provides it with the condition necessary for autonomy. The space of the tactic is the space of the other. Thus it must play on and with a terrain imposed on it and organized by the law of a foreign power. It does not have the means to keep to itself, at a distance, in a position of withdrawal, foresight, and self-collection" (*Practice*, 37).

34. See Unruh's *Performing Women and Modern Literary Culture in Latin America: Intervening Acts*, as well as chapter 5 of this book.

35. See "Mass Culture as Woman: Modernism's Other" in Huyssen's *After the Great Divide*.

36. In a chronicle called "Paris," published in Rio de Janeiro's *Diário de Notícias* on March 31, 1940, Mário explains the status of Paris among Brazilian artists and reviews a book published by Dante Costa in 1940, *Itinerário de Paris*.

37. Novo traveled as a delegate to a conference on education, held in Hawaii in 1927, which he chronicled in "Return Ticket." In 1934 he went to the International American Conference in Buenos Aires, where he met Federico García Lorca. Both trips were financed by Mexico's ministry of education and ministry of foreign affairs.

38. See "Intellectuals and Educators" in *The Antonio Gramsci Reader: Selected Writings, 1916–1935*, 300–322.

39. Although little work has been done on reading publics in Latin America, and data are hard to come by, certain assumptions can be made. The growth and heterogeneity of reading publics in the early twentieth century varied greatly from city to

city and hence had various effects on how popular publications imagined their target audience. For instance, the larger audience of Buenos Aires enabled, according to Beatriz Sarlo, the establishment of various publications dedicated to specific segments of the population, thus dividing readers into less heterogeneous groups that were self-selecting (*El Imperio*). A newspaper such as *El Mundo*, however, where Roberto Arlt published, had a wide enough circulation to encompass a broader sector of the middle and working classes. I would argue that in Mexico City, where readers were comparatively scarce, a publication such as the *Ilustrado* had to pragmatically target upper social circles as well as the middle and lower middle class.

40. See Kernan, "Idea of Literature."

41. See Nestor García Canclini's *Consumers and Citizens: Globalization and Multicultural Conflicts*, 37–48.

42. In *Performing Women*, Unruh similarly builds on Bourdieu's notion of "the art of living" (Bourdieu, *Rules of Art*, 54–57) and focuses on the creation of public personas by woman writers in the early twentieth century.

Chapter 2

1. For a concise overview of this period of Argentine history, see "Four Seasons of Democracy, 1890–1930" in David Rock's *Argentina, 1516–1987: From Spanish Colonization to Alfonsín*.

2. The Encyclopaedia Britannica defines an etching as follows: "A method of making prints from a metal plate, usually copper, onto which the design has been incised by acid. The copperplate is first coated with an acid-resistant substance, called the etching ground, through which the design is drawn with a sharp tool. The ground is usually a compound of beeswax, bitumen, and resin. The plate is then exposed to nitric acid or dutch mordant, which eats away those areas of the plate unprotected by the ground, forming a pattern of recessed lines. These lines hold the ink, and, when the plate is applied to moist paper, the design transfers to the paper, making a finished print (Encyclopaedia Britannica Online, s.v. "Etching," accessed April 29, 2009, http://www.search.eb.com/eb/article-9033116.

3. See Huyssen's *After the Great Divide* (especially 3–15). *Lunfardo* refers to the popular slang, or argot, spoken in Buenos Aires and Montevideo at the end of the nineteenth century and the beginning of the twentieth, that developed as a result of the arrival of European immigrants.

4. Arlt was often criticized for his inability to spell, his ungrammatical sentences, and his poor vocabulary. This aspect of his persona is rescued in Ricardo Piglia's novel *Respiración artificial* (Artificial Respiration). However, Sylvia Saítta points out that Arlt often exaggerated his lack of formal education. Although he claimed to have studied only until the third grade, he actually studied until the fifth grade and left school at age fourteen (Saítta, *Escritor*, 17).

5. See Josefina Ludmer's The Gaucho Genre: *A Treatise on the Motherland* for the importance of the figure of the gaucho in Argentine national identity, especially as depicted in José Hernández' *El gaucho Martín Fierro*. See also Angel Rama's *The Lettered City*, in particular the chapter "The Modernized City," for the importance of folk traditions in national identity.

6. For an analysis of the chronicles Arlt wrote later in his career, see Fernando Rosenberg's *The Avant-Garde and Geopolitics in Latin America*, in particular chapter 5, "Leaving Home: Cosmopolitanism and Travel."

7. For more on crowds in the city, see David Riesman, *The Lonely Crowd*, as well as Richard Sennet's *The Fall of Public Man*.

8. See Alfredo R. Lattes and Ruth Sautu, *Inmigración, cambio demográfico y desarrollo industrial en la Argentina*, Cuadernos del CENEP, no. 5 (Buenos Aires, 1978), quoted in Sarlo, *La modernidad periférica*, 17.

9. For an overview of the history of Buenos Aires, see Richard Walter's *Politics and Urban Growth in Buenos Aires, 1910–1940*; see also José Luis Romero and Luis Alberto Romero's *Buenos Aires: Historia de cuatro siglos*. For a more contemporary picture, see David William Foster's *Buenos Aires: Perspectives on the City and Cultural Production*.

10. Beatriz Sarlo documents the cultural and technological importance of the radio in Buenos Aires during the 1920s: "A veritable rage for radios developed, with great expectations of radio technology feeding both a thriving market for imported radios and kits and a rash of home-made sets and research projects" ("In Pursuit of the Popular Imaginary," 576).

11. Quotation is from Silvia Saítta's introduction to *Aguafuertes porteñas: Buenos Aires, vida cotidiana*. The numbers appeared in *El Mundo* on May 14, 1929. Although they might not be reliable, they still serve to illustrate the extent of this newspaper's presence in Buenos Aires. Saítta described *El Mundo* in this way: "The recently inaugurated tabloid in Argentina, a showy cover, photographs and large captions, brief and easy-to-read articles that resembled in no way the lengthy and confusing articles of other morning newspapers. Office employees, housewives and storekeepers, had, at last, their newspaper" (I).

12. Some dramatic changes to the Buenos Aires cityscape are chronicled in other articles by Arlt published in *El Mundo*, such as "New Aspects of Demolitions" (June 28, 1937), "The Skyscraper and the Plaza" (May 20, 1937).

13. Most of the articles that stem from interruptions come from Arlt's early years as a chronicler, from 1928 to the early 1930s, when he was still a newcomer to the newspaper and was forming his public persona. Before writing for *El Mundo*, he had already made incursions into journalism, although he had not reached the continuity and visibility that he obtained through his *Aguafuertes*. He had published articles in *Don Goyo* and *Última Hora* and, most notably, had worked for the crime section of the popular daily *Crítica*.

14. The structural interruption that begins this chronicle is repeated in many of Arlt's texts. Here are a few examples: "Golden Crib and Silk Diapers" starts with "I was on the streetcar the other day when I heard that a *fulano* [guy] told another . . ."(Arlt, *Aguafuertes porteñas*, 124). "Love in Rivadavia Park" begins: "I was crossing the park, like a little saint, the hands submerged in the pockets of my raincoat, and my eyes alert. All of a sudden . . ." (37).

15. Concrete spatial referents abound in Arlt's *aguafuertes* and sometimes are indicated from the very title of the text. A few examples: "Storekeepers of Libertad, Cerrito and Talcahuano," "Abandoned Cranes on Maciel Island," "Canning and Rivera."

16. "No one ignores that the South begins at the other side of Rivadavia," mentions Borges (*Ficciones*, 198).

17. For more, see "Panopticism," in Michel Foucault's *Discipline and Punish: The Birth of the Prison*.

18. A few of Arlt's titles can illustrate his interest in urban types and his interest in disappearing lifestyles: "The Sinister Voyeur," "The Doctor's Wife," "The Watchmaker," "The Neighbor Who Dies."

19. The principal traits of *costumbrismo* are described in *Periodismo y costumbrismo en el siglo XIX*, by José Manuel Pérez Carrera. See also the chapter "The Modernized City" in Angel Rama's *Lettered City*.

20. The weekly *Caras y Caretas* was founded in 1898 by Eustaquio Pellicier, Manuel Mayol, and Bartolomé Mitre. It was an artistic and literary publication that focused on daily life in Buenos Aires, and was illustrated with photographs, etchings, and caricatures. Other Argentine *costumbristas* of the nineteenth and early twentieth centuries are included in *Fray Mocho, Felix Lima y otros: Los costumbristas del 900*.

21. This argument, however, does not intend to simplify the flaneur's interaction with the city. There are many varieties of flaneurs, and many also dwell on the overwhelming aspects of urban modernization. It is more a question of considering which tradition of the flaneur Arlt chooses to continue, as well as what this choice signifies in terms of his relationship to Buenos Aires and to a literary tradition of writing about the city. For an excellent drawing out of the intricacies of the flaneur in modern French culture, see Mary Gluck's *Popular Bohemia: Modernism and Urban Culture in Nineteenth-Century Paris*.

22. See Josefina Ludmer's *El cuerpo del delito: Un manual* for an analysis of delinquency in Roberto Arlt's work. Especially interesting is her close reading of his 1930 article "This Is Souza Reilly"; she parallels Arlt's initiation to literature with an introduction to delinquency and treason.

23. The relationship between the chronicle and advertising is explored further in chapter 3.

24. For more, see Borré, *Roberto Arlt y la crítica*.

25. Ricardo Piglia's novel *Artificial Respiration* touches on the importance of technology and invention in Buenos Aires and offers a fascinating profile on Arlt's

participation in this frenzy. Also see Saítta's excellent biography of Arlt, *El escritor en el bosque de ladrillos*.

26. In *Roberto Arlt y la crítica*, Borré dwells on Arlt's spelling problems and the critical reaction it provoked in other contemporary writers.

· 27. Ibid.

28. Alfonsina Storni's chronicles offer a radically different perspective on commerce and the street Florida. For more, see chapter 5 of this volume.

29. "Roberto Arlt asked Borges if he liked the neighborhood Villa Luro, and Borges answered that he did not know where that neighborhood was, and since then, Arlt never greeted him again" (Borré, *Roberto Arlt y la crítica*, 32). One must take this anecdote with a grain of salt, both because of its exaggeration and because it came from an interview given by Borges, famous for his purposeful misquotes. However, it does give a clear example of the different social connotations of the various neighborhoods of Buenos Aires. While Arlt frequented marginal neighborhoods such as Villa Luro, Borges preferred the more traditional Palermo.

30. For a detailed analysis of the Argentine vanguards, and in particular the different currents Boedo and Florida, see Francine Masiello's *Lenguaje e ideología: Las escuelas argentinas de vanguardia*; and Christopher Towne Leland's *The Last Happy Men: The Generation of 1922, Fiction, and the Argentine Reality* (more specifically, his chapters "The Movements" and "Treason and Transformation: Roberto Arlt's *El juguete rabioso*").

31. For more on tango in Buenos Aires, see Garramuño, *Modernidades primitivas*.

32. In "El Teatro del Pueblo va al Teatro Corrientes" (*RA II*, 444), Arlt explains the different locations of the fledgling company directed by Leónidas Barreta. It was first opened in 1928 at an abandoned theater at Corrientes #500, then it moved around the corner to the avenue Carlos Pellegrini. Finally, in the late 1930s the municipality donated the Corrientes theater to the company. Today the Teatro del Pueblo is located on the avenue Roque Saenz Peña, near the street Corrientes.

33. For more on the relationship between masculinity and the popular in Arlt's writings, see Civantos, "Language, Literary Legitimacy and Masculinity in the Writings of Roberto Arlt."

34. Borges described his own wanderings as "callejero no hacer nada" (street idleness). Quoted in Sylvia Molloy's " Flanerias textuales: Borges, Benjamin y Baudelaire," an article that offers an excellent reading of Borges' relationship with the city.

35. Another possible explanation for the differences between Arlt's and Girondo's dialogic relationships to urban space lies in the formal constraints of poetry. Girondo's poetic voice does not have the hybrid flexibility that Arlt constantly brings into play as a chronicler. A thorough close reading of these two figures, however, would warrant a comparative reflection on the differences between poetry and the chronicle that falls beyond the scope of this project.

36. I would like to thank Ricardo Piglia for this information, from a conversation in Buenos Aires, July 1999.

37. For more on Arlt and the cinema, see Saítta, *Escritor*, as well as the collection of Arlt's chronicles on film, *Notas sobre el cinematógrafo*.

38. In *Communication, Culture and Hegemony: From the Media to Mediations*, Jesús Martín-Barbero coined the term mediation to argue that mass media interpellates an audience through the process of self-recognition. Something similar is at stake through Arlt's *Aguafuertes*. However, Martín-Barbero links interpellation to the creation of a national community, a "pueblo," and Arlt stops short of calling for a national identity, a national sentiment. The similar caveat I have pointed out in regard to Anderson's "imagined communities" applies here.

39. In *The Culture of Time and Space*, Stephen Kern describes the effect of speed (electricity, motorized vehicles, telephone, telegraph, etc.) on European modern life and gives an excellent overview of the cultural reactions (both favorable and alarmist) to these technological changes.

40. In the chronicle "Don Juan Tenorio and Ten Cents," Arlt tells of the plight of a friend who wants to follow a woman onto a streetcar but discovers that he lacks the ten cents to pay the fare.

41. The speed of the chronicle's transition from personal experience to published text resembles another form of media that was increasingly popular in Buenos Aires and of great interest to Arlt and the other chroniclers composing this study: the radio. For more on the radio during the avant-garde times, see Gallo, *Mexican Modernity*, and Birkenmaier.

42. As chapter 5 shows, women chroniclers had to circumvent additional hurdles to obtain recognition as writers and public figures.

43. See Enzensberger's "Constituents of a Theory of the Media."

44. Clifford points to a similar situation in his essay "On Collecting Art and Culture": "Whether a child collects dinosaurs or dolls, sooner or later she or he will be encouraged to keep the possessions on a shelf or in a special box or to set up a doll house. Personal treasures will be made public" (60).

45. As Beatriz Sarlo comments, the high price that scientific books fetched indicated the importance of science, technology, and invention in Buenos Aires of the 1920s ("In Pursuit of the Popular Imaginary"). Also see Vicky Unruh's *Latin American Vanguards*, in which she provides a provocative reading of *Mad Toy* and considers Silvio Astier's character in the light of other vanguardist representations of the artist.

Chapter 3

1. Mostly known as a poet, Manuel Bandeira also published chronicles in the *Diario Nacional* in the 1930s along with Mário de Andrade and Luis da Câmara Cascudo. He had a long and frequent correspondence with Mário, to the extent that the latter named his first typewriter "Manuela," in honor of his interlocutor. Bandeira collaborated in the modernist magazines *Klaxon* and *Revista de Antropofagia* and also wrote on music for *A Idéia Ilustrada* and *Ariel*. In 1937 he published *Crônicas da Província do Brasil*.

2. Rio De Janeiro's Olavo Bilac, for example, held in contempt his work as chronicler and once asked: "What are we all, journalists and *cronistas*, if not desecrators of art and journeymen of literature?" (Süssekind, *Cinematograph*, 7). See Flora Süssekind's *Cinematograph of Words*, in particular her chapter "The Hand and the Machine," for more on the relationship between literature and technology for Brazilian chroniclers of the early twentieth century.

3. Mário de Andrade made two significant trips chronicled in *O turista aprendiz*. The first trip, in 1927, took him to the Amazon (he made particular note of Belém). This trip was projected as part of a "caravan for the discovery of Brazil," a continuation of a first trip made with fellow modernists to Minas Gerais in honor of the poet Blaise Cendrars' visit to Brazil. However, at the last minute, the travelers were reduced to Dona Olívia Guedes Penteado of the coffee aristocracy, Dulce do Amaral Pinto (Tarsila do Amaral's niece), and Mário de Andrade himself, an uncomfortable situation for the apprentice ethnographer. The second trip, from December 1928 to March 1929, took him to the northeast and was partly financed by the *Diario Nacional*, where he published his chronicles of the journey in the column *O turista aprendiz* and dedicated many chronicles to Recife, Natal, and Paraiba. For more on these two trips and for bibliographic references, see Telê Porto Ancona Lopez' introduction to the 1976 edition of *O turista aprendiz*. See also Rosenberg, *Avant-Garde and Geopolitics*, and Gabara, *Errant Modernism*.

4. Paulo Prado was one of the main patrons of São Paulo arts, and the one to invite poet Blaise Cendrars to Brazil.

5. Mário de Andrade was a participant in the drive toward a "rehumanization of art," the reengagement between art and experience that has generally characterized the Latin American vanguards (Unruh, *Vanguards*, 21–29). Vicky Unruh contends that the Latin American vanguards' drive toward a "rehumanization of art" responds in part to José Ortega y Gasset's essay *La deshumanización del arte*. The main points of her argument, which guide her book *Latin American Vanguards: The Art of Contentious Encounters*, are "(1) that Latin America's vanguards sought a reengagement between art and experience; (2) that Latin American writers often sought to reshape and redefine, with various purposes in mind, what Ortega had identified as the dehumanized quality of modern art; and (3) that Latin American vanguardist activity sometimes recast vanguardism itself, in particular, the defamiliarizing features encompassed in Ortega's word *dehumanized*, as peculiarly Latin American phenomena" (26). Although Mário de Andrade's description of his cultural contributions as a humanizing labor coincides with Unruh's argument, his thoughts respond more to concerns stemming from his own vanguardist practice than to Ortega y Gasset's essay.

6. This newspaper ran from June 1927 to 1932. It was linked to the Democratic Party and was always in a tight financial situation. For more on the *Diario Nacional*, read Telê Porto Ancona Lopez' introduction to Mário's *Táxi*.

7. Mário de Andrade was a founder of and a regular participant in the modernist magazine *Klaxon*. He contributed many chronicles, especially on music, and

commented on musical performances in São Paulo. Vicky Unruh lists many magazines whose titles are associated with modernity (*Vanguards*, 80), from among which I have chosen to quote these few.

8. Mário de Andrade's description of Oswald reads as follows:

—Abade Liszt da minha filha monja,
na Cadillac mansa e glauca de ilusão,
passa o Oswald de Andrade
mariscando gênios entre a multidão! (*Poesías completas*, 94)
[Abbé Liszt of my daughter the nun, in the gentle sea-green Cadillac of illusion, Oswald de Andrade goes by fishing for geniuses in the crowd!] (Brotherston, *Latin American Poetry*, 80)

9. These figures are taken from Queiroz, *São Paulo*, and Sevcenko, "Blaise Cendrars."

10. The figure for cars in São Paulo is from Queiroz, *São Paulo*, 187, and the figure for taxis is from Correa Stiel, *História dos transportes colectivos*, 17.

11. See chapter 2. For more on the streetcar as represented by the modernists, see Roberto Schwarz' article, "The Cart, the Tram and the Modernist Poet" in *Misplaced Ideas*. Also see Antonio Luciano Tosta, "Exchanging Glances: The Streetcar, Modernity, and the Metropolis in Brazilian Literature."

12. References to movement (be it of texts, vehicles, images, or even gossip) surface in the works of many Brazilian chroniclers as they define their practice. In 1909, João do Rio titled the first volume of his chronicles *Cinematógrafo: Crônicas cariocas*. Being in the city, for this writer, is likened to being in a cinema, and his work as a chronicler is analogous to that of a filmmaker (Süssekind, *Cinematograph*, 27). Carlos Drummond de Andrade, a contemporary of Mário's based in Rio de Janeiro, also appealed to movement and intimacy when introducing one of his many books of chronicles, *Cadeira de balanço* (Rocking Chair, 1966): "The rocking chair is a traditionally Brazilian piece of furniture that does not look bad in a modern apartment. It favors repose and stimulates the serene contemplation of life, without abolishing the pleasure of movement. Whoever is installed in it can read these pages more comfortably." By evoking the coexistence of tranquility and movement, Drummond's description of the chronicle connotes intimacy and solitude at the same time as it invites the reader to a virtual journey through city life. Like João do Rio, Drummond describes the chronicle as a path toward a particular way of reading and seeing, which in this case rocks back and forth between what is defined as traditionally Brazilian and the modern and cosmopolitan street life of Río de Janeiro.

13. "A Ciranda" originated in the northern state of Pernambuco. It is a dance in which anyone can join or leave a circle of dancers, in the middle of which are the musicians, while the master, or *cirandeiro*, improvises the verses sung. "Bumba meu boi" is a Brazilian tradition that originated at the end of the eighteenth century; it tells the story of the death and the resurrection of an ox through popular parades, music, and dancing. Depending on the region, it takes place either during the Christmas

season or in June. These are both musical festivals, pointing once more to Mário's interest in popular musical traditions.

14. For more on speed, see Kern, *Culture of Time and Space*.

15. These examples come from the collection *Os filhos da Candinha*.

16. Aníbal González traces the influence of oratory on the Spanish American modernist chronicle. Not only was oratory indicative of the "literary" style of these chronicles, but it was also closely linked to "journalism of opinion," which expressed ideological criticism of the government (*Journalism*, 88).

17. In his introduction to *Contos: Uma antologia*, John Gledson describes the importance of a female audience for Machado de Assis' short stories. Almost all of them were initially published in newspapers and magazines, and some of the publications that gave greater space to his works were "feminine" magazines, such as *O Jornal das Famílias* and *A Estação*.

18. For more on Gutiérrez Nájera's "La novela del tranvía," see chapter 2.

19. Michael Warner defines gossip in relation to public discourse: "Gossip might seem to be the perfect instance of public discourse. It circulates widely among a social network, beyond the control of private individuals. It sets norms of membership in a diffuse way that cannot be controlled by a central authority" (*Publics and Counterpublics*, 78). Warner, however, also highlights that gossip can be divisive, bringing in issues of trust, relative standing, and measurements of group membership; if one does not follow the unspoken rules of gossip, it is easy to slide into being considered slanderous.

20. Mário de Andrade's concept of nationalism differs substantially from the regionalism of Gilberto Freyre. Based in Recife, Freyre established the Regionalist Center of the Northeast and in 1926 published the Regionalist Manifesto. In contrast to the modernist movement of São Paulo, which saw nationalism as a step toward a greater universalism, the Regionalist Manifesto "developed two interlinked themes: the defense of the region as a unit of national organization and the preservation of the regional and traditional values of Brazil in general and the northeast in particular" (Oliven, "Brazil," 59). In the words of Beatriz Resende, "Gilberto Freyre would be responsible for the formulation of the theory of miscegenation, according to which racial mixture in Brazil is the product of the cultural peculiarities and modes of behavior characteristic of the country" ("Brazilian Modernism," 203).

21. For more on the *Diario Nacional*, see Telê Porto Ancona Lopez' introduction to *Táxi e crónicas no Diario Nacional*.

22. See Unruh's *Latin American Vanguards*, 224–231, for an overview of linguistic activities in the Latin American avant-gardes.

23. For two recent compelling readings of *Macunaíma*, see Rosenberg, *Avant-Garde and Geopolitics*, and Gabara, *Errant Modernism*.

24. This ideal sensibility was expressed through the metaphor of cannibalism in Oswald de Andrade's Cannibalist Manifesto, which was published in the *Revista de Antropofagia* in May 1928.

25. "A linguagem," I and II, and "Ortografia," I and II, written in 1929, and "Ortografia," I and II, written in 1930, are some of Mário de Andrade's chronicles on the subject of spoken Brazilian Portuguese.

26. The Academia Brasileira de Letras was founded in 1896 and represented one of the academic perspectives that the modernists questioned with most persistence.

27. For more on Arlt and his conceptualization of street language, see Civantos, "Language, Literary Legitimacy and Masculinity."

28. Mário de Andrade's references to grammar in his column *Táxi* can be traced back to some of his statements in *Hallucinated City*: "You will easily note that if grammar is sometimes scorned in my poetry, it does not suffer serious insults in this extremely interesting preface" (16); and "Pronouns? I write Brazilian. If I use Portuguese orthography, it is because it furnishes me an orthography without altering the result" (16).

29. No information is available on the circulation of the *Diario Nacional*.

30. Angel Rama singles out Sílvio Romero, and in particular his "Estudos sobre a poesia popular no Brasil," to describe the incorporation of orality in Brazilian literary tradition in the nineteenth century. It is worth quoting Rama on this point: "Literature was considered an autonomous field of knowledge as a consequence of—or, at least, enhanced by—the humble oral productions of rural cultures whose long history and conservatism provided a broad legitimating foundation for conceptions of nationality" (*Lettered City*, 65).

31. Rio's pedestrian Rua do Ouvidor was a busy street in the city's commercial district where political and intellectual discussions took place in some of its numerous cafés.

32. For more on Novo's fascination with chauffeurs, see his erotic autobiography, *La estatua de sal*.

33. In a speech marking the twentieth anniversary of Modern Art Week, Mário de Andrade highlighted the differences between Rio and São Paulo in the 1920s: "There was a great difference, already today less marked, between Rio and São Paulo. Rio was much more international, as a norm of exterior life. It is clear: seaport and capital of the country, Rio possessed an innate internationalism. São Paulo was spiritually much more modern, however, a necessary result of the coffee economy and its consequent industrialization. Hillbilly from *serra-acima* [above the mountains], conserving until now a provincial subservience, well disclosed by its politics, São Paulo was at the same time, because of its commercial actuality and its industrialization, in more spiritual and technical contact with the actuality of the world" (*Mário de Andrade hoje*, 20).

34. In 1890, Rio's population was 552,651, growing to 1,157,873 in 1920. São Paulo went from 64,935 to 579,033 in the same years (Burns, *History of Brazil*, 271).

35. In *Errant Modernism*, Esther Gabara refers to the double implications of *errar* (to err, both to wander and to be mistaken) in regard to the ethnographic impulse of Brazilian modernism. The discomfort that Mário expresses with regard to travel, in her convincing reading, is intrinsically linked to the ethos of modernism.

36. Clifford describes this alienation in the European city after World War I: "Reality is no longer a given, natural, familiar environment. The self, cut loose from its attachments, must discover meaning where it may—a predicament, evoked at its most nihilistic, that underlies both surrealism and modern ethnography" (*Predicament*, 119).

Chapter 4

1. In 1928 the title of *El Universal Ilustrado* was shortened to *Ilustrado*. For simplicity's sake, I will use the shortened version of the title throughout the next two chapters, for this is how the magazine was informally called by its contributors even before the name was officially changed.

2. The essayist and teacher Julio Torri (1889–1970) was a member of the Ateneo de la Juventud. Novo knew him well. It was Torri who introduced Novo to Pedro Henríquez Ureña, who would become his intellectual mentor and who would encourage him to develop his skills as an essayist.

3. Novo uses an epigraph from his short story "El joven" in his essay "Nuestra ciudad mía" (*VE I*, 107). He adds this same short story as an appendix to his book-length chronicle on Mexico City, *Nueva grandeza mexicana*, published in 1946. In this way, he becomes the core of his genealogy of influences, designating himself as his own inspiration.

4. At the start of *Hallucinated City*, Mário de Andrade includes a letter signed with his name and dedicated to Mário de Andrade, whom he refers to respectfully as his teacher. With false modesty, he claims: "I do not know, Master, whether you will forgive me the distance that lies between these poems and your noblest lessons" (3).

5. Knowing Novo's humor, it might not be coincidental that "El maestro," an essay preceding Torri's "Del epigrafe" in *Ensayos y poemas*, is introduced by an epigraph from Shakespeare's *King Lear*.

6. The decision to include this image of Barbara La Marr was not external to Novo, for he refers to the photograph at the end of his essay. However, he does not refer to her by name in this text, so perhaps he was more interested in the pose rather than in the background of this specific film star.

7. The Tupi are a Brazilian indigenous group from the Amazon who supposedly practiced anthropophagy; hence Oswald de Andrade's inclusion of them in his Cannibalist Manifesto.

8. I here take from Judith Butler's argument that a performative act takes place within a recognizable formula that "conceals or dissimulates the conventions of which it is a repetition" (*Bodies*, 12). Novo demonstrates that he is acquainted with and can follow the unspoken codes of literary conventions, but he chooses to authorize himself by giving a mocking twist to their accepted use. In other words, he reveals what Butler calls "the hidden conventions of performativity."

9. Novo also participated in advertising and in theater, directing the department of theater in the Palacio de Bellas Artes in Mexico City in 1947.

10. Novo was not always as intimate with official power as he would be later in his career. In *Lo marginal en el centro*, Monsiváis details the hostility of the Cardenas government toward Novo in the 1930s, which led to his short-lived exile in Los Angeles.

11. Following are only a sample of the many columns Novo published during his career as a chronicler: *Consultorio a cargo del niño Fidencio* (*Excélsior, edición de la tarde*, January–April 1929); *Perifonemas* (*Últimas Noticias*, 1937); *La semana pasada* (*Hoy*, 1938); *Sidecar* (*Excélsior*, 1940); *Ventana* (*Novedades*, 1943); *Diario* (*Mañana*, 1943); *Cartas viejas y nuevas* (*Mañana*, 1950). Most of his chronicles have now been regrouped into the series *La vida en México*, edited by José Emilio Pacheco.

12. The publication of Novo's explicitly erotic memoirs, *La estatua de sal* (1998), followed by Carlos Monsiváis' intellectual biography, *Salvador Novo: Lo marginal en el centro* (2000), spearheaded this revaluation of Novo's work. More of an erotic bildungsroman than an autobiography, *La estatua de sal* focuses on Novo's youth and his coming of age. It was long deemed too scandalous to publish, as it outed many of Mexico's prominent intellectuals and functionaries.

13. In this chapter, I concentrate on Novo's reflections on the genre of the chronicle and his engagement with literary debates, rather than looking primarily at ways the chronicler interacts with the space of the city, a perspective I privilege in my earlier chapters on Roberto Arlt and Mário de Andrade. Many interesting studies dealing with the relationship between Novo and the city have been made. Mary K. Long's dissertation on Novo dedicates a chapter entitled "Writing the City" to this subject. Vicente Quirarte's *Biografía literaria de la ciudad de México* gives a solid overview of the Contemporáneos' relationship with Mexico City. See also Juan Gelpí's article "Walking in the Modern City: Subjectivity and Cultural Contacts in the Urban *Crónicas* of Salvador Novo and Carlos Monsiváis."

14. In "Walking in the Modern City," Gelpí mentions an example of another "doubling" performed by Salvador Novo, this time with José Joaquín Fernández de Lizardi, who like Sor Juana, had suffered from intellectual persecution.

15. For further reading, see Daniel Balderston's article "Poetry, Revolution, Homophobia: Polemics from the Mexican Revolution" and Robert McKee Irwin's *Mexican Masculinities*.

16. This preoccupation with sexual orientation can be traced back to the famous "baile del 41," when forty-one men were arrested in Mexico City in November 1901 for dancing in drag in a private home. This event was widely reported in the press and became a common reference to designate homosexuality. See Ben Sifuentes-Jáuregui's chapter "Nation and the Scandal of Effeminacy: Rereading los 41," in *Transvestism, Masculinity, and Latin American Literature: Genders Share Flesh*.

17. See Sheridan's *Los Contemporáneos ayer* and *México en 1932: La polémica nacionalista*, as well as González Rodríguez' "Usos amorosos del joven Novo," in *Cuidado con el corazón: Los usos amorosos en el México moderno*, for more on Novo's

tense relationship with official discourse during the political climate of the 1920s and 1930s.

18. Novo recounts his erotic adventures in detail in *La estatua de sal*. Some similar anecdotes appear in *Elías Nandino: Una vida no/velada*, by Enrique Aguilar.

19. For more on posing as a contestatory cultural statement, see Sylvia Molloy's "The Politics of Posing." This article is particularly relevant to my reading of Salvador Novo, because of its focus on the influence of Oscar Wilde in Latin America, and as I have commented here, Novo was a great reader and admirer of Wilde. Novo's interpretation of Wilde, in particular when thought about in terms of posing, would warrant further study.

20. For Eve Kosofsky Sedgwick, the closet is a space that condenses problems associated with representation, making visible the role of the secret in the process of self-definition. In this manner, the closet thus functions as a space of homo/heterosexual definition, framing many of the major structures of thought and knowledge in contemporary Western culture (*Epistemology*, 71). Novo's strength, to follow Sedgwick's terminology, lies in that he neither comes out of the closet nor stays within it, choosing instead to sidestep a definition of his sexuality in absolute terms.

21. Novo's penchant for the excess can be read as a form of baroque. For an analysis of the writing of Novo and his fellow Contemporáneos as an expression of neobaroque literature, see Salvador Oropesa's *The Contemporáneos Group: Rewriting Mexico in the Thirties and Forties*.

22. See Julio Ramos' chapter "Decorating the City" in *Divergent Modernities*. Also see chapter 1 of this volume for an analysis comparing the chronicles of *modernismo* with the *aguafuertes* of Roberto Arlt.

23. Bernardo de Balbuena's *Grandeza mexicana* was written between 1602 and 1603. It is addressed to Doña Isabel de Tovar and describes Mexico City in paradisiacal terms. Novo's epigraph to *Nueva grandeza mexicana* reads as follows:

> Caballos, calles, trato, cumplimiento,
> regalos, ocasiones de contento,
> letras, virtudes, variedad de oficios,
> origen y grandeza de edificios,
> gobierno ilustre, religión, estado,
> primavera inmortal y sus indicios,
> todo en este discurso está cifrado. (*VE I*, 165)
> [Horses, streets, negotiations, compliance,
> gifts, occasions for contentment,
> letters, virtues, variety of trades,
> origin and grandeur of edifices,
> illustrious government, religion, state,

> immortal spring and its signs,
> everything in this speech is encoded]

24. Salvador Novo and Dolores del Río were, in fact, neighbors in the southern Mexico City neighborhood of Coyoacán. The street where Novo used to live was renamed after him in March 1968. Dolores del Río, María Félix, and Novo's mother were present at the naming ceremony.

25. In *The Contemporáneos Group*, Oropesa analyzes Novo's articles from the 1940s in the light of the construction of his celebrity. He especially insists on how Novo would repeatedly highlight his intimate friendship with Dolores del Río, to the point that he accompanied her to the premiere of the film *María Candelaria* (1944) and held her nervous hand during the preview.

26. This caricature was cut out by Novo himself and pasted without a date in his "Recortes de prensa," a personal scrapbook in which he kept photographs and drawings of himself that had appeared in the press (Centro de Estudios de Historia de México Carso, Archivo Salvador Novo, Fondo Antonio López Mancera, without a date). The reference to Novo's status as "an employee of public education" suggests that this document dates from approximately 1924. See Monsiváis' *Lo marginal en el centro* and Novo's autobiography, *La estatua de sal*, for more on Novo's tense relation with official circles as a result of his homosexuality.

27. "We do not create newspapers for a determined social elite, and it is our pleasure to create a 'magazine for barbershops'—as used to say an excellent writer, who today honors us with his writings" (unsigned editorial note probably written by the director, Carlos Noriega Hope, from the column "La flecha en el blanco," *Ilustrado*, January 22, 1925, 13).

28. Vasconcelos develops these ideas in *La raza cósmica*. José Joaquín Blanco's *Se llamaba Vasconcelos* gives a detailed overview of Vasconcelos' educational and political philosophy.

29. *El Universal Ilustrado* was founded in 1916 as a weekly supplement to the newspaper *El Universal*. It was under the direction of Carlos Noriega Hope from 1920 to 1934. Novo was a frequent contributor to this magazine during the mid- to late 1920s.

30. For more on the designation of Azuela's *The Underdogs* as the quintessential novel of the Mexican Revolution, see Jorge Aguilar Mora's *Una muerte sencilla, justa, eterna: Cultura y guerra durante la revolución mexicana*, especially the chapter "Primero una novela y al final un ensayo."

31. Especially important was the supplement to *Ilustrado*, *La novela semanal*, where short novels by a various young writers were published. Francisco Monterde, Arqueles Vela, Carlos Noriega Hope himself, and others published there.

32. Julio Ruelas (1870–1907) was an artist affiliated with *modernismo* who drew many of the covers and illustrations for the *Revista Moderna de México* (*VE II*, 396).

33. See Mary K. Long's analysis of Novo's take on folklore in "Nota introductoria" to *VE II*.

34. The format of this essay implies that it was originally a piece Novo read on the radio and then published.

35. See Peter Bürger's *Theory of the Avant-Garde*. What Novo contends is that art cannot afford to be autonomous, because it needs to reach out to the public (to society) and be "used" in order to evolve. Also see Hannah Arendt's *Lectures on Kant's Political Philosophy*, especially "10th Session," in which she describes the originality of the artist in terms of his or her ability to be understood by an audience (58–65).

36. In her doctoral thesis, Mary K. Long defines Novo's intellectual posture as "introductory"; that is, he presents ideas but avoids constructing a particular analysis or position from his observations. José Joaquín Blanco similarly picks up on Novo's avoidance of the didactic: "What stands out for a reader familiar with [Novo's work] is that everything he says is a lie, or better yet, that he has also written the opposite" ("Contemporáneos," 4).

37. Novo's column "Consultorio a cargo del Niño Fidencio" appeared in 1929 in the daily *Excélsior*. Still today, the followers of Niño Fidencio, the "Fidencistas," pay homage to this unofficial saint with yearly pilgrimages.

38. *Ilustrado*'s choice of articles often reflected the growing importance of female readers in the 1920s and 1930s, for some of its "frivolous" sections (dealing with fashion or the lives of movie stars) were directed specifically toward women. For more on this magazine's female readership, see chapter 5.

39. Despite the relatively small number of readers in Mexico City after the revolution, Aurrecoechea and Bartra estimate that the public for the popular press was becoming increasingly hybrid and that by the 1930s there existed a thriving business of secondhand newspapers and illustrated magazines, especially in the Lagunilla market (*Puros cuentos*, 205).

40. Just to give a couple of examples among many, Novo's articles "Desventajas del pan francés" (The Disadvantages of French Bread) and "Mis sólidos conceptos sobre la leche" (My Solid Ideas regarding Milk), published in 1929 as part of his column "Consultorio a cargo del Niño Fidencio," refer to current events that were discussed in the daily press.

41. See Andreas Huyssen's chapter "Mass Culture as Woman: Modernism's Other," in *After the Great Divide: Modernism, Mass Culture, Postmodernism*, where he traces the association between women and mass culture, as opposed to men and "authentic" culture: "Time and time again documents from the late 19th century ascribe pejorative feminine characteristics to mass culture—and by mass culture here I mean serialized feuilleton novels, popular and family magazines, the stuff of lending libraries, fictional bestsellers and the like—not, however, working-class culture or residual forms of older popular or folk cultures" (49).

42. In his introduction to his collection *Ensayos*, Novo compares his texts to children and the present anthology to a family reunion (*VE II*, 25).

43. Novo's comment on prostitution has become one of his most recognizable statements. In the prologue to his only anthology of chronicles, *Historia de lo inmediato*,

Renato Leduc paraphrases Novo to explain his hesitance to group his journalistic texts in an anthology with literary pretensions: "The friends and readers who have urged me to write novels, essays, theater . . . that is, something of quality, and who have asked me why I do not do so, are not few. I haven't dared give them the response that Salvador Novo (RIP) used to give to the same instance and the same question: 'Because one cannot alternate the sacred ministry of maternity with the exercise of prostitution that is journalism'" (8).

Chapter 5

1. For a more in-depth perspective on women's social and cultural roles in modern Argentina, see Francine Masiello's *Between Civilization and Barbarism: Women, Nation and Literary Culture in Modern Argentina*. For an overview of women in Mexico, see Jean Franco's *Plotting Women: Gender and Representation in Mexico*, and Julia Tuñón Pablos's *Women in Mexico: A Past Unveiled*. For a more comprehensive analysis of popular iconography depicting women in the Mexican press of the 1920s, see Joanne Hershfield's *Imagining la Chica Moderna: Women, Nation, and Visual Culture in Mexico, 1917–1936*. The latter analyzes many images from the *Ilustrado*.

2. Such discussions regarding taste were not necessarily new in the 1920s, as they had already been very much linked to nineteenth-century *modernismo*. The early twentieth century, however, saw an exacerbation of the question of taste as a social marker, probably as a result of the wider choices in reading materials available to cultural consumers, who were becoming more diverse in terms of social class.

3. It is uncertain if Storni's chronicles were ever published in the Mexican press. Many of her poems, however, were printed and discussed in Mexico, as were a few longer essays dealing with women's issues.

4. See "Las poetisas americanas" for Storni's disparaging comments on *poetisas* and women writers (*AS II*, 1017). While she has favorable opinions of figures such as Gabriela Mistral, Juana de Ibarbourou, and Delmira Agustini, Storni's article implies that *poetisas* lacked the constructive rigor and long-term vision necessary for drama or the novel.

5. I do not agree with certain readings that differentiate strongly Storni's poetry from her prose (see Diz, *Alfonsina periodista*). I am more in line with Gwen Kirkpatrick's reading in the article "Alfonsina Storni as Tao Lao," where the critic connects Storni's poetic sentimentalism to commercial motivations.

6. For more on the distance that *modernistas* reinforced between journalism and their poetic work, see chapter 1.

7. Vicky Unruh has convincingly argued that Storni was extremely conscious of the performativity inherent to the creation of any public persona, an awareness that was honed through the notorious theatricality of her poetic readings. For a compelling and detailed reading of Storni's *poetisa* persona, see "Alfonsina Storni's Misfits" in Unruh's *Performing Women*.

8. There is speculation that Storni herself wrote these articles and used "La niña boba" as a pseudonym, but there is no confirming documentation (see Diz, *Alfonsina periodista*; and Kirkpatrick, "Journalism").

9. For more on the parallels between Arlt and Storni, see Diz, *Alfonsina periodista*, 80–96.

10. Both Kirkpatrick and Unruh point out Storni's ambivalent relationship to feminism. According to Kirkpatrick, Storni proposed an idiosyncratic version of feminism ("Journalism," 105); in Unruh's view, Storni's ambivalent feminism contained underhanded critiques of women's intellectual endeavors (*Performing Women*).

11. Storni's self-description as a working woman who rides in public transportation indicates another factor that distanced her from intellectual and avant-garde circles—that of class. Norah Lange, who drove around Buenos Aires in her flamboyant vehicle and hosted *tertulias* (literary salons) in her family home, would perhaps be the best counterexample to Storni, who consistently defined herself through her need to earn a living.

12. Carlos Noriega Hope was an eager cinephile who spent time in Hollywood and published various short stories and chronicles related to this experience before beginning to direct the *Ilustrado* in 1921. As director of the weekly, he consistently gave space to film criticism and interviews with actors and directors. Noriega Hope would also write the script for *Santa* (1931), the film adapted from Federico Gamboa's novel of the same name.

13. In her chronicle "Vanity of Vanities," Bonifant mentions the criticism that she received from a male reader for posing in so many pictures, and she defends her right to be photographed. Yet she concludes her article by suggesting that her defense was in jest and that her desire to be photographed is a lie: "Truths are like some men: pleasant but uninteresting. However, lies are pleasant, interesting and useful" (*Marquesa*, 77). This playful ambivalence reveals what was at stake regarding the bodily representation of women in this period, while also providing an early explanation for Bonifant's growing reluctance to be photographed alongside her articles.

14. As a film critic, Bonifant was remarkably harsh with Mexican films, frequently denouncing their lack of technical rigor and the limited acting skills of their stars. Her posture was in contrast to the majority of critics of the period, who defended Mexican film out of nationalist solidarity. In terms of international cinematography, Bonifant was extremely dismissive of Hollywood (with the rare exceptions of Chaplin and Disney, whom she admired) and often praised Russian filmmakers, especially Sergei Eisenstein.

15. This declaration was made by the chronicler Antonio Medina in "Seis años de anécdotas del *Ilustrado*."

16. Bonifant refers to the sentimental novel *María* (1867), by Jorge Isaacs, and *Carmen* (1845), by Prosper Mérimée.

17. For more on the *Revista Moderna* and decadentism, see Pineda Franco, *Geopolíticas de la cultura finisecular en Buenos Aires, París y México*.

18. After the revolution, and with the presidencies of Álvaro Obregón (1920–1924) and Plutarco Elías Calles (1924–1928), both of whom were military men from Sonora, the ruling class in Mexico City shifted from the traditional Porfirian networks to the Sonoran politicians and their families. Bonifant's "Notes of a Married Woman" caricaturizes this new elite and denounces the blatant political abuses that were taking place on a daily basis by a supposedly revolutionary government.

19. In their introduction to their coedited volume *Unfolding the City: Women Write the City in Latin America*, Guerrero and Lambright comment on the "socially constitutive role of public space" (xi) and reflect on the gendering of space in the Latin American city: "A woman artist or writer who traverses the city may not play the same role as a man. She may not have easy or secure access to certain streets or buildings, such as the soccer field, the pub, or a poorly lit avenue; furthermore, she cannot be a detached observer distanced from her surroundings, as she can rarely escape the gaze of others" (xiv).

20. It must be noted, however, that by the early 1930s Bonifant had acquired remarkable prestige and influence among the *Ilustrado*'s contributors. When Noriega Hope stepped down as director in 1934, just a few months before his untimely death, she formed part of the consortium of directors that took over the magazine and she directed a few issues herself. Furthermore, by the early 1930s Bonifant's film column, which she signed "Luz Alba" (Light of Dawn), did not have any visible gender markers and was directed to the *Ilustrado*'s general public. This journalistic recognition did not, however, lead to a broader acceptance within literary circles.

21. For more on the influence of Hollywood on the construction of literary celebrity in the 1920s and 1930s, see Hammill, *Women, Celebrity and Literary Culture between the Wars*.

22. One can cite as an example Arlt's chronicles on marriage, which provoked the anger of many of his women readers. While these articles spurred the interest of women in his column, their satirical element can also be read as a form of discomfort with and even resentment of women readers.

23. Arlt's second wife, Elizabeth Mary Shine, was the secretary of León Bouché, the director of the weekly *El Hogar*. Noriega Hope's play *La señorita voluntad* (Miss Strong-Will, 1917) is set in a newspaper room, where the female love interest of the protagonist works as a secretary.

24. Chroniclers were paid by the article, and I have not found whether there was a difference in the payment men and women received. However, one can assume that regular columnists, regardless of gender, earned more than anonymous reporters.

25. This information comes from Guisti's eulogy of Storni, published shortly after her death in *Nosotros* (November 1938, 372–397).

26. "Oscar Leblanc" was the alias of journalist Demetrio Bolaños Espinosa. He referred to Bonifant in his article "El *Ilustrado* por dentro" (*Ilustrado*, May 17, 1934, 13, 38). This was one of the many introspective articles published by the weekly that

detailed how journalists worked and what cultural projects they envisioned through this publication.

27. Masiello, Kirkpatrick, and Unruh coincide in this point. Masiello defines avant-garde women in Argentina, such as Norah Lange and Victoria Ocampo as "bridge figures" in the avant-garde: "both function as translators of the ideas of others, as sifters of alien discursive material, but both are equally important in their revision of women's language and subjectivity" (*Civilization and Barbarism*, 147).

28. In *Women, Celebrity, and Literary Culture between the Wars*, Faye Hammill describes middlebrow writing in terms that could easily apply to the chronicle: "Middlebrow fiction did not always simply 'lay claim' to the highbrow, it frequently expanded and challenged earlier definitions of art and intellectual work. In borrowing from both modernist and mass cultural forms, it diminished the apparent distance between them" (11).

Afterword

1. This gritty realism is part of the aesthetics promoted by the publishing house Alfaguara, which has headquarters in fourteen countries throughout Latin America, as well as in the United States and Spain. Alfaguara has had an enormous influence in promoting new Latin American writers, especially through its literary prize, Premio Alfaguara de Novela, which recently has been won by young writers such as Xavier Velasco (Mexico, 2003) and Santiago Roncagliolo (Peru, 2006). A similar aesthetics of the real can be perceived in recent successful films such as *Amores perros* (Mexico, 2000) and *City of God* (Brazil, 2002).

2. I here take from Lyotard's notion of the "petite histoire" or "micronarrative" in *The Postmodern Condition*.

3. In "Walking in the Modern City," Juan Gelpí compellingly explores the distance between the chronicler and the traditional *letrado* by reflecting on the difference between the chronicle and the essay.

4. For more on the chronicle and the ethics of writing, see Aníbal González' *Journalism and the Development of Spanish American Narrative* (especially chapter 6), as well as his recent *Killer Books: Writing, Violence, and Ethics in Modern Spanish American Narrative*.

5. Corona and Jörgensen make this point in their coauthored introduction to *The Contemporary Mexican Chronicle*, commenting that "the contemporary chronicle reproduces popular speech and emphasizes listening over looking, the voice over the scene" (11). While I agree with their point in some instances, such as with Poniatowska's testimonial chronicles, I do not think that one can go so far as to state that the gaze has lost its predominance in the contemporary chronicle.

Bibliography

Aguilar, Enrique. *Elías Nandino: Una vida no/velada*. Mexico City: Grijalbo, 1986.

Aguilar Mora, Jorge. *Una muerte sencilla, justa, eternal: Cultura y guerra durante la revolución mexicana*. Mexico City: ERA, 1990.

Alonso, Carlos. *The Burden of Modernity: The Rhetoric of Cultural Discourse in Spanish America*. New York: Oxford University Press, 1998.

Anderson, Benedict. *Imagined Communities: Reflections on the Origin and Spread of Nationalism*. London and New York: Verso, 1991.

Andrade, Carlos Drummond de. *Cadeira de balanço: Crônicas*. Rio de Janeiro: Olympio, 1982.

Andrade, Mário de. *Correspondência Mário de Andrade e Manuel Bandeira*. Ed. Marcos Antonio de Moraes. São Paulo: Instituto de Estudios Brasileiros, 2000.

———. *Fotógrafo e turista aprendiz*. São Paulo: Instituto de Estudios Brasileiros, Universidade de São Paulo, 1993.

———. *Hallucinated City*. Nashville, TN: Vanderbilt University Press, 1968. Originally published as *Paulicéia desvairada*.

———. *Macunaíma*. Trans. E. A. Goodland. New York: Random House, 1984.

———. *Mário de Andrade hoje*. Ed. Carlos E. O. Berriel. São Paulo: Ensaio, 1990.

———. *Os filhos da Candinha*. São Paulo: Livraría Martins, 1963.

———. *O turista aprendiz*. São Paulo: Secretaria da Cultura, Ciência e Tecnologia, 1976.

———. *Poesías completas*. Ed. Dílea Zanotto Manfio. Belo Horizonte and Rio de Janeiro: Villa Rica, 1993.

———. *Táxi e crônicas do Diario Nacional*. São Paulo: Duas Cidades, 1976.

———. *Vida literária*. Ed. Sonia Sachs. São Paulo: EDUSP, 1993.

Arendt, Hannah. *Lectures on Kant's Political Philosophy*. Chicago: University of Chicago Press, 1992.

Arlt, Roberto. *Aguafuertes porteñas*. Buenos Aires: Hyspamerica, 1986.

———. *Al margen del cable: Crónicas publicadas en El Nacional, México, 1937–1941*. Ed. Rose Corral. Buenos Aires: Losada, 2001.

———. *Notas sobre el cinematógrafo*. Buenos Aires: Simurg, 1997.

———. *Obras*. Vol. 2. Buenos Aires: Losada, 1998.

———. *Los siete locos: Los lanzallamas*. Caracas: Ayacucho, 1978.

Assis, Machado de. *Crônicas de bond*. Ed. Ana Luiza Andrade. Chapecó: Argos Editora Universitária, 2001.

———. *Crônicas escolhidas*. São Paulo: Editora Atica, 1994.

Augé, Marc. *In the Metro*. Trans. Tom Conley. Minneapolis: University of Minnesota Press, 2002.

Aurrecoechea, Juan Manuel, and Armando Bartra. *Puros cuentos: La historia de la historieta en México, 1874–1934*. Mexico City: CONACULTA; Museo Nacional de Culturas Populares; Grijalbo, 1988.

Bakhtin, M. M. *The Dialogic Imagination: Four Essays*. Trans. Caryl Emerson and Michael Holquist; ed. Michael Holquist. Austin: University of Texas Press, 1981.

Balderston, Daniel. "Poetry, Revolution, Homophobia: Polemics from the Mexican Revolution." In *Hispanisms and Homosexualities*, ed. Sylvia Molloy and Robert McKee Irwin, 57–75. Durham, NC: Duke University Press, 1998.

———. *Sex and Sexuality in Latin America*. New York: NYU Press, 1997.

Barrera, Reyna. *Salvador Novo: Navaja de la inteligencia*. Mexico City: Plaza y Valdés, 1990.

Bencomo, Anadeli. *Voces y voceros de la megalopolis: La crónica periodística-literaria en México*. Frankfurt: Iberoamericana/Vervuert, 2002.

Benjamin, Walter. *The Arcades Project*. Cambridge, MA: Belknap Press of Harvard University Press, 1999.

———. "The Author as Producer." In *Reflections*, 220–238. New York: Schocken Books, 1968.

———. *Charles Baudelaire: A Lyric Poet in the Era of High Capitalism*. London and New York: Verso, 1997.

———. "The Work of Art in the Age of Mechanical Reproduction." In *Illuminations*, 217–251. New York: Schocken Books, 1968.

Berman, Marshall. *All That Is Solid Melts into the Air: The Experience of Modernity*. New York: Penguin, 1989.

Berriel, Carlos E. O., ed. *Mário de Andrade hoje*. São Paulo: Editora Ensaio, 1990.

Birkenmaier, Anke. *Alejo Carpentier y la cultura del surrealismo en América Latina*. Madrid and Frankfurt: Iberoamericana/Vervuert, 2006.

Blanco, José Joaquín. "Contemporáneos: Juventud y obra crítica." *Nexos*, March 1, 1978.

———. *Se llamaba Vasconcelos: Una evocación crítica*. Mexico City: Fondo de Cultura Económica, 1977.

Bonifant, Cube. *Una pequeña Marquesa de Sade: Crónicas selectas, 1921–1948*. Ed. Viviane Mahieux. Mexico City: DGE/Equilibrista; UNAM; CONACULTA, 2009.

Borges, Jorge Luis. *Fervor de Buenos Aires*. Buenos Aires: Emecé, 1969.

———. *Ficciones*. Buenos Aires: EDA, 1987.

———. "Sur." In *Ficciones*. Buenos Aires: EDA, 1987.

Borré, Omar. *Roberto Arlt y la crítica, 1926–1990: Estudio, cronología y bibliografía*. Ediciones América Libre, 1996.

Bourdieu, Pierre. *The Field of Cultural Production: Essays on Art and Literature*. New York: Columbia University Press, 1993.

———. *The Rules of Art: Genesis and Structure of the Literary Field*. Stanford, CA: Stanford University Press, 1996.

Brotherston, Gordon. *Latin American Poetry: Origins and Presence*. Cambridge and New York: Cambridge University Press, 1975.

Buck-Morss, Susan. *The Dialectics of Seeing: Walter Benjamin and the Arcades Project*. Cambridge, MA, and London: MIT Press, 1999.

Bürger, Peter. *Theory of the Avant-Garde*. Minneapolis: University of Minnesota Press, 1984.

Burns, E. Bradford. *A History of Brazil*. New York: Columbia University Press, 1980.

Butler, Judith. *Bodies That Matter: On the Discursive Limits of "Sex."* New York and London: Routledge, 1993.

Campos, Rubén. "La 'novísima' espuma literaria." In *Viajes y ensayos II*, by Salvador Novo, 400–401. Mexico City: Fondo de cultura económica, 1999.

Cândido, Antonio. Introduction to *A crônica: O gênero, sua fixação es suas transformações no Brasil*, 13–37. Campinas: UNICAMP, 1992.

Capistrán, Miguel. "Notas para un posible estudio de las relaciones entre Alfonso Reyes y los Contemporáneos: El caso de Don Alfonso y Novo." *Nueva Revista de Filología Hispánica* 37, no. 2 (1989): 339–363.

Castillo, Debra. *Easy Women: Sex and Gender in Modern Mexican Fiction*. Minneapolis: University of Minnesota Press, 1998.

Charney, Leo, and Vanessa Schwartz. *Cinema and the Invention of Modern Life*. Berkeley: University of California Press, 1995.

Chazkel, Amy. "The Crônica, the City and the Invention of the Underworld: Rio de Janeiro, 1889–1922." *Estudios Interdisciplinarios de América Latina y el Caribe* 12, no. 1 (2001).

Civantos, Christina. "Language, Literary Legitimacy and Masculinity in the Writings of Roberto Arlt." *Latin American Literary Review* 33, no. 65 (2005): 109–134.

Clifford, James. "On Collecting Art and Culture." In *The Cultural Studies Reader*, ed. Simon During, 57–76. London and New York: Routledge, 1999.

———. *The Predicament of Culture: Twentieth Century Ethnography, Literature and Art.* Cambridge, MA, and London: Harvard University Press, 1988.

Corona, Ignacio, and Beth E. Jörgensen, eds. *The Contemporary Mexican Chronicle: Theoretical Perspectives on the Liminal Genre.* Albany: SUNY Press, 2002.

Correa Stiel, Waldemar. *História dos transportes colectivos em São Paulo.* São Paulo: Editora McGraw-Hill do Brasil, 1978.

Debord, Guy. *La société du spectacle.* Paris: Gallimard, 1992.

De Certeau, Michel. *The Practice of Everyday Life.* Berkeley: University of California Press, 1984.

Deleuze, Gilles. *The Logic of Sense.* Trans. Mark Lester with Charles Stiyale; ed. Constantin V. Boundas. New York: Columbia University Press, 1990.

Díaz Arciniega, Victor. *Querella por la cultura "revolucionaria" (1925).* Mexico City: Fondo de Cultura Económica, 1989.

Diz, Tania. *Alfonsina periodista: Ironía y sexualidad en la prensa argentina (1915–1925).* Buenos Aires: Libros del Rojas, 2006.

Duarte, Paulo. Mário de Andrade por ele mesmo. São Paulo: HUCITEC, 1985.

Egan, Linda. *Carlos Monsiváis: Culture and Chronicle in Contemporary Mexico.* Tucson: University of Arizona Press, 2001.

Enzensberger, Hans Magnus. "Constituents of a Theory of the Media." *New Left Review* 60 (1970): 13–36.

Ewen, Stuart. *All Consuming Images: The Politics of Style in Contemporary Culture.* New York: Basic Books, 1999.

"¿Existe una literatura mexicana moderna?" *El Universal Ilustrado,* January 22, 1925, 30–31.

Faria Cruz, Heloisa. *São Paulo em papel e tinta: Periodismo e vida urbana, 1890–1915.* São Paulo: EDUC, 2000.

Fernandes Lopes, Dirceu, José Coelho Sobrinho, and José Luiz Proença, eds. *A evolução do jornalismo em São Paulo.* São Paulo: Edicon, 1996.

"La flecha en el blanco." *El Universal Ilustrado,* January 22, 1925, 13.

Forster, Merlin H. *Los contemporáneos, 1920–1932: Perfil de un experimento vanguardista mexicano.* Mexico City: Andrea, 1964.

Foster, David William. *Bodies and Biases: Sexualities in Hispanic Cultures and Literatures.* Minneapolis: University of Minnesota Press, 1996.

———. *Buenos Aires: Perspectives on the City and Cultural Production.* Gainesville: University of Florida Press, 1998.

Foster, Hal, ed. *The Anti-Aesthetic: Essays on Postmodern Culture.* New York: New Press, 1998.

Foucault, Michel. *Discipline and Punish: The Birth of the Prison.* New York: Vintage Books, 1995.

Franco, Jean. *Plotting Women: Gender and Representation in Mexico*. New York: Columbia University Press, 1989.

Fray Mocho, Felix Lima y otros: Los costumbristas del 900. Buenos Aires: Centro Editor de América Latina, 1992.

Freud, Sigmund. *The Joke and Its Relation to the Unconscious*. Trans. Joyce Crick. Introduction by John Carey. Penguin Books, 2003.

Fritzsche, Peter. *Reading Berlin 1900*. Cambridge, MA, and London: Harvard University Press, 1996.

Gabara, Esther. *Errant Modernism: The Ethos of Photography in Mexico and Brazil*. Durham, NC, and London: Duke University Press, 2008.

Gallo, Rubén. *Mexican Modernity: The Avant-Garde and the Technical Revolution*. Cambridge, MA: MIT Press, 2005.

Garber, Marjorie. *Vested Interests: Cross-dressing and Cultural Anxiety*. New York: Routledge, 1997.

García Canclini, Nestor. *Consumers and Citizens: Globalization and Multicultural Conflicts*. Trans. and ed. George Yúdice. Minneapolis and London: University of Minnesota Press, 2001.

———. *Hybrid Cultures: Strategies for Entering and Leaving Modernity*. Minneapolis: University of Minnesota Press, 2005.

Garramuño, Florencia. *Modernidades primitivas: Tango, samba y nación*. Buenos Aires: Fondo de Cultura Económica, 2007.

Gelpí, Juan. "Paseo por la crónica urbana de México: Carlos Monsiváis y José Joaquín Blanco." *Nómada* 3 (July 1997): 83–88.

———. "Walking in the Modern City: Subjectivity and Cultural Contacts in the Urban *Crónicas* of Salvador Novo and Carlos Monsiváis." In *The Contemporary Mexican Chronicle: Theoretical Perspectives on the Liminal Genre*, 201–220. Albany: SUNY Press, 2002.

Girondo, Oliveiro. *Veinte poemas para ser leídos en el tranvía*. Madrid: Visor, 1989.

Gledson, John. "Os contos de Machado de Assis: O machete e o violoncelo." Introduction to *Contos: Uma antologia*, by Machado de Assis, 83–88. São Paulo: Companhia das Letras, 1998.

Gluck, Mary. *Popular Bohemia: Modernism and Urban Culture in Nineteenth-Century Paris*. Cambridge, MA, and London: Harvard University Press, 2005.

Gramsci, Antonio. *The Antonio Gramsci Reader: Selected Writings, 1916–1935*. Ed. David Forgacs. New York: New York University Press, 2000.

Grángia, Lúcia. *Machado de Assis: Escritor em formação (à roda dos jornais)*. São Paulo: FADESP/Mercado de Letras, 2000.

González, Aníbal. *La crónica modernista hispanoamericana*. Madrid: Porrúa Turanzas, 1983.

———. *Journalism and the Development of Spanish American Narrative*. New York: Cambridge University Press, 1993.

————. *Killer Books: Writing, Violence, and Ethics in Modern Spanish American Narrative.* Austin: University of Texas Press, 2001.

González Rodríguez, Sergio. "Usos amorosos del joven Novo." In *Cuidado con el corazón: Los usos amorosos en el México moderno*, 65–80. Mexico City: Instituto Nacional de Antropología e Historia, 1995.

Gorelik, Adrián. "El color del barrio: Mitología barrial y conflicto cultural en la Buenos Aires de los años veinte." *Variaciones Borges: Journal of the Jorge Luis Borges Center for Studies and Documentation* 8 (1999): 36–68.

Greenblatt, Stephen. *Renaissance Self-Fashioning: From More to Shakespeare.* Chicago: University of Chicago Press, 2005.

Guerrero, Elizabeth, and Anne Lambright. Introduction to *Unfolding the City: Women Write the City in Latin America.* Ed. Anne Lambright and Elizabeth Guerrero, xi–xxxii. Minneapolis: University of Minnesota Press, 2007.

Güiraldes, Ricardo. *Don Segundo Sombra.* Madrid: Cátreda, 1995.

Gutiérrez Nájera, Manuel. *Cuentos completos y otras narraciones.* Mexico City: Fondo de Cultura Económica, 1987.

————. *Obras inéditas: Crónicas de Puck.* New York: Hispanic Institute of the United States, 1943.

Habermas, Jürgen. *The Structural Transformation of the Public Sphere: An Inquiry into a Category of Bourgeois Society.* Trans. Thomas Burger and Frederick Lawrence. Cambridge, MA: MIT Press, 2001.

Hammill, Faye. *Women, Celebrity, and Literary Culture between the Wars.* Austin: University of Texas Press, 2007.

Hershfield, Joanne. *Imagining la Chica Moderna: Women, Nation and Visual Culture in Mexico, 1917–1936.* Durham, NC, and London: Duke University Press, 2008.

Huyssen, Andreas. *After the Great Divide: Modernism, Mass Culture, Postmodernism.* Bloomington: Indiana University Press, 1986.

Irwin, Robert McKee. *Mexican Masculinities.* Minneapolis: University of Minnesota Press, 2003.

Jay, Martin. *Downcast Eyes: The Denigration of Vision in Twentieth-Century French Thought.* Berkeley: University of California Press, 1993.

Jrade, Cathy. *Modernismo, Modernity, and the Development of Spanish American Literature.* Austin: University of Texas Press, 1998.

Kern, Stephen. *The Culture of Time and Space, 1880–1918.* Cambridge, MA: Harvard University Press, 1983.

Kernan, Alvin B. "The Idea of Literature." *New Literary History* 1 (1973): 31–40.

Kiernan, Fernando. "Roberto Arlt, periodista." *Contorno*, no. 2, ed. Ismael and David Viñas (May 1954): 10–11.

Kirkpatrick, Gwen. "Alfonsina Storni as 'Tao Lao': The Confessional 'I' and the Roving Eye." In *Reinterpreting the Spanish American Essay*, ed. Doris Meyer, 135–147. Austin: University of Texas Press, 1995.

————. "The Journalism of Alfonsina Storni: A New Approach to Women's History." *Women, Culture and Politics in Latin America*, ed. Seminar on Feminism and Culture in Latin America, 105–129. Berkeley: University of California Press, 1990.

Kittler, Friedrich. *Gramophone, Film, Typewriter*. Trans. Geoffrey Winthrop-Young and Michael Wutz. Stanford, CA: Stanford University Press, 1999.

Krauze, Enrique. *Caudillos culturales en la revolución mexicana*. Mexico City: Siglo XXI, 1976.

Leduc, Renato. *Cuando éramos menos*. Mexico City: Cal y Arena, 1989.

————. *Historia de lo inmediato*. Mexico City: Fondo de Cultura Económica, 1997.

————. *Obra literaria*. Mexico City: Fondo de Cultura Económica, 2000.

Leland, Christopher T. *The Last Happy Men: The Generation of 1922, Fiction, and the Argentine Reality*. Syracuse, NY: Syracuse University Press, 1986.

Lomelí Castro, Lligani. "Salvador Novo y el carnaval de los seudónimos." In *Un recorrido por bibliotecas y archivos privados III*, 217–223. Mexico City: Fondo de Cultura Económica.

Long, Mary K. "Nota introductoria." In *Viajes y ensayos II*, by Salvador Novo. Mexico City: Fondo de Cultura Económica, 1996.

————. *Salvador Novo: Between the Avant-Garde and the Nation*. Diss., Princeton University, 1995. (Ann Arbor: UMI, 1995. AAT 9527854.)

————. "Writing the City: The Chronicles of Salvador Novo." In *The Contemporary Mexican Chronicle: Theoretical Perspectives on the Liminal Genre*, ed. Ignacio Corona and Beth Jörgensen, 181–200. Albany: SUNY Press, 2002.

Lopez, Telê Porto Ancona. "A crônica de Mário de Andrade: Impressões que historiam." In *A crônica: O gênero, sua fixação, e suas transformações no Brasil*, ed. Antonio Cândido, 165–180. Rio de Janeiro: Fundação Casa de Rui Barbosa, 1989.

————. Introduction to *O turista aprendiz*, by Mário de Andrade, ed. Telê Porto Ancona Lopez. São Paulo: Duas Cidades, 1976.

————. Introduction to *Táxi e crônicas no Diario Nacional*, by Mário de Andrade, ed. Telê Porto Ancona Lopez, 15–57. São Paulo: Duas Cidades, 1976.

————. *Mariodeandradeando*. São Paulo: Editora Hucitec, 1996.

Ludmer, Josefina. *El cuerpo del delito: Un manual*. Buenos Aires: Perfil Libros, 1999.

————. *The Gaucho Genre: A Treatise on the Motherland*. Trans. Molly Weigel. Durham, NC, and London: Duke University Press, 2002.

————. "Las tretas del débil." In *La sartén por el mango*, ed. Patricia González and Eliana Ortega, 47–54. Rio Piedras, Puerto Rico: Huracán, 1984.

Mahieux, Viviane. "Nota introductoria: Una pequeña Marquesa de Sade en la crónica mexicana." In *Una pequeña Marquesa de Sade: Crónicas selectas, 1921–1948*, by Cube Bonifant. Mexico City: DGE/Equilibrista; UNAM; CONACULTA, 2009.

Man, Paul de. *Blindness and Insight: Essays in the Rhetoric of Contemporary Criticism*. Minneapolis: University of Minnesota Press, 1983.

Martín-Barbero, Jesús. *Communication, Culture and Hegemony: From the Media to Mediations.* London: Sage, 1993.

Martínez Estrada, Ezequiel. *Radiografía de la pampa.* Buenos Aires: Editorial Losada, 1983.

Martins, Wilson. *The Modernist Idea: A Critical Survey of Brazilian Writing in the Twentieth Century.* Trans. Jack. E. Tomlins. New York: New York University Press, 1970.

Masiello, Francine. *Between Civilization and Barbarism: Women, Nation and Literary Culture in Modern Argentina.* Lincoln and London: University of Nebraska Press, 1992.

————. *Lenguaje e ideología: Las escuelas argentinas de vanguardia.* Buenos Aires: Hachette, 1986.

Medina, Antonio. "Seis años de anécdotas del *Ilustrado.*" *El Universal Ilustrado,* May 17, 1934, 17, 38.

Meyer, Marlise. "Voláteis e versáteis: De variedades e folhetins se fez a chronica." In *A crônica: O gênero, sua fixação, e suas transformações no Brasil,* ed. Antonio Cândido, 93–133. Rio de Janeiro: Fundação Casa de Rui Barbosa, 1989.

Molloy, Sylvia. "Flânerias textuales: Borges, Benjamin y Baudelaire." In *Homenaje a Ana María Berrenechea,* ed. Lia Schwartz Lerner and Isaias Lerner. Madrid: Castalia, 1984.

————. "The Politics of Posing." In *Hispanisms and Homosexualities,* ed. Sylvia Molloy and Robert McKee Irwin, 141–161. Durham, NC: Duke University Press, 1998.

Monsiváis, Carlos. *A ustedes les consta: Antología de la crónica en México.* Mexico City: Ediciones Era, 1980.

————. "De la santa doctrina al espíritu público (sobre las funciones de la crónica en México)." *Nueva Revista de Filología Hispánica* 35 (1987): 753–771.

————. *Salvador Novo: Lo marginal en el centro.* Mexico City: Editorial Era, 2000.

Morris, Meaghan. "Banality in Cultural Studies." In *What Is Cultural Studies? A Reader,* ed. John Storey, 147–168. London: Edward Arnold, 1996.

Novo, Salvador. *La estatua de sal.* Mexico City: CONACULTA, 1998.

————. *Viajes y ensayos I.* Mexico City: Fondo de Cultura Económica, 1996.

————. *Viajes y ensayos II.* Mexico City: Fondo de Cultura Económica, 1999.

————. *La vida en México en el periodo presidencial de Manuel Avila Camacho.* Ed. José Emilio Pacheco. Mexico City: Consejo Nacional para la Cultura y las Artes, 1994.

Nunes, Aparecida Maria. *Clarice Lispector jornalista: Páginas femeninas e outras páginas.* São Paulo: Senac, 2006.

Oliven, Ruben George. "Brazil: The Modern in the Tropics." In *Through the Kaleidoscope: The Experience of Modernity in Latin America,* ed. Vivian Schelling, 53–71. London and New York: Verso, 2000.

Oropesa, Salvador. *The Contemporáneos Group: Rewriting Mexico in the Thirties and Forties.* Austin: University of Texas Press, 2003.

Ortega, Febronio (alias Aldebarán). "¿Cuál género de revista prefiere usted?" *El Universal Ilustrado*, May 22, 1924.

Ortega y Gasset, José. *La deshumanización del arte*. Madrid: Alianza Editorial, 1996.

Ortiz, Renato. "Popular Culture, Modernity and Nation." In *Through the Kaleidoscope: The Experience of Modernity in Latin America*, ed. Vivian Schelling, 127–147. London and New York: Verso, 2000.

Pastor, Beatriz. *Roberto Arlt y la rebelión alienada*. Gaithersburg, MD: Hispamérica, 1980.

Paz, Octavio. *Sor Juana Inés de la Cruz o las trampas de la fe*. Mexico City: Fondo de Cultura Económica, 1985.

Pérez Carrera, José Manuel. *Periodismo y costumbrismo en el siglo XIX*. Madrid: Santillana, 1996.

Piglia, Ricardo. *Respiración artificial*. Barcelona: Anagrama, 2001.

Pineda Franco, Adela. *Geopolíticas de la cultura finisecular en Buenos Aires, París y México: Las revistas literarias y el modernismo*. Pittsburg: Instituto Internacional de Literatura Iberoamericana, 2006.

Queiroz, Suely Robles Reis de. *São Paulo*. Madrid: Editorial Mapfre, 1992.

Quirarte, Vicente. *Elogio de la calle: Biografía literaria de la ciudad de México*. Mexico City: Cal y Arena, 2001.

Rama, Angel. *The Lettered City*. Ed. and trans. John Charles Chasteen. Durham, NC: Duke University Press, 1996.

Ramos, Julio. *Desencuentros de la modernidad en América Latina: Literatura y política en el siglo XIX*. Mexico City: Fondo de Cultura Económica, 1989.

———. *Divergent Modernities: Culture and Politics in Nineteenth-Century Latin America*. Trans. John D. Blanco. Durham, NC, and London: Duke University Press, 2001.

Resende, Beatriz. "Brazilian Modernism: The Canonized Revolution." In *Through the Kaleidoscope: The Experience of Modernity in Latin America*, ed. Vivian Schelling, 199–216. London and New York: Verso, 2000.

———. Introduction to *Cronistas do Rio*, 11–13. Rio de Janeiro: José Olympio, 1995.

Riesman, David. *The Lonely Crowd: A Study of the Changing American Character*. New Haven, CT: Yale University Press, 1969.

Rivera, Jorge B. *El escritor y la industria cultural*. Buenos Aires: Atuel, 1998.

Rock, David. *Argentina, 1516–1987: From Spanish Colonization to Alfonsín*. Berkeley and Los Angeles: University of California Press, 1987.

Romero, José Luis. *Las ciudades y las ideas*. Argentina: Siglo XXI, 1976.

Romero, José Luis, and Luis Alberto Romero. *Buenos Aires: Historia de cuatro siglos; Desde la ciudad burguesa (1880–1930) hasta la ciudad de masas (1930–2000)*. Buenos Aires: Altamira, 2000.

Romero, Luis Alberto. *Libros baratos y cultura de los sectores populares: Buenos Aires en la entreguerra*. Buenos Aires: Centro de Investigaciones Sociales sobre el Estado y la Administración, 1986.

Rosenberg, Fernando. *The Avant-Garde and Geopolitics in Latin America*. Pittsburgh: University of Pittsburgh Press, 2006.

Rotker, Susana. *The American Chronicles of José Martí: Journalism and Modernity in Spanish America*. Hanover, NH: University Press of New England, 2000.

———. *La invención de la crónica*. Buenos Aires: Edición Letra Buena, 1992.

Sá, Jorge. *A Crônica*. São Paulo: Editora Atica, 1985.

Said, Edward. *Representations of the Intellectual*. New York: Vintage Books, 1994.

Saítta, Sylvia. *El escritor en el bosque de ladrillos: Una biografía de Roberto Arlt*. Buenos Aires: Editorial Sudamericana, 2000.

———. Introducción. In *Aguafuertes porteñas: Buenos Aires, vida cotidiana*, by Roberto Arlt. Buenos Aires and Madrid: Alianza Editorial, 1993.

———. *Regueros de tinta: El diario Crítica en la década de 1920*. Editorial Sudamericana, 1998.

Sarlo, Beatriz. *El imperio de los sentimientos: Narraciones de la circulación periódica en la Argentina*. Buenos Aires: Catálogos, 1985.

———. "In Pursuit of the Popular Imaginary: From Sentimentalism to Technical Skill." In "Loci of Enunciation and Imaginary Constructions: The Case of (Latin) America, I," special issue, *Poetics Today* 15, no. 4 (Winter, 1994): 569–585.

———. *La modernidad periférica: Buenos Aires, 1920–1930*. Buenos Aires: Nueva Visión, 1988.

———. *The Technical Imagination: Argentine Culture's Modern Dreams*. Trans. Xavier Callahan. Stanford, CA: Stanford University Press, 2008.

Schelling, Vivian. *A presença do povo na cultura brasileira: Ensaio sobre o pensamento de Mário de Andrade e Paulo Freire*. Campinas, Brazil: Editora da Unicamp, 1991.

Schneider, Luis Mario, ed. *El estridentismo: México, 1921–1927*. Mexico City: UNAM, 1985.

———. *México y el surrealismo (1925–1950)*. Mexico City: Arte y Libros, 1978.

———. *Ruptura y continuidad: La literatura mexicana en polémica*. Mexico City: Fondo de Cultura Económica, 1975.

Schwartz, Roberto. *Misplaced Ideas: Essays on Brazilian Culture*. Ed. John Gledson. London and New York: Verso, 1992.

Sedgwick, Eve Kosofsky. *Epistemology of the Closet*. Berkeley and Los Angeles: University of California Press, 1990.

Sennet, Richard. *The Fall of Public Man*. New York and London: W. W. Norton, 1996.

Sevcenko, Nicolau. *Orfeu extático na metrópole: São Paulo, sociedade e cultura nos frementes anhos 20*. São Paulo: Companhia das Letras, 1992.

———. "São Paulo: The Quintessential, Uninhibited Megalopolis as Seen by Blaise Cendrars in the 1920s." In *Megalopolis: The Giant City in History*, ed. Theo Barker and Anthony Sutcliffe, 175–193. New York: St. Martin's Press, 1993.

Sheridan, Guillermo. *Los Contemporáneos ayer*. Mexico City: Fondo de Cultura Económica, 1985.

————. *México en 1932: La polémica nacionalista*. Mexico City: Fondo de Cultura Económica, 1999.

Sifuentes-Jáuregui, Ben. *Transvestism, Masculinity, and Latin American Literature: Genders Share Flesh*. New York: Palgrave, 2002.

Simmel, Georg. *Simmel on Culture: Selected Writings*. Ed. David Frisby and Mike Featherstone. London: Sage, 1997.

Sontag, Susan. *Against Interpretation, and Other Essays*. New York: Anchor Books, 1990.

Souza Neves, Margarida. "História da crônica, crônica da história." In *Cronistas do Rio*, ed. Beatriz Resende, 15–31. Rio de Janeiro: José Olympio, 1995.

Storni, Alfonsina. *Nosotras . . . y la piel: Selección de ensayos de Alfonsina Storni*. Comp. Mariela Méndez, Graciela Queirolo, and Alicia Salomone. Buenos Aires: Alfaguara, 1998.

————. *Obras: Prosa; Narraciones, periodismo, ensayo, teatro*. Vol. 2. Buenos Aires: Losada, 2002.

Süssekind, Flora. *A Cinematograph of Words: Literature, Technique, and Modernization in Brazil*. Trans. Paulo Henriques Britto. Stanford, CA: Stanford University Press, 1997.

Torri, Julio. *Ensayos y poemas*. Mexico City: Planeta/Joaquín Mortiz, 2002.

Tosta, Antonio Luciano. "Exchanging Glances: The Streetcar, Modernity, and the Metropolis in Brazilian Literature." *Chasqui: Revista de Literatura Latinoamericana* 32 (2003): 35–52.

Tuñón Pablos, Julia. *Women in Mexico: A Past Unveiled*. Trans. Alan Hynds. Austin: University of Texas Press, 1987.

Unruh, Vicky. *Latin American Vanguards: The Art of Contentious Encounters*. Berkeley, Los Angeles, and London: University of California Press, 1994.

————. *Performing Women and Modern Literary Culture in Latin America: Intervening Acts*. Austin: University of Texas Press, 2006.

Vasconcelos, José. *La raza cósmica*. Mexico City: Austral, 1997.

Walter, Richard. *Politics and Urban Growth in Buenos Aires, 1910–1942*. Cambridge and New York: Cambridge University Press, 1993.

Warner, Michael. *Publics and Counterpublics*. New York and Cambridge, UK: Zone Books, 2002.

"Fala brasileira" (Brazilian Speech)
(M. de Andrade), 84
"Falação" (Chat). *See* Brazilwood
Manifesto
Fall of Public Man, The (R. Sennet), 75
fashion(s), 20, 50, 108, 110, 113, 118,
127, 145, 146, 147, 156; "flapper,"
119
Félix, María, 110, 111; La Doña, 111
Feminine Sketches (A. Storni), 135–137
Femininities (A. Storni), 130, 151;
"Femininities," 129, 131, 134, 137,
140
femininity, 15, 105, 110, 128, 138–
139, 143, 149, 152, 156, 158;
"feminization," 9, 107, 122, 150;
masculinity and, 150; masculinity versus, 111; modern, 126, 146;
urban, 138;
feminist, 126, 136, 138, 148–150;
"valiant feminist," 136, 148
"Feminization of Mexican Literature,
The" (J. Jiménez Rueda), 100
Fernández, Emilio, 110
Fernández de Lizardi, José Joaquín, 96
Fernández de Santa Cruz, Manuel,
98, 99
Fervor de Buenos Aires (J. L. Borges), 48
fetish, 59–62, 90, 115; ephemeral, 61;
film as, 59; "modern" as, 90
fetishism, 60–61
feuilleton, 72; folletín, 60, 134; folhetim, 72;
Figaro, Le (Paris), 16
filhos da Candinha, Os (The Children of
Candinha) (M. de Andrade), 65, 68,
69, 81, 82, 85
flaneur, 39–40, 42, 48–50, 52, 54, 87,
89; Baudelairean, 42
flapper, 119, 126, 146, 147, 149,
194n21

folklore, 66, 73, 88, 98, 114; folkloric
traditions, 74; folklorist, 114
France, Anatole, 13
Fray Mocho. *See* Álvarez, José S.
Freud, Sigmund, 13, 54
Freyre, Gilberto, 82, 199n20
Fritzsche, Peter, 37, 62
frivolity, 25, 106, 113, 116, 120, 154;
tone; 101; topics, 151
Frivolous Commentaries (Arqueles Vela),
156
"Full-blown Feminism" (C. Bonifant),
148–149
Función de medianoche (J. J. Blanco), 166

Gamboa, Federico, 114
Garber, Marjorie, 104
García Cabral, Ernesto "El Chango,"
156
García Canclini, Néstor, 30
Gastélum, Bernardo, 103
gay, 97, 125, 166
gaze, 20, 32, 39, 40, 49, 51, 52, 55, 81,
119, 163, 209n5; aesthetic, 63; critical, 143; ethnographic, 55; indigenous, 119; satirical, 148
Gelpí, Juan, 124
gender, 25, 48, 96, 104–106, 119, 122,
128, 136, 139, 146, 149–150, 152–
153, 157–159, 166; of the chronicle,
58, 80; markers, 25, 139
"Generación anecdótica" (Anecdotal
Generation) (S. Novo), 97, 114, 121
genre(s), 14, 16–20, 22–30, 40, 42, 63,
65, 66, 68–70, 72–73, 78, 80–81,
87, 101, 107, 109, 128, 157–158,
163–167; minor, 17
Gentlemen Prefer Blondes (A. Loos), 146
Gide, André, 101
Girondo, Oliverio, 49, 71, 113, 195n35
Giusti, Roberto, 156

masculinity, 158; Mexican, 103–106, 112, 122–124, 149; "literature under pressure," 16, 75, 164

Loco afán (P. Lemebel), 166

"Long Hair and Short Ideas" (C. Bonifant), 147–148

Loos, Anita, 146

López, Rafael, 98

Lopez, Telê Porto Ancona, 81

López Obrador, Andrés Manuel, 161

Ludmer, Josefina, 141

Lugones, Leopoldo, 151

lunfardo, 34, 85, 192n3

luxury, 115; and literature, 42–43

Machado de Assis, Joachim Maria, 17, 26, 80–81, 87

Macunaíma (M. de Andrade), 66, 83

maestro (teacher), 131, 136, 139, 143; *maestra rural* (rural schoolteacher), 130

magazine, 36, 113–114, 118, 136–138, 149–150, 151–152, 154, 156; American, 102–103; middlebrow, 131

male: chroniclers, 25–26, 80, 152–153; community, 48–49; reader, 152, 154; universality, 156; writers, 151, 155; and writing, 58

Man, Paul de, 29, 31

Manhã, A, 67

manifesto(es), 21, 82, 101

manliness, 102, 105, 107, 118, 158

map, 39; cultural, 163; literary, 92; mapping, 39, 40

margins, 27, 39, 41, 164; marginal neighborhoods, 46

market, 16, 18, 21, 23, 89; cultural, 23, 60, 122; economy, 60; global, 15; literary marketplace, 48; marketing, 158

marriage, 33, 48, 56, 58, 134, 136

Martí, José, 15, 17–18, 42, 64, 78

Martínez Estrada, Ezequiel, 39

Martínez, Mariano, 111

Martín Fierro (J. Hernández), 47, 172

Martins, Wilson, 71

Marx, Karl, 60

masculinity, 48, 58, 100–102, 105, 106, 111, 138, 150–151, 154, 158, 166

Masiello, Francine, 158

Massacre in Mexico (E. Poniatowska), 165

mass culture, 21, 22, 53

mechanical reproduction, 28, 33

media, 13, 14, 16, 19–22, 30, 35, 50, 58, 86, 97, 112, 116, 128, 159, 161, 165; egalitarian potential of, 59; mass, 20, 25–26, 29, 50, 119, 122, 155, 164, 165

"médica, La" (The Woman Doctor) (A. Storni), 135

"Meditation on Eyeglasses" (S. Novo), 117, 119

melodrama, 52, 54, 133–134, 144

Metz, Christian, 59

Mexicanness, 104, 106

Mexican Revolution, 19, 100, 112–114

middlebrow, 158–159; press, 150; publications, 28, 151, 154; readers, 144; writing, 159

Milenio, 160

Milliet, Sérgio, 71

mise en abîme, 52, 55, 57, 58

Mistral, Gabriela, 13, 113, 131, 143

mobility, 13, 73, 90, 152, 153, 165

mockery, 35, 54–55, 154

Modern Art Week, 65, 89

modernism, Brazilian, 65–67, 82, 88, 89–90

modernismo, 20, 21, 98, 100, 132, 188n5; Mexican, 100, 144; Spanish American, 15